ROMAN COOKERY

MARK GRANT teaches classics and is the editor and translator of culinary works by Anthimus and Oribasius. Inspired by working as a cook, he spent a year training in catering management. He has been researching the cooking of the ancient world for more than twenty years as well as writing and lecturing on the subject.

D1335890

BY THE SAME AUTHOR

Anthimus:
On the Observance of Foods

Dieting for an Emperor:
A Translation of Books 1 and 4 of Oribasius' Medical Compilations
with an Introduction and Commentary

ROMAN COOKERY

ANCIENT RECIPES *for* MODERN KITCHENS

Mark Grant

DECORATIONS *by* JANE SMITH

Serif
London

First published 1999 by
Serif
47 Strahan Road
London E3 5DA

British Library Cataloguing-in-Publication Data.
A catalogue record for this book is available from the British Library.

Library of Congress Cataloging in Publication Data.
A catalog record for this book is available from the Library of Congress.

ISBN 1 897959 39 7

Designed by Sue Lamble
Printed and bound in Malaysia by Forum

CONTENTS

To the memory of
Piroska Sternberg (née Szántó)
1908-1979
who inspired me when I was small
with her Central European cooking

ACKNOWLEDGEMENTS

Many years ago I organised and cooked an ancient banquet to raise money for the St Andrews branch of the Scottish Hellenic Society. This event was advertised under the name 'Alexandrian Delicacies' because the recipes came from such a wide variety of ancient sources, Alexandria representing both the cultural diversity of the Roman Empire and the academic resources of the great museum where, amongst other books, cookery manuals of all ages would have been kept. Two other such banquets followed, and these led my starting to collect recipes from outside the pages of the celebrated book by Apicius, supplemented by practical research for many other festive occasions.

These recipes are now published here in a collected form for the first time, adapted for use in the modern kitchen and to serve as a complement to Apicius. I would like to thank Elizabeth Craik for her original idea about Alexandrian Delicacies and numerous friends who have been subjected to strange smells and flavours over the years. That they have returned for more shows that ancient food is not a cuisine to ignore. Duncan Ross of Poyntzfield Herb Nursery has been of invaluable assistance in tracking down some of the more unusual herbs and spices. John Davis encouraged my first tentative steps towards the realisation of this book and has kept me abreast of all things Greek. Stephen Hayward has been a most caring and thoughtful editor. This book is dedicated to my dear Alison, Anna and Toby for their many critical suggestions over improving the presentation of these ancient dishes; without their support this work would never have been completed.

Haileybury College,
January 1999

INTRODUCTION

So I got myself ready for dinner. There I found a large number of guests, the cream of society in fact, something not wholly unexpected considering our hostess was the leading lady of the city. The tables were of citron wood and shone with ivory, the couches were draped in cloth sparkling with gold, the large wine cups were stunning in their variety but equal in their extravagance. Over here a glass cup was decorated with figures in relief, over there was a cup of incised crystal, over here was a gleaming silver cup, over there a glittering gold cup, another cup was of skilfully carved amber, whilst others were of semi-precious stones that could be drunk from. It would be impossible to imagine what was there. Numerous waiters, who deftly served a whole range of dishes, were drawn up in smart uniforms, whilst beautifully dressed boys with their hair specially curled filled the semi-precious stones hollowed out as cups with vintage wine.

This description of a banquet, in Apuleius' second-century AD novel *The Golden Ass*, paints the popular picture of Roman eating habits as unceasing gluttony in sumptuous marble dining-rooms filled with large numbers of guests and attendant slaves. We read of Trimalchio's vulgar culinary creations in the pages of Petronius, we see portraits of the wobbling bulk of the gourmet emperor Vitellius staring grossly from coins and we recall Seneca's dictum that people ate to vomit and vomited to eat. Having ploughed violently through dinners of many courses, consuming as they went daintily baked dormice, tender larks' tongues, roasted flamingo and parrot, viciously spiced stews and sweet poppy-seed concoctions sticky with honey, the poor Romans could do little but drag themselves, helped by slaves, to small rooms set aside for this purpose and relieve their overladen stomachs of their disgusting burdens. Certainly a few very wealthy and bored Romans indulged in these excesses, and thereby gave moralists and satirists something to moan about, yet the ordinary Roman did nothing of the sort. And this is where there are problems of source materials, for it is easy to discourse about the extraordinary side of Roman diet since the Romans themselves liked to describe it at great length – it was, after all, sensational. But there are just passing references to the humble wine bars, fried-fish shops and backstreet restaurants which catered for the majority of the population, and these are often derogatory.

The theme of this book is everyday Roman food. That does not necessarily imply food just for the ordinary person, because the great and famous ate straightforward food as well as attending extravagant banquets, so I have included references to emperors as well as to plebs. In fact, Stoic philosophy, to which many Romans adhered in the first two centuries AD, advocated a simple lifestyle so as to afford the mind strength of purpose and freedom from unnecessary distractions.

Roman food is exciting because it is the recognisable source of modern European cooking, yet it also surprises with its unfamiliar combinations of ingredients. There are, of course, fundamental differences between the Mediterranean cooking of today and that of ancient times, not only in the range of ingredients but also in the technology used to process and cook the food, although there is also much that is familiar. This tension between the strange and the recognisable often makes it difficult to reconcile the available evidence, whether literary or archaeological, so as to reconstruct a realistic outline of Roman cooking.

But what do we mean by 'Roman cookery'? It would be wrong to presume a national cuisine. From the very beginning of their imperial expansion the Romans borrowed from and adapted to suit their own circumstances the cultures of the nations they conquered.

Greek philosophy and medicine, Gallic farming methods and foreign deities such as the Egyptian goddess Isis were all assimilated and quickly regarded as Roman. The different languages of the Empire were allowed to exist alongside Latin, so that in Britain, for example, the provincials continued to speak the Celtic dialect which is the ancestor of modern Welsh. In this polyglot empire, however, there was one language that was equal in status to Latin and which was spoken fluently by all educated Romans. From the eighth century BC Greek colonists had spread their language and civilisation from the shores of the Black Sea to southern Spain, and Greece had generally been venerated by the Romans as a source of high culture. Two famous examples of this colonisation were Naples and Marseilles, both of which were still very much Greek cities in the Roman period. Alexander the Great's conquest of the Middle East in the fourth century BC further spread the Greek language and way of life. In this way Greece permeated the Mediterranean world, and when Julius Caesar was assassinated his dying words were not the Latin 'Et tu Brute', as Shakespeare has persuaded the English-speaking world, but the Greek 'Kai su teknon'. This bilingualism can be seen in the names of a number of the recipes in this book, some of which date from the second century BC or earlier and are described by Greek writers, but they may still be called Roman, for many of the cooks in Rome were Greek and most wealthy Romans travelled to Greece for their higher education. That older Greek recipes were cooked in the later Roman Empire can be judged from their appearance in novels, letters and encyclopaedias.

'The temptation to equate the Roman past as much as possible with our own world (or with what we would like our world to be) has been strong. It has produced much apologetic writing, but little history.' These strong words from Willem Jongman's book on Pompeii are as applicable to our attempts to understand Roman cooking as to our efforts at comprehending the ancient world more generally. The reconstruction of a Roman kitchen at the museum at Cirencester, for example, with its neatly painted walls, bundles of herbs hanging from rafters, ingredients lying on a table and jars and pots of olive oil and wine stacked ready for pouring is reminiscent of the farmhouse scenes in evocative photographic books of Mediterranean lands that soothe northern spirits on dark winter evenings. The reality, however, was rather more harsh. Archaeology is normally able only to present the foundations of walls and ovens, but at Pompeii and Herculaneum, both buried by the eruption of Vesuvius in AD 79, we can catch a glimpse of the shabbiness and primitiveness of the ancient kitchen. There was rarely a supply of fresh water – a bucket would have been fetched from a public fountain in the street – and the lack of ventilation would have caused a smoky atmosphere. Classical writers comment in passing on these attributes: Martial tells of a black kitchen, Horace moans about smoke from the kitchen causing his eyes to water and Seneca often refers to the city of Rome as if it were little more than an agglomeration of charcoal stoves. The kitchen fire could, when out of hand, threaten the whole house. Horace describes how, when dining out at Beneventum, the kitchen caught fire, causing guests and slaves to panic in their efforts to extinguish the blaze.

The preparation of food centred on the knife and the pestle and mortar. Every archaeological site contains fragments of mortars, heavy clay bowls with a lip for pouring which often had grit baked into the bottom to facilitate grinding. As food was eaten at the table with fingers and bread, everything was either chopped into manageable chunks or puréed before serving. Spoons were the only pieces of cutlery that seem to have been used regularly. Their handles, which had sharp, pointed ends, are commonly thought to have been used for hooking snails out of their shells. On the other hand, virtually raw eggs heated quickly in boiling water were a popular delicacy and pointed spoon handles may have been used to puncture the shell and allow the contents to be sucked out. Two-pronged forks certainly existed, and the archaeological museum at Pula in Slovenia has some fine examples, but their use at the table is not confirmed in the surviving literature. It is possible that they appeared at restaurants and bars where customers wanted to eat their food quickly without dirtying their hands. Double-handed blades were used for mincing and the range of cooking pots and baking trays would have done justice to a modern kitchen.

During the Roman Empire flour could be bought, as could loaves of bread, from the local miller and baker. Mills in the shape of an hour-glass turned by blindfolded donkeys are depicted on numerous reliefs and the remains of bakeries have been found at various ancient sites. Some flour, however, was ground at home by hand, as hand-held querns testify. With the cost of fuel being comparatively high, bakers probably cooked in one large batch loaves made by their customers, as still happened in some parts of Greece until recently. Those breads and the foods that were enjoyed with them are the subject of this book.

Wealthy households owned cooks as slaves. Martial remarks that a cook must possess the same tastes as his master. A good cook was expensive. In fact, the historian Livy is very precise in dating the decline in moral standards at Rome that led to the permissiveness of the Late Republic to 187 BC, when the value of cooks rose steeply and cooking moved from being a necessary service to an art form. Cicero, writing a little earlier than Livy, listed cookery and baking under the heading of vulgar arts; Seneca, a century later, excluded cooks and other purveyors of pleasure from what he termed the liberal arts, in other words those arts suitable for a free person rather than a slave. No doubt the earlier reputation of cooks had lingered on, for the practice had been for chefs to hang around the market-places in cities and advertise themselves to potential customers. They would then be hired for specific occasions, such as an engagement party or a wedding or birthday feast, before returning to the marketplace and hawking their skills again. This temporary relationship between cook and customer was the subject of many scenes in comic plays of the second century BC. The cook in *The Liar* by Plautus is a complete charlatan, fabricating ridiculous names for the exotic spices he pretends to use in preference to the common seasonings employed by other cooks. When accused by his potential employer of charging exorbitant prices, he admits that he is a rather expensive cook, but insists that price means quality. He even claims to be able, like the sorceress Medea with the aged Pelias, to rejuvenate with his dishes. Cooks in classical Greece were of a low status: Plato in *The Republic* lists them with wet nurses, barbers and beauticians, while in Persia they were exchanged as gifts, which perhaps indicates that they occupied a higher position in people's estimation. The Scythians, however, who lived in what is now the Republic of Georgia, took a somewhat more callous view of chefs: Herodotus tells us that they strangled their concubines, cup-bearers and cooks to lay in the tombs of their kings.

Not everyone ate at home. There were places in the cities of the Roman Empire where either a full meal or a snack could be eaten. Fast-food establishments called *popinae* served fried fish, ham and sausages, as well as other delicacies, and Catullus mentions the pages of an unfortunate historian as being so useless as to be fit only for wrapping up mackerel, so a take-away service was also available. But *popinae* had a reputation as the haunt of drunks, thieves, prostitutes and lazy slaves. Juvenal describes in passing an all-night *popina* where debauched insomniacs could fritter away the small hours. This literary evidence comes from an upper-class perspective, however, and the greasy restaurants, as Horace described them, were probably enjoyed by a large part of the population. The remains of these restaurants can be seen at Pompeii and have been studied closely by archaeologists.

Similar to the *popina* was the *thermopolium* or, in a literal translation, a 'place where hot things are sold'. Asellina's *thermopolium*, for example, had an assortment of amphorae and jugs for the serving of hot and cold drinks. There were also cosy corners and upper rooms which bear out the suggestion made by certain writers that bars and fast-food restaurants were used for other purposes besides eating, and in fact the names of prostitutes are found scrawled on the outside of the shop. At the inn near the corner of Mercury Street the walls are decorated with paintings depicting people seated around tables, with sausages, strings of onions and cheeses hanging from the rafters. Ovid in his *Metamorphoses* writes of a ham, covered in soot from the fire, hanging in the hovel of a poor elderly couple, whilst Virgil has a round cheese pierced through the middle with a string and a bunch of dried dill hanging in the hut of his peasant Simulus. Tenant farmers and freeholders like Simulus had been regarded from earliest times as the backbone of the Roman state. Their service in the army brought them government grants of land and legal protection from the encroachments of the aristocratic latifundia that were worked by slaves.

Cookery books formed an extensive branch of literature in the ancient world. Athenaeus, in *The Partying Professors* of the third century AD, records among other works *The Art of Dining* in epic verse by Clearchus, *The Banquet* by Philoxenus of Leucas, *Breadmaking* by Chrysippus of Tyana, *Cookery* by Simus, *On Cakes* by Iatrocles and *The Art of Dining* by Archestratus. But medieval scribes were not interested in copying these treatises, for other than *The Art of Cookery* by Apicius, no cookery book from the ancient world survives in its entirety, and a great deal of delving is required to winkle out recipes from the other sources. Marcus Porcius Cato, for example, a Roman statesman of the second century BC, wrote a short work called *On Agriculture* and amongst this jumbled collection of advice and recommendations a number of recipes for breads and cakes are to be found. Alexandrian and Roman grammarians added notes to texts of early authors such as the epic poet Homer, author of *The Iliad* and *The Odyssey*, and the fifth-century BC comic playwright Aristophanes, author of *Lysistrata* and *Women at the Assembly*, in order to elucidate strange terms, and these notes sometimes take the form of recipes. There are also papyrus fragments from cookery books that have been found in Egypt where the dry sands have preserved both them and other documents.

From a purely culinary point of view, the most valuable book to have survived from the Roman Empire is the treatise on cooking that bears the name of Apicius. This was probably compiled in the fifth century AD amidst the political upheavals of barbarian invasion. A celebrated gourmet called Marcus Gavius Apicius is known to have lived during the reign of the emperor Tiberius (AD 14-37) and various stories have been handed down to illustrate his devotion to the pleasures of the table. He was spending some time at Minturnae, a city in Campania where he indulged himself on giant prawns, when a report came to him that the prawns off the North African coast were even larger and juicier, so he hired a ship and, after a rough voyage, arrived at his destination. The locals, who had heard reports of his great wealth, sailed out in their fishing boats to meet him with samples of their catches. Apicius took one look at their offerings, decided that the prawns of Minturnae were of superior quality and sailed back home again. Some time later he took stock of his assets and, finding a mere thirty million *sesterces* to his account (at this time an aqueduct to supply a city with water cost just over three million *sesterces* to build), he decided to end his life rather than live off ordinary fare. It appears that an anonymous writer of the fifth century AD, taking advantage of Apicius' reputation as a *bon vivant*, used his name to sell the book, in much the same way as modern cookery books bear the name of Mrs Beeton although being far removed from the Victorian original.

Up to now books about ancient cooking have either relied solely on Apicius or they have interspersed his ideas with just a few recipes from other sources. None of the recipes in this book come from the pages of Apicius, something which has not been attempted before. Sufficient has been written about Apicius and enough books have been published to allow anyone interested to follow that unique manual. What has not been possible before now is to eat the ordinary food of the Roman Empire.

The distinction between what was and was not luxurious is vital for an understanding of food in antiquity. The ancient world lived for the most part at subsistence level, as did all societies up until the modern age. Food shortages were frequent, doctors not finding anything strange in recording what poor people ate and suffered during a time of want. Galen actually begins his work *On Foods that Produce Good and Bad Humours* with the statement that many shortages had occurred in the Roman Empire at the time of writing and that people had been forced to cook roots, bulbs and shoots that would otherwise have been avoided. Seneca attacks the fashion for fattening birds so efficiently that they almost ooze grease and castigates the apparent need to farm estates in Sicily and Africa just to satisfy the belly of one senator. He also fantasises about the plain diet of ancient times and metaphorically considers simple pastry with honey as being like thinking of friends who are alive and well.

Peter Garnsey, in his book on famine and food supply in the Graeco-Roman world, concludes that food crises were common but that famine was rare. Famine could be defined as a critical shortage of essential foodstuffs, whilst shortage was a temporary reduction in the amount of available foodstuffs leading to rising prices, hunger, riots and the possibility of starvation. It was generally the people in the country who starved after a poor harvest, while city dwellers were cushioned by grain stored in government granaries or in private hands, for the tax collector and landlord during the imperial period extracted their due from the peasantry with ruthless efficiency.

The basic ingredients for any Roman meal were olive oil and wine, two of the cornerstones of what we now think of as the Mediterranean diet. Regional styles of cooking existed and these took up the native cuisine which existed prior to the Roman conquest and also adapted Roman recipes to the ingredients that were available locally. Thus in Britain and Germany long halls in some villas attest to the survival of Celtic feasting around meat roasted on a spit, whilst in northern Gaul butter and cream were incorporated into Roman dishes. Pliny in his *Natural History* remarks on butter being eaten by barbarians – that is people who did not speak Latin and lived beyond the frontiers – and used for rubbing into the skin instead of olive oil. This barbarian ingredient was, no doubt, an important element in the heavier meals needed for sustenance during northern winters.

Any account of food in the Roman world has to take account of these geographical factors, which are well illustrated by the coins issued by the southern British tribes in the early years of the first century AD. The Trinovantes in Essex, who were supported by the Romans, stamped their coins with the legend of a vine leaf; their rivals in Hertfordshire, the Catuvellauni, pronounced their freedom from Roman influence with their motif of a barley ear. Beer drinkers therefore competed with the imbibers of wine, the barbarian with Roman civilisation. When the emperor Claudius invaded Britain in AD 43, however, the propaganda quickly gave way to the simple fact that Roman soldiers enjoyed drinking beer. At Canterbury olive oil from Spain was imported on a regular basis until the third century AD, according to the testimony of amphora shards, but then a series of barbarian incursions into the Iberian peninsula put an end to this trade and from then until the demise of the province in the early fifth century AD only a few imports of North African oil appear.

Wine carried with it as much linguistic baggage as it does today, with accolades bandied about of vintages being heavy-bodied, fine-nosed and possessing aromatic qualities. Two Falernian wines from northern Campania, a sweet red and a dry white, were the yardstick by which to judge other wines. Writers often discussed their preferences in passing: Marcus Aurelius, who became emperor in AD 161, remarked that he enjoyed reading his friend Fronto's letters more than quaffing Massic wine, Aulus Gellius celebrated the vintage season with the poet Annianus in the Faliscan district and Horace wanted to forget about the winter's chill over a glass of Sabine wine that had aged for four years. Like fish sauce and olive oil, wine was shipped all over the Roman Empire. Whilst literary evidence can say much about an individual's taste and the received wisdom about regional wines, archaeology can show general trends in consumption: for example, towards the close of the Roman Empire in western Europe wine from the Abruzzo was popular, accounting for almost a fifth of all the shards at Marseilles. Especially popular were sweet white wines, which were generally held to be the ideal aperitif, and sweet red wines, which were drunk with a meal. This penchant for sweetness survives in Greece today with the rich, fruity Mavrodaphe wine, although it is of course impossible to say exactly how an ancient wine would have tasted. Locally grown wines were also drunk: grape pips have been discovered among the Roman sites of southern Britain, and while these may be no more than evidence of table grapes, medieval documents lend some clues as to the volume of wine that might have been produced in Roman times under similar agricultural and climatic conditions.

The Romans and Greeks watered their wine, not because it was any more alcoholic than modern wine but because it was not right for a sensible citizen to be seen drunk. In classical Greece the proportions of water to wine ranged from three to one, five to three and three to two, all of which were harmonic balances in Greek music. The Greeks held wine to be at the same time both dangerous and beneficial: it could act as a drug, reveal the truth and temporarily suppress the misery of the human condition. The Romans do not appear to have imbued wine with such religiosity – it was something to enjoy at a meal or to add to sauces. Wine could be drunk hot or chilled with ice and Plutarch records how ice was wrapped in an insulating layer of straw and unfulled wool to keep it from melting. It was for the individual palate to decide the temperature at which wine should be served. Indeed, personal and local taste was the arbiter as to what type of drink might accompany a meal, since although shipping was effective enough to distribute in bulk wines from all over the Roman world, local preferences might still captivate. Beer, for instance, was drunk in the northern provinces by civilians and soldiers alike, as the documents from Vindolanda reveal. This fort on the Stanegate border road that was the predecessor of Hadrian's Wall has preserved in its rubbish pits the thin wooden sheets on which personal letters and lists drawn up by the commissariat were written. Beer and wine are juxtaposed, a happy union of barbarian and Roman. Otherwise there are no surprises on the lists, for even the deliveries of lard to the fort can be paralleled by the use of this ingredient in everyday recipes, and the supply of olive oil shows that the soldiers had not lost sight of Mediterranean cooking, even if the majority of them were recruited from the northern provinces.

Some Romans railed against *garum*, Ancient Rome's famous fish sauce, dubbing it an expensive and poisonous ichthyological extract that shrivelled the stomach with its salty rottenness. Nevertheless, huge quantities were shipped in amphorae all over the Mediterranean, proudly bearing labels advertising the manufacturer's name, and cities like Pompeii grew rich on the proceeds of the trade. The demand for *garum* was so great that it was made even in places that were not wholly suitable for its production: amphorae used for bottling fish sauce, together with considerable quantities of herring and sprat, have been found by the Roman dockyards in London and similar finds point to exports from Brittany. Most of the recipes in Apicius call for the addition of fish *garum*, whether as a constituent of a more complex sauce or on its own for sprinkling over a boiled egg. Yet with simpler Roman food it is not *garum* that is featured, but salt, which calls into question the price, availability and so the social class of those who ate this condiment. Amphora shards are, after all, virtually indestructible and will therefore leave the sort of record that makes for a convenient link with Apicius.

Meat was also expensive. One of the many strands of satirical humour in Petronius is the serving of meat at every course of Trimalchio's banquet, for this would have appeared vulgar even to a wealthy senator. Pork was the most popular meat in Rome, since pigs can eat virtually anything and convert what is otherwise waste into flesh. When the emperor Severus Alexander expressed a year in advance his intention of visiting Egypt in AD 233, some forty pigs were made ready for the imperial court in the district of Oxyrhynchus. In all, approximately 2,000 pounds of pork were to be served, although it is frustrating that we do not know the number of courtiers or the sort of meals they were expecting to eat, beyond the fact that such imperial journeys were ruinously expensive for the local inhabitants because of the size of the emperor's entourage.

Interestingly, the figures allow for an average weight of 35 pounds for an individual pig, approximately the same as the pigs which scavenge in the streets of Coptic villages in Egypt today.

Michael Jameson suggests that the Greeks, on the other hand, derived virtually all their meat – apart from game – from the ritual of sacrifice, and adds that sheep and goats were the most commonly kept animals in classical Greece. In Homer's writing sheep certainly feature predominantly in feasts, eaten with bread and wine. Archaeology has furnished evidence for the consumption in Roman Britain of ox, sheep, goat, pig, bear, deer and boar. There are, however, few meat or fish dishes in this book. This is partly a reflection of the fact that most Romans only ate meat on special occasions – in literature chickens and hams appear for birthdays or dinner parties with important guests – and partly a reminder that meat and fish were generally eaten grilled and so do not merit a description in the surviving literary sources.

Fish was probably in the same price bracket as meat, although the evidence is awkward to judge. Fish bones and oyster shells are found among the remains at archaeological sites, but questions must be asked about how frequently these foods were eaten and by whom. After all, it does not take a great many oyster shells to create a substantial deposit, so these finds could illustrate just the food of the minority. Impoverished characters in Roman literature are depicted as wholly resigned to just an occasional taste of fish. There is, however, one further piece of evidence. Early in AD 301 the emperor Diocletian published his Decree on Maximum Prices in an attempt to stop the rampant inflation that was ruining the economy. For the historian this may be a problematic document, but it does at least have the merit of showing the comparative prices of various foodstuffs. Twelve *denarii* would buy a pound of either pork, venison or best quality freshwater fish. By way of contrast, the same sum could purchase nearly three pounds of beans or barley. A farm labourer could expect to earn 25 *denarii* as a daily wage, a baker 50 *denarii* and an interior decorator 75 *denarii*. How often these people bought meat or fish is impossible to say, but the relative expense of such a purchase is clear. Even the depictions of fish on mosaics and wall paintings are now generally interpreted as symbolising the beneficence and importance of the owner rather than items from the menu. Yet the huge shopping complex in Rome constructed by the emperor Trajan in the second century AD incorporated on its fifth floor special facilities for selling fish, and two channels were built specifically to provide the water in which the fish were kept, one linked to an aqueduct conveying fresh water and the other to a supply of salt water from Ostia. At Ostia itself water tanks and marble slabs have been unearthed from the premises of a fishmonger, so it seems probable that the concentration of wealth in the large cities allowed for a thriving fish market.

Vegetables, especially pulses, were universally eaten as an accompaniment to the staple bread, and were referred to generically in Greek as *opson* and in Latin as *pulmentum* or *pulmentarium*. The dictionaries translate these words as 'relish', although this does cover the whole range of the ancient terms, the nearest equivalent being the Italian *companatico* or 'something eaten with bread'. Olive oil was relatively expensive: Cato provided the slaves who worked on his farm with about one pint a month and lighting a room with olive-oil lamps was almost certainly the prerogative of the more wealthy, the poor having to work by daylight alone. Using the evidence of wooden tablets carbonised in the eruption of Vesuvius, Robert Etienne gives the daily shopping list of a Pompeian family: bread features heavily, the slave of course receiving a rougher loaf than the freeborn. Olive oil and wine occur frequently, as does cheese. Onions, dates and pears also appear, but fish is listed only once and there is no meat. The list is extant for just over a week's shopping, but the pattern of the diet seems clear, although more meat and fish would surely have been bought if a dinner was being given for friends.

Since fish and meat were expensive, most Romans relied on bread, pulses and vegetables, but although they were not vegetarian by choice, this philosophy was by no means alien to the ancient world. Seneca espoused the avoidance of animal flesh: 'I began to avoid food derived from animals. By the end of the year this diet was as pleasant as it was easy. I began to think that my mind was more active, although today I could not say for certain whether it really was or not.' Plutarch wrote an entire book on vegetarianism entitled *On the Eating of Meat*, and there are numerous other references to works on diets devoid of meat. Most Romans were more than aware of the difficulty and expense involved in producing meat, which explains both the thrill of serving exotic birds and beasts at a banquet and also the numerous references to ersatz dishes involving nuts and root vegetables. Apicius, for example, includes a recipe for salt fish substituted by ground walnuts, and when King Nicomedes of Bithynia (now northern Turkey) was travelling in the late fourth century BC far from the coast and developed a craving for anchovy, his cook served him thin slices of turnip sprinkled with salt and poppy seeds. Colin Spencer understandably expresses his astonishment that anyone became a committed vegetarian in Rome, given the people's bloodthirsty appetite for gladiator and animal shows. Yet Plutarch is perhaps a rather more lonely voice than is generally assumed. The words Ovid gives in his *Metamorphoses* to Pythagoras may be less a defence of vegetarianism than a gentle satire on the Golden Age when life was supposed to be so simple and carefree, and Seneca did not hold to his new diet for long, for vegetarianism in the ancient world was complicated by its frequent association with magic and foreign cults. The Romans were a superstitious people and the Senate often passed laws banning practices associated with the occult. Seneca quickly abandoned his vegetarianism in AD 19 when the emperor Tiberius banned Egyptian and Jewish religious rites from being performed in Rome. Abstinence from pork would have suggested to government informers that Seneca had been proselytised and as a consequence his future might have been in jeopardy.

Willem Jongman argues in his fascinating book on Pompeii that cereals provided the greater part of the ancient diet, perhaps even as much as seventy per cent. Most of these cereals were consumed in the region in which they were grown. Only the large cities of Rome, Carthage (modern Tunis), Alexandria in Egypt and Antioch in Syria had the means to import grain in bulk. Occasionally relief was offered during famine. In AD 99 the Nile did not rise as much as normal, and consequently the harvest was poor. The emperor Trajan ordered the ships transporting wheat from Egypt to Rome to return fully laden so that the Egyptians would not starve. In the Mediterranean wheat and barley were the main cereals. Millet was sometimes sown after a failure in the harvest: it can be sown in spring and has a high yield ratio, so only a small stock of emergency seed need be kept. Barley does not require as much rainfall as wheat and does not demand such fertile soil. The Romans made barley into porridge, but because of its low gluten content it could not easily be made into bread, so a variety of spelt wheat called *triticum vulgare* was grown for this purpose. In Etruria and Campania farmers sowed this crop extensively during the empire. Teams of oxen were as familiar a sight on ancient farms as tractors are today. Columella, an agricultural writer of the first century AD, stressed the importance of oxen for the farmer: he even says that the Greeks used to call them *italos*, and so the peninsula was named after its plough teams. Some might dispute the etymology, but the importance of cereals in everyday fare cannot be doubted.

As Colin Spencer says, the Mediterranean diet with its healthy emphasis on fresh fruit and vegetables appears in a recognisable form by the fourth century BC. The Roman legacy was to spread this knowledge into northern Europe and to transmit it beyond the fall of the empire. Texts of Apicius may have been copied by medieval monks for use in the abbot's sophisticated kitchen, but alongside this literary transmission there must have run an oral tradition for the simpler recipes. In his study of medieval cooking, Helmut Birkhan rightly acknowledges the broad affiliation between the piquant flavours of modern French cuisine and the sweet and sour basis of so many Roman recipes. What is fascinating about everyday Roman cookery is not just this broad affiliation, but also the obvious ancestry of modern Mediterranean dishes such as pesto, soufflé, pasta, pizza, baklava and pancakes, early versions of which are to be found in the pages that follow. Cooking Roman food illuminates the social history of the empire which laid the foundations of European culture, a unique claim that rewards investigation both in the kitchen and when travelling. All roads do indeed lead to Rome.

INGREDIENTS

The classical Roman diet was in many respects much like its modern Mediterranean counterpart, but without New World ingredients like potatoes, tomatoes, peppers, maize and chillies, and those from Africa and the eastern parts of the Old World like coffee, tea, lemons and oranges. Good olive oil was essential to flavour simple dishes, while pepper and herbs were employed to season wine-based sauces. Bread provided the basic accompaniment to any meal, even more so than today when rice, potatoes and other alternatives are to hand.

A present-day kitchen cupboard will contain ketchup, tabasco and a variety of other sauces, and the Roman kitchen was little different: prepared sauces could be purchased in the market or else made at home. In the classical sources a complicated set of instruct-ions is often followed by a simple recipe, and the latter must surely be the domestic version in which the months the ingredients were supposed to be left to mature in the sun are compressed into a few hours of boiling and grilling.

The food was cooked in kitchens which are well illustrated by those excavated at Pompeii. Their most recognisable feature is the masonry platform, sometimes edged with a low guard at the top.

Arched openings at the front of the platform allowed for the storage of fuel. Stone supports for the wooden tables used for food preparation have been discovered. Much of the cooking was carried out on small iron tripods and gridirons over burning charcoal. Many kitchens were probably unroofed, apart from canvas awnings that could be unfurled in bad weather, so that the smoke could escape easily.

Bronze strainers with holes arranged in ornamental patterns were used to serve wine, although the sieving was concerned less with catching the lees than the herbs and spices that were frequently added to impart extra flavour to an average vintage. When the food was ready to serve there was a variety of dishes to use: large platters and shallow bowls of silver, bronze, pewter or fine pottery, often decorated with incised patterns or designs in relief. From the first century BC each course was brought into the dining room on a tray, generally made of wood but sometimes of silver, depending on wealth and the complexity or otherwise of the meal. Small tables made trays essential even in humble houses. Before this date the courses were placed on three-legged tables and carried in to the banqueters, hence the expressions 'first tables' for the first course and 'second tables' for the second. A restaurant would no doubt have followed the same pattern of serving as at a private house.

For the most part the identification of the ingredients is reasonably certain, following extensive research over the past fifty years, although there are still occasional problems. Plants, animals, herbs and spices are described by such authors as Pliny, Theophrastus and Palladius, and from their detailed descriptions and references by other authors to the particular properties of ingredients we can nearly always say for certain what ingredients are required in ancient recipes. Take, for instance, the Latin word *piper*, or *peperi* in Greek. Pliny writes that trees resembling junipers bore *piper*. The seeds, he adds, are contained in small pods which, when plucked before they are open and dried in the sun, produce black *piper*, but if left to open gradually when ripe, disclose white *piper*. Theophrastus describes *peperi* as being like bay berries, and both writers say that *piper/peperi* is pungent and heating, as does Celsus. *Piper* must be pepper: no other berry matches the description. It would be wrong to adjust the ancient recipes by substituting other flavours for pepper just because it seems jarring to modern tastes, as many recipes call for the juxtaposition of honey and pepper. If tasted, this combination is pleasantly pungent and spicy, the heat of the pepper heightened by the sweetness of honey. Latin names can sometimes be confusing, however. *Apium* can refer to both celery and parsley, a surprising match, until it is remembered that wild celery is not too dissimilar in appearance to flat-leaved parsley. Since the Roman period some plants have evolved either naturally or through human intervention: for example, *pastinaca* can denote both the carrot and the parsnip, the ambiguity lying in the then virtually identical appearance of the two roots. It was not until the thirteenth century that the familiar orange carrot appeared through cross-breeding between the ancient European white carrot and a red species from Afghanistan.

To create a brief repertoire of Roman condiments is not difficult, although substitutes can be devised if cooking time is of the essence. Some old jam jars sterilised in the oven should be used to store these sauces, which will keep safely for several months without refrigeration. Reduced wine was one such condiment. The manufacture and storage of this seasoning literally caused the Romans a headache, for the glaze applied to the earthenware jars used for both processes leached lead through its reaction with the acidity of the wine. Lead pipes were recognised as injurious to the health and Roman engineers recommended that water should be run through them for several weeks until they were furred up with calcium deposits; glaze was not considered to pose such a hazard, but chemical analysis has shown that many Roman skeletons harbour an extremely high proportion of lead.

The charcoal used on the stoves must have given Roman food a smoky tang, although I do not suggest its use in the recipes which follow. The ancient world relied on this fuel for cooking because it can be produced locally using fairly simple technology, its lightness ensures low transport costs and it gives a more even and controllable heat than wood. But wood was also used, especially to impart a special savour to particular dishes: apple, pear, plum and apricot wood are fragrant, for example, whilst olive wood fuels an incandescent braise.

Most of the herbs and spices used in Roman cooking can be bought fresh or dried in supermarkets and health food shops. A handful may cause problems, namely savory, pennyroyal, costmary, spikenard and sumach. One solution is to grow these in the garden or on the window-sill; the other is to substitute. The recipes themselves suggest the latter, with their frequent parallel listings of ingredients. If something could not be procured, whether as a result of erratic supply, crop failure or barbarian rampaging, then what was to hand was added. One renowned case of substitution occurs with silphium. This spice was grown in what is now Libya, its exquisite taste inflating its price to such an extent that the growers became very wealthy. But for some reason intensive farming caused its demise, perhaps through disease, so by the first century AD it was supposedly extinct, although there is some evidence to suggest that it might have survived until later. To take its place asafoetida, a spice immediately recognisable from its distinctive use in curries, was employed.

Roman cooks were used to substituting ingredients, as Apicius' illustrations show: 'To which you should add the reduced juice of quinces, further reduced to the consistency of honey by exposure to a blazing sun. If you do not have reduced quince juice, you should use the reduced juice of dried figs, which the Romans call "colour".' Anthimus was also familiar with the problem of availability: 'Although cucumbers at present cannot be procured here, when they are available the seeds that are inside them may be eaten.'

I have made suggestions in the recipes as to what ingredients can be added instead of their more exotic counterparts, but if an interest does develop it is more than worth trying to achieve as authentic a taste as possible. Garden centres can usually supply the names of specialist seed companies, whilst grocers specialising in ethnic ingredients or food halls in large department stores may stock unusual herbs and spices.

An ingredient that does cause controversy is cheese. As with ancient wine, it is impossible to know exactly how Roman cheese would have tasted. So with many of the recipes that call for just cheese, without any qualifying words such as goat's or cow's, I have chosen a straightforward modern variety, although there is in fact more than just convenience or whim behind this choice. My experiments with making cheese the Roman way, curdling cow's milk with fig sap and employing for a press a cake tin weighted with bricks, produced a cheese full of flavour and with a texture not too dissimilar from Cheddar. Since there was no refrigeration, such cheeses were bottled in brine or vinegar, dipped in salt, smoked or packed with crushed pulses. I have therefore interpreted references to the freshness or newness of a cheese as the absence of any subsequent preserving processes. There is no reason, however, why other sorts of cheese cannot be substituted to lend variety to the recipes, the only caveat being that where cheese provides the only flavouring, a good strong type ought to be used. Chefs in the ancient world appreciated the ease with which grated cheese can be incorporated into a sauce or dough, and graters are commonly found on archaeological sites, whilst in Aristophanes' play *Lysistrata* there is an intriguing reference to a sexual position known as the 'lioness on a cheese-grater'.

Recipes in Apicius often specify *liquamen* or *garum*. This salty sauce was usually manufactured from mackerel and other fish. The fish, pressed with salt in large vats, were left for several months in the sun and the fermented liquid that resulted was drained off and bottled. Factories for this process were established in Spain and North Africa. What is intriguing is the discrepancy between the widespread finds of *garum* containers and the relative absence of the sauce from the ordinary recipes. Presumably *garum* was an expensive commodity, both to manufacture and transport, since a bag of salt will season far more dishes than its equivalent weight of *garum* and the earthenware containers for the *garum* would have been heavy and needed careful packing to avoid breakages. Unfortunately, Diocletian's Decree on Maximum Prices does not record *garum*, although it does list both ordinary and seasoned salt at 6 and 8 *denarii* per pint respectively, extremely modest sums even for the lowest paid worker. If *garum* has in the past been instantly associated with the elaborate Roman cooking of Apicius, then the recipes in this book show that salt was just as important a commodity in the more humble kitchen.

FISH SAUCE

Garum

'*A recipe for* garum. *What is called* liquamen *is made like this. Fish guts are put into a pot and salt is added. Use small fish, particularly smelt, red mullet, sprats or anchovies, although any other fish is fine. Salt all these fish in the same way and leave to ferment in the sun, shaking the pot frequently. When it has fermented in the heat, draw the* garum *from the pot like this: a big sieve with a fine mesh should be placed in the middle of the pot containing the fish and the* garum *strained into the sieve. Whatever passes through the sieve is called* liquamen *and the remaining sludge is called* allec. *The people of Bithynia have this recipe: ideally take large or small sprats, but otherwise anchovies, horse mackerel or mackerel, pile them up together and put into the sort of trough which bakers use to knead dough. To each* modius *of fish add 2 Italian* sextarii *of salt and mix together. Leave overnight and then put into an earthenware pot. Place the open pot in the sun for two to three months and stir with a pole from time to time. Then take the pot, cover with a lid and store. Some people also add two* sextarii *of old wine to each* sextarius *of fish.*

If you want to make the garum *at once, that is without leaving it in the sun, but instead boiling it, the recipe is as follows: when brine has been tested for strength by seeing if an egg floats on it – if it sinks the brine is not sufficiently salty – using a new earthenware pot add the fish and some oregano. Place on a decent flame so that it boils, or in other words until it begins to reduce. Some people also add reduced wine. Then leave it to cool and strain two or three times until it is clear. Cover with a lid and store.'*

[*Bassus* Country Matters]

A factory making *garum* would have employed Bassus' first two recipes, since the operations described are elaborate and lengthy, while the third recipe with its comparative ease of preparation was probably for household use, although manufacturers of *garum* in the northern provinces would also have had to use fire.

1 jar of salted anchovies (100 g / 3 oz)
700 ml / 24 fl oz water
400 g / 14 oz sea salt
A pinch of dried oregano
1 tbsp sapa *(see p.33)*

I use dried oregano in this recipe because its taste is more concentrated than the fresh herb and because it is available to hand in most kitchens. Dissolve the salt in the water over a low heat. Add the anchovies to the salted water with the oregano and *sapa*. Simmer gently for 20 minutes and then leave to cool. Strain the *garum* through a fine sieve or muslin cloth and store in a jar ready for use.

PIQUANT PEAR SAUCE

Liquamen ex Piris

'A liquamen from pears suitable for those avoiding meat can be made like this: the ripest pears are mashed with pure salt. When their flesh has been pulped, leave to mature either in small wooden tubs or in earthenware pots that have been treated with pitch. After the third month the suspended flesh releases a juice of pleasant taste and of whitish colour. Alternatively, the following works well: at the moment when the pears are being salted you should stir in some rather dark wine.'

[*Palladius* On Agriculture]

My suggestion for a vegetarian *garum* is based on the ingredients listed by Palladius, but uses the rapid cooking method described in the preceding recipe. The result is a pleasant piquant sauce that affords an interesting background taste to various dishes.

125 ml / 1/4 pint red wine
6 large pears
700 ml / 24 fl oz water
400 g / 14 oz sea salt

Take a large pan and pour in the water and sea salt. Dissolve the sea salt in the water over a low heat, stirring occasionally to prevent a crust from building up on the side of the pan. Meanwhile core the pears and pulp them in a blender. When the salt has dissolved in the water, add the pear pulp and the wine. Simmer gently for half an hour, giving the mixture a stir once or twice, then leave to cool. When cold, decant into sterilised jars ready for use in cooking.

SPICED SAUCE

Garon tou Ioachou

'A recipe for garum *by Ioachos of Martyropolis. Take 1 pound of breadcrumbs from a stale loaf that has not been leavened or seasoned; half a pound each of crushed mint, calamint and dried turnip; 40 measures each of rue, wild thyme and fennel; 30 measures each of dill, plump black raisins, stoned dates and pure honey; 100 measures each of sugar and dried roses or rose extract. These should be put in a jar with water and left in the sun for forty days. To these should be added in a clean linen bag: 5 measures of aloes, 6 of spikenard, 2 of cloves, 3 of saffron, 9 of mastich, 10 of myrrh, 15 of cinnamon, 1 of musk, 2 of amber. Put all these ingredients together in the linen cloth, place in the middle of the juice and squeeze each day for forty days. When the forty days are up, pour off the water that is on the surface of the juice and put in another jar; pour more water on the juice and leave both out in the sun. After all the juice has thickened, put into another container, either a clean saucepan or a casserole, and boil down; fill with ripe quinces, but never withdraw the linen bag from the middle of the* garum, *and you should get an excellent* garum *that is beneficial to everyone.'*

[*Galen* On Quick Remedies]

Ioachos seems to have been detailing a *garum* that was more medicinal than culinary, for sugar rarely strayed beyond the confines of the

Roman surgery. The treatise from which this recipe is taken is unlikely to be by Galen himself, but it was certainly written under the Roman Empire, perhaps in the fifth century AD. A slightly simplified version of the recipe yields a sauce that could accompany a rice pudding or serve for dunking biscuits. Its taste is reminiscent of mulled wine. Rose water can been found in many supermarkets as it is an essential ingredient in modern Middle Eastern cooking.

1 apple or quince
1 plum (fresh or dried)
60 g/2 oz breadcrumbs
1 tsp mint
30 g/1 oz turnip
A sprig each of fresh rue and thyme
1/2 tsp fennel seeds
1/2 tsp dill tops
30 g/1 oz raisins
30 g/1 oz dates
2 tbsp clear honey
100 g/3 oz muscovado sugar
1 tbsp rose water
2 cloves
A pinch of saffron
1 cinnamon stick

Core and dice the apple or quince; stone and dice the plum. Combine all the ingredients in a pan with 2 pints of water, bring to the boil and simmer for 40 minutes. Allow to cool before straining through muslin and storing in a glass bottle.

REDUCED WINE SAUCE

Sapa

'*But* siraeum, *which those other people call* hepsema, *but which we Romans call* sapa, *an artificial rather than a natural product, calls for must reduced to a third part of its original volume.*'
[*Pliny* Natural History]

Cooks in the ancient world reduced their wine before adding it to sauces, rather than, as today, reducing the wine after it has been added to a sauce. Pliny was an officer and a gentleman, serving in particular the emperor Vespasian. Both men died in AD 79, Vespasian of natural causes, Pliny of suffocation whilst trying to observe the famous eruption of Vesuvius that buried the cities of Pompeii and Herculaneum. Of all Pliny's prolific writings, only his *Natural History* survives, an encyclopaedia of everything from medicine to astronomy, and from geography to reduced wine preparations.

1 litre/2 pints red grape juice

Pour the grape juice into a saucepan and boil vigorously whilst stirring until one-third remains. Leave to cool and decant into a sterilised bottle.

A NOTE ON THE RECIPES

Cookery writers in the ancient world tended to be extremely laconic and it is rare, even with the more detailed recipes, to find much more than a list of ingredients. In their original form, some of the recipes in this book comprise just one enigmatic sentence quoted out of context by another author who may have been interested in food but was certainly not a cook. This inevitably prompts questions about the relative proportions of the ingredients and the accuracy of the perceived methods.

Perhaps there can be no definitive solution to the problems raised by such source material, but a claim can still be made for authenticity. The methodology I have employed belongs to experimental archaeology, in which the various pieces of surviving evidence are used to provide a viable blueprint for a working reconstruction. It was once thought, for example, that without stirrups Roman cavalrymen were limited as to what they could achieve in battle, but by actually making a saddle in Roman style, basing the design on ancient accounts and material finds, it has been shown that a cavalryman could remain on his horse even after striking an enemy hard with his lance.

The evidence for Roman cooking is purely literary, and only through constant testing of the texts can this evidence hold any meaning. By practising with those recipes for which a relatively full set of instructions was given, a clear picture of the methodology can be obtained, whilst making recipes for which precise quantities are listed gives an idea of the force of the flavours that were enjoyed. These two approaches work well with the savoury dishes, because there is extensive support from the cookery book by Apicius and the agricultural treatises by authors such as Cato and Columella. Where a gap still remains, medieval and modern recipes can be of assistance if they possess an historical affinity with the ancient recipe. This approach lies behind many of the sweet dishes, an area that is hardly covered by Apicius, and I have frequently used cake and biscuit recipes from contemporary Greece and the Middle East to help to decipher and reconstruct terse remarks about honey, nuts and flour made by ancient Greek and Roman writers.

In order to allow the reader to judge the recipes independently, I first give my own translation of the Latin or Greek original, then something of the culinary background and finally my thoughts on the amounts and methods adapted for the modern kitchen. Further adjustments are of course possible, and no doubt readers will wish to increase or decrease particular flavours, but I have aimed for a taste commensurate with a knowledge of Roman cooking as a whole.

A cookery book like this one certainly allows for an ancient meal to be recreated very realistically, but there is also no reason why something Roman should not be served alongside a modern dish, Pork in a Piquant Sauce or *psoia* (p.126) going equally well with anachronistic couscous as with historically accurate barley and fried carrots. Both paths have given me immense pleasure, whether experiencing an intimate glimpse at the past or startling friends with some surprisingly modern and fresh ideas.

BREAKFAST

Breakfasts are mentioned only rarely by ancient authors. No doubt some people waited until lunchtime before they ate, as is occasionally the case in the Mediterranean today. If breakfast was taken, the time for eating was sunrise. Homer describes how Telemachus found his father Odysseus, who had just returned after an eventful voyage following the siege of Troy, preparing breakfast by the light of the dawn with a swineherd in a hut. A fire had been lit, but unfortunately Homer does not go on to mention the food that was to be cooked. The swineherd Eumaeus is, however, depicted as mixing wine with water.

Galen, the Greek doctor of the second century AD, says that hunger caused the body to tremble and grow cold, and it would seem strange, therefore, if the Greeks and Romans went to work on empty stomachs. In classical Athens the citizens would certainly have had some sort of breakfast before attending the Assembly or the Festival of Dionysus at which plays were performed. The military writer Vegetius of the fifth century AD stresses the importance of adequate nourishment for soldiers so that, in a prolonged struggle, they would not faint from hunger. Yet Simulus, the humble farmer in Virgil's poem The Ploughman's Lunch, waits until midday before consuming his vegetable purée and home-made bread, although he has risen at cockcrow to knead the dough and mash his cabbage and leeks. Perhaps the most that can be said is that breakfasts were usually frugal and sometimes overlooked. The Byzantine lexicographer Photius of the ninth century AD glosses breakfast merely as 'a bit to eat before lunch'.

Wine, as Homer noted, was one of the chief components of breakfast. In fact, the Greek word for breakfast, *akratisma*, was supposedly derived from *akratos* meaning 'unmixed wine'. The reason for this was that the meal was often no more than bread dipped in wine. The Romans similarly derived their word *ientaculum* from *ieiunus* meaning 'hungry' or 'fasting'. Menander, the Athenian comic playwright, wrote a play entitled *The Women at Breakfast* and a surviving fragment has someone asking for another drink and being told in what seems an aggrieved tone that the maid, because she was foreign, had carried off the wine along with the food.

Bread was the other main component of breakfast. In big cities a snack of bread could be bought from boys selling loaves in the streets at dawn, but meat and cheese might be eaten as well. There were numerous types of bread in the ancient world and some of these have survived into the modern world, for example *dipyros*, which was preserved by the monks of the Orthodox church. This was bread that was baked twice and eaten hot, either on its own or with a sliced egg. A lexicon of the Byzantine period called *The Suda* or *Fortress* glosses the Greek word *paxamas* as a Latin term for *dipyros* bread. Patrick Leigh Fermor, in his book *Mani*, describes how he ate *paximadia* with a peasant called Yorgo: the dark brown pumices of bread were soaked in a spring and then eaten with garlic. Chris Connell, who recorded his experiences of travelling around the islands of the Cyclades in the 1970s and sketched the age-old crafts and way of life, writes that small loaves called *pauloi* were broken into five pieces and returned to the oven to cook overnight. In the Britain of the post-Roman period, the monk Gildas, who lived in the sixth century, advises the eating of *paxmatum* as plain fare for clergy who had transgressed church laws by having intercourse either 'normally or in the manner of a sodomite'.

Breakfasts were not always rushed or solitary occasions, as two examples from the Greek world show. The first is an inscription from Priene on the Aegean coast of what is now Turkey which specifies a communal breakfast after a procession to mark the new moon at the end of September, the beginning of the ancient Greek month of Boedromion. The second is Herodas, writing in the third century BC, who describes a domestic scene in which several women, together with their children, visited each other for breakfast, the account perhaps describing a religious feast, although this is not certain. Religious rituals are remarkably durable, and a record of their existence in the Hellenistic period can be taken as implying their continuation under the Roman empire. In the later Roman world breakfast was taken to signify the end of fasting before the Pascal feast. Religious breakfasts are in fact attested: for example Lucius, the hero of Apuleius's novel *The Golden Ass*, eats a religious breakfast as part of his initiation into the worship of the goddess Isis. Invitations to breakfast are also recorded: Martial wrote a poem about a breakfast for a certain Caecilianus, but his guest did not turn up until lunchtime and Martial wondered why he had bothered being friendly. Elsewhere Martial ridiculed Fescennia, who desperately chewed expensively flavoured pastilles for breakfast in order to cover up the smell of his excessive drinking the day before.

It can be seen that the evidence for breakfast in the Roman world is disparate and dispersed. This may be ascribed to the nature of the sources, breakfast containing little that was worthy of comment or reflection. When Suetonius alleges that the gluttonous emperor Vitellius consumed four sumptuous meals a day, he is merely playing on the idea that breakfast was for many people a simple occasion. The following recipes are typical of this simplicity.

CARTHAGINIAN PORRIDGE

Puls Punica

'Cook Carthaginian porridge like this. Put a pound of emmer groats into water and ensure that they are properly soaked. Pour the emmer groats into a clean bowl, add three pounds of fresh cheese, half a pound of honey and one egg, and mix everything together well. Transfer to a new pot.'

[*Cato* On Agriculture]

This recipe seems to break off before it has finished its descriptive task, for the expectation is for a cooking process to be mentioned, yet there is none. Groats are cereal grains that have had their husks removed. The term used here is *alica*, which are specifically groats from emmer wheat. My version of this recipe employs flattened wheat grains that are sold in most health food shops. In taste they are similar to groats, but their thinness obviates the need for soaking. Porridge is perhaps a misnomer, because the consistency of the dish is more pudding-like, but its substantial nature is more appropriate for beginning a working day than rounding off a meal.

300 g/10 oz Cheddar cheese (see pp.27–8)
100 g/3 oz wheat flakes
60 g/2 oz clear honey
1 egg

Grate the cheese and mix it together with the wheat flakes together in a heavy casserole. Stir in the honey so that it is well distributed. Whisk the egg and fold it into the cheese and wheat mixture. Gently press the mixture down so that the surface is even. Put a lid on the casserole and place in an oven pre-heated to 190°C/380°F/gas mark 5 for 30 minutes. Serve immediately with a spoonful of honey if you wish. The texture of this dish is soft and spongy, the taste extremely cheesy.

CREAMED WHEAT

Granea Triticea

'Make wheat grain like this. Put half a pound of clean wheat into a clean bowl, wash well and both remove the husks and rinse well. Next put it with clean water into a pot and cook. When it has been cooked, gradually add enough milk to make a thick cream.'

[*Cato* On Agriculture]

This bland dish calls for salt or honey or an accompanying savoury sauce. As a breakfast with salt it is not unlike the porridge served in Scotland, and using processed wheat flakes means that the details about cleaning and husking can be ignored.

100 g/3 oz wheat flakes
250 ml/¹/₂ pint milk

Boil the wheat flakes in 1 pint of water for 10 minutes, stirring occasionally. Then add the milk and simmer very gently for a further ten minutes. Serve hot.

MILLET PORRIDGE

Milium in Aqua

'First boil the millet in fresh hot water and, when the grains begin to split open, cook them in the water with the addition of goat's milk. Cook them slowly in the same way as I detailed above for rice.'

[*Anthimus* On Foods]

When prepared like this, millet does in fact taste remarkably like rice. Rice had been cooked in classical Greece, although it was an expensive commodity imported from India. Presumably millet furnished a useful substitute, for at the time of Anthimus writing his treatise the trade routes from the Middle East and further afield into northern Europe had been disrupted by the collapse of Roman imperial rule. J.M. Renfrew suggests that millet was cultivated in central Greece as early as 5,000 BC, whereas rice does not make an appearance even in Egypt until Arabic times.

150 g/5 oz millet
600 ml/1 ¹/4 pints goat's milk
1 tsp sea salt (optional)

Put the millet and 1 pint of water in a pan, bring to the boil, then lower the flame and simmer with the lid on for 30 minutes, or until the millet grains are soft and begin to split. Then add the goat's milk and simmer gently for a further 30 minutes, stirring occasionally to prevent any sticking to the bottom of the pan. Add the sea salt if required just before serving; this is not in the original recipe, but seems necessary to add flavour to the dish. Serve either on its own, or use as an accompaniment to other recipes, for example stews, sweet biscuits or flavoured honey.

BARLEY PORRIDGE

Polenta de Hordeo

'However, whatever sort of barley has been prepared, people mix in a mill twenty pounds of barley, three pounds of linseed, half a pound of coriander seed and a cup of salt, toasting all these things beforehand.'

[*Pliny* Natural History]

The inclusion of linseed provides a rather subtle nutty taste to the porridge. It can be eaten on its own or used to accompany a stew or vegetables.

150 g / 5 oz pearl barley
1 1/2 tsp linseed
2 tbsp ground coriander
1 tsp sea salt

Soak the barley and linseed in water overnight. Rinse and put in a heavy pan with 2 1/2 pints of water, ground coriander seeds and sea salt. Bring to the boil and then simmer gently for at least an hour, checking occasionally in case further water has to be added. Taste to see if any more salt is needed. Serve hot.

PYRAMID CAKES

Pyramides

'In his book On Cakes, *Iatrokles makes mention of* khoirinai *and what are called* pyramous, *which he says are no different from what people call* pyramis. *For these are made from toasted wheat soaked in honey. They are served to those who have stayed up all night for religious festivals.'*
[*Athenaeus* The Partying Professors]

I have fought battles with this recipe, staying up late at night to contemplate not prayer but the oven. Should the wheat be toasted before being soaked in honey? Or after? My experiments have resulted either in brittle cakes that endanger the teeth or soggy lumps that do not hold together. The latter point is important, for the name of the cake refers to those famous pointed Egyptian monuments. The Greeks lent humorous sobriquets to everything the Pharoahs had earlier constructed: obelisk means 'small kebab stick' and pyramid probably derives from this ridiculous cake. The version that I present here does work and will not affect delicate dentistry, although the wheat flakes are toasted after being soaked in honey rather than before.

100 g/3 oz wheat flakes
100 g/3 oz white flour
100 g/3 oz clear honey
2 tbsp water
1 tbsp olive oil

Soak the wheat flakes in the honey for 6 hours or overnight. Then combine all the ingredients and knead into a sticky dough. Smear a baking tray thoroughly with olive oil. Use your fingers to shape a spoonful of the mixture into a little pyramid about 1 inch in height. Arrange the pyramids on a baking tray. Bake for 15 minutes in an oven pre-heated to 200°C/400°F/gas mark 6. Take out and stand to cool.

ROSE HONEY

Rhodomeli

'Recipe for rose honey: fine roses, wild ones if possible. Cut away the white part at the end of the rose petals, squeeze them in a press and take two pints of the juice and one pint of honey. Skim off the froth on the honey, add the honey to the rose juice and put in a storage jar; stir vigorously and store away in a place that is not damp.'
[*Bassus* Country Matters]

Roses are often used in Middle Eastern cooking and Arto der Haroutunian gives details of a recipe called *varti-anoush* which consists of fresh rose petals, lemon juice, sugar and water. The ancient recipe is simpler and of greater rosy redolence. Bottled rose water can be bought from supermarkets and health food shops.

75 g/2 oz honey
125 ml/¼ pint rose water

Stir the rose water into the honey and store in a sterilised jar. It will keep for several months. Use to flavour porridges or as a dip for fresh bread.

LUNCH

Lunch was not eaten by everyone in the ancient world, so doctors were at pains to explain why someone unused to this meal could fall ill as a result of eating in the middle of the day. It would be foolish to ignore medicine when examining Roman diet, partly because so much of our evidence derives from medical writers, and also because the kitchen and the surgery were so closely interlinked. Galen stresses throughout his works that a good doctor must also have a sound knowledge of cooking. The situation today is not dissimilar, with dietitians issuing guidelines on the amount of fruit and vegetables needed for protection against various diseases. The difference lies in the ideas involved between the current preoccupation with anti-oxidants and dietary fibre and the ancient insistence on the balancing of the four humours and qualities. In a world without effective treatment for many illnesses, recourse in the first instance was always to food and diet. *On Ancient Medicine*, a key text which illustrates this close relationship and has an immediate bearing on the eating of lunch, was written by Hippocrates in the fifth century BC.

> That over-eating should cause no less sickness than excessive fasting is easily understood by reference to healthy people. Some find it better to eat but once a day and consequently make this their

habit. Others similarly find it better for them to have a meal both at noon and in the evening. Then there are some who adopt one or other of these habits merely because it pleases them or because of chance circumstances. On the grounds of health it matters little to most people whether they take one meal a day or two. But there are some who, if they do not follow their usual custom, do not escape the result and they may be stricken with a serious illness within a day. There are some who, if they take lunch when this custom does not agree with them, at once become both mentally and physically dull; they yawn and grow drowsy and thirsty. If subsequently they should have dinner as well, they suffer from wind, indigestion and diarrhoea and, not infrequently, this has been the start of a serious illness even though they have taken no more than twice the amount of food they have been accustomed to. In the same way a man, who is used to having lunch because he finds this agrees with him, cannot omit the meal without suffering great weakness, panic attacks and faintness.

Hippocrates continues by saying that those who usually eat only once a day suffer when taking an extra meal because the stomach has not yet had time to digest or evacuate the previous meal. Such stomachs, being slow in digestion, need rest and relaxation. Those who are in the habit of having a meal at midday suffer when they have to go without, for their bodies require nourishment and the food taken at the previous meal has been used up.

Hippocrates says as much in *Diet in Acute Diseases*, but with considerably more emphasis. If someone who normally has two meals a day omits lunch, he will find himself weak, feeble, averse to all exertion and the victim of heart-burn. On the other hand, if anyone who is not accustomed to lunch eats at midday, he will feel bloated and heavy in his stomach, as well as drowsy. All this is not as far-fetched as it seems: the gurgling and rumbling of midday stomachs in any office or classroom testify to the truth of Hippocrates' first declaration, whilst the tendency to nod off after a particularly large lunch supports the second.

For doctors in the ancient world, change meant disease, there being four simple and four composite classes of disease. As regards the former, there were hot, cold, wet and dry diseases; whilst of the latter there were hot and dry, cold and dry, hot and moist or cold and moist diseases. The body was regulated by the four qualities – hot, cold, wet and dry – and the four humours, for Hippocrates wrote in his *Nature of Man* that the body contained blood, phlegm, yellow bile and black bile, through which pain is felt or health enjoyed. Galen elaborates on this idea in *On Humours* in which he states that health can be characterised by the equality and symmetry of these humours. Diseases arose whenever these humours were deficient or excessive in quantity, quality, shifting of position, irregular combination or putrefaction. Health could be restored by the removal and the addition and by the thinning and thickening of the humours, and generally through their mildness and symmetry. When a person fell ill, the aim of the doctor was to restore this equilibrium through diet, which not only included the sense of the modern term, but also physical exercise, as Hippocrates says in his work *On Diet*.

Galen explains the diet necessary to restore a person to health who, though unused to lunch, has nevertheless eaten some. First a bath was prescribed, then sleep, after which a long slow walk was to be taken. If an evacuation of the bowels then occurred, a patient was permitted to have dinner and to drink a little wine; if, however, the bowels remained unmoved, then the patient's body was to be rubbed down with warm olive oil and a glass of watery white or sweet wine was to be drunk before sleep. Doctors hoped to restore the natural balance of the body with the aid of food and drink. Bread baked in the ashes, because it was the driest of all breads, was useful in combating 'moist bowels and indigestion and all those things that have phlegm'. Bitter almonds and garlic cut through phlegm, cabbages reduced black bile, honey and other sweet liquids furnished material for yellow bile, beef and bread made from bran engendered black bile whilst unripe apples produced phlegm. Food not only provided nourishment, but also strengthened or weakened the health, saturating the body with one humour or depriving it of another.

Breakfast, as has been seen, was a very simple affair, so lunch was of immense importance for health and energy and it is understandable that our sources sometimes suggest different times, for an early start to the day would necessitate an earlier lunch. It was generally taken around midday, as Martial says in a poem about the times of the different activities of the day. The emperor Claudius, according to the biographer Suetonius, took such pleasure in the combats with wild beasts, and in particular those that were fought at midday, that he would go down to the amphitheatre at daybreak and, after dismissing the people for lunch at noon, would remain in his seat to munch on his own repast. Galen used to have a simple lunch of just bread after visiting his patients or attending to some civic duties, and this he ate round about the fourth hour of the day, or about ten o'clock, earlier than most people. On the other hand, the doctor Antiochus, a contemporary of Galen, used to have breakfast of bread with boiled Attic honey around the third hour, or at the latest at the fourth hour. His lunch was at the seventh hour, or two o'clock. Antiochus proved how balanced and symmetrical his diet was by living into his eighties. Telephus the grammarian was, at the time of Galen writing his *On the Preservation of Health*, almost a hundred; he ate porridge mixed with honey for breakfast at the third hour and had lunch at the seventh hour or a little earlier. It was not the time of eating that mattered but the adherence to a precise pattern for, as has been seen, change engendered disease. The Roman doctor Celsus, however, allowed some variation so long as it was occasional. He stated that no harm would come if one attended a banquet, ate more than was sufficient or took food twice rather than once a day, provided one did not do these things regularly.

What people ate for lunch also varied considerably. As has been noted, Galen used to eat bread on its own for lunch, but he adds that some people liked to have it with dates, olives, honey or salt, and some even had a drink. Provided what they ate could be digested by the tenth hour, or in other words by dinner time, no harm would result. Since many people exercised in the afternoon, an excess of food at lunch could cause severe problems. The doctor Antiochus was served rock and sea fish for lunch to relax his bowels, whilst Telephus the grammar teacher enjoyed vegetables as a first course and fish or fowl as a second course. He balanced this lavish lunch with a frugal evening meal of bread soaked in diluted wine. Seneca, in one of his letters, reminds Lucilius of his simple lifestyle, munching his way through dry bread that did not even require him to wash his hands afterwards. Pliny the Elder reserved his appetite for the evening. Pliny the Younger, writing to Babius Macer of his uncle, said:

When he got home he gave over any spare time to his work. After having something to eat – his meals during the day were light, simple and old-fashioned – he would in the summer often lie in the sun when not too busy, and a book was read aloud while he made notes and extracts.

Plutarch remarks on this ancient habit of the Romans of taking their early meals alone but eating dinner with their friends. Fronto wrote to Marcus Aurelius of his 'tiny piece of bread' at lunch, compared to the boiled beans, onions and fish of his companions. Martial describes a huge cheese stamped with the image of the moon that was sufficient for a thousand lunches for slaves. In the time of Plautus – that is the second century BC – cooked lunches seem to have been slightly unusual, to judge from the surprised questions of the characters in his plays. In *The Little Carthaginian*, for example, Lycus asks Agorastocles: 'Have you eaten a hot lunch today? Tell me!' And Pliny in his *Natural History* tells of the frugal Catus Aelius who, when consul in 198 BC, did not accept the silver plate presented to him by envoys from the Greek state of Aetolia, preferring to eat his lunch off earthenware. Presumably his food was as modest as his crockery, although Pliny declines to comment here on such mundane matters as bread and beans.

Cicero, in his speech *Against Piso*, reproaches his opponent for having lunch in a *caupona*, the equivalent of a fast-food restaurant serving fried foods:

> Do you remember, you foul creature, when I visited you at about the fifth hour with Gaius Piso, how you were just coming out of some rough dive with a hood over your head and slippers on your feet? And how, when from your stinking mouth you had breathed over us the fumes of that disgusting bar, you gave as your excuse troubled health, claiming you usually took for it some medicine helped down with a drop of wine.

The Roman attitude to these bars is discussed in the introduction to the following chapter, but Cicero's comments show that the typical time for lunch was midday and that the serving of wine was common at these establishments. Martial says that for lunch workmen had beet, which cooks tried in vain to liven up with pepper, and he speaks elsewhere of wild game being eaten for the midday meal. The sons of Quintus Arrius even lunched on nightingales, Horace exclaims with horror, but this is surely for mock effect since birds like this cannot have been such a rare item on the menu. Even in twentieth-century Italy, as Elizabeth David recorded in her *Italian Food*, all kinds of small birds such as thrushes, larks, robins, blackbirds and quails are eaten roasted or grilled, and Charles Edwards in *Sardinia and the Sardes*, published in 1889, recalls how the epicures of Cagliari were fond of larks and nightingales, consuming thousands of these little birds year by year. How many more birds were available to the Romans when the population of Italy was much smaller and the natural habitat of the birds more extensive? The Greek and Latin phrasebook known as *The Monaco Conversations* lists things to be bought for lunch: fish, vegetables, mushrooms, figs, peaches, pears and apples. Horace quotes an Epicurean philosopher saying that to remain healthy in summer one ought to eat blackberries after lunch before the sun gets too hot. The many *popinae* and *cauponae* in Roman cities must have served a wide variety of lunches, from fried fish and stews to bread and cheese. Galen describes a popular snack in the cities of Asia: bread hot from the oven eaten with a mild fresh cheese called *oxygalaktinos*.

Seneca disapproved of drinking after lunch, as did Cicero, but the emperor Nero enjoyed a few glasses of wine at lunch and *The Monaco Conversations* has some phrases for asking a guest to lunch 'frugally', which does not excluded the tasting of some 'good everyday wine'. Apuleius in his *The Golden Ass* tells the story of the wife of a poor craftsman, who compares her lot in life, despite her own adultery, to that of her neighbour enjoying some wine before lunch before staggering off to bed with her lover. Juvenal mocks the preposterous Greek stories of how whole streams were drained dry when the Persian army under Xerxes had lunch during its invasion of Greece.

Where did people eat their lunches? Pliny the Elder has been mentioned reclining outside and listening to a book being read aloud, and there were the *cauponae* and *popinae* where people stood to eat, or sat at stools and benches. Cicero, in a letter to his friend Atticus, describes how he and his family had lunch at a farm at Arcanum, reclining to eat as at a dinner. Seneca enjoyed picnics: he and his friend Maximus took a few slaves – a mere carriage load – and had lunch lying on mattresses. According to Seneca, nothing could have been subtracted from this lunch, for all they took with them were the clothes they were wearing and some bread and dried figs, but considering this took an hour to prepare, it might be suspected that perhaps they ate a little more elaborately. There were wedding lunches and lunches to commemorate military victories such as those of Julius Caesar in Spain. Farmers and shepherds carried their lunches in a leather bag. Theocritus paints a picture of a little boy sitting on a dry-stone wall guarding a vineyard loaded with reddening clusters, but he is distracted from his task because he is weaving cages in which to catch cicadas, and one of the foxes plunders the ripe grapes while the other uses all her ingenuity to rob the boy of his lunch. In Babrius there is a tale of a fox eating a goatherd's pouch full of the previous day's meat and bread. The goatherd Daphnis, in the novel by Longus, always carried with him his satchel for lunch. A rustic lunch could consist of bread with wild vegetables, figs or grapes. Provided the siesta did not extend too long, it was probably safe to drink Mendaean wine, an Egyptian beverage made with dates: Hermippus said that it was so good that even the gods wet themselves in their soft beds because of it, a most embarrassing side-effect.

The Greeks and Romans generally slept in the afternoon following their lunch, although for Cicero this was a novel experience brought about by his lack of work after his retirement from public life. Even Seneca dozed a little after his lunch of dry bread, whilst Horace enjoyed pottering around the house after eating 'not greedily'. Ovid, however, enjoyed more exciting afternoons making love with his girlfriend Corinna in a shaded room, the afternoon sun filtering through a half-open shutter, until they both collapsed exhausted. Catullus hoped for more with his 'sweet Ipsithilla', for as he lies prostrate on his bed, feeling full after lunch, he hopes for *nouem continuas fututiones* or 'nine consecutive fucks' at her house, the Latin vernacular perhaps lending a note of desperation to his predicament. Whether she invited him that afternoon we do not know. Aristotle recommended a large lunch and a light dinner if the *fututiones* were to be in the evening.

For the Roman legions lunch was important for sustaining bodily strength and energy during a battle. Livy tells of the consul Aemilius ensuring that his troops had eaten a good lunch before facing the

Etruscan army at the battle for Sutrium in 311 BC. His dietary tactics paid off, for the Romans won despite the enemy force being superior in numbers. Sometimes, however, having lunch was dangerous, as the Spartans discovered to their cost when facing the Argive army at Sepeia near Tiryns. The Argives attacked while the Spartans were eating lunch and many of them were killed, the remainder only just escaping to a small wood nearby.

Lunch, in conclusion, was on the whole simple, but the evidence is scanty, and while Seneca could manage on a piece of dry bread at lunch, it seems obvious that workmen and farm labourers would have required something more substantial. Martial hints at this when he describes the giant cheese already mentioned as being suitable for one thousand lunches for slaves. Pliny in his *Natural History* informs us that such cheeses could weigh up to one thousand pounds. A lump of cheese, some bread and some olives and fruit were probably what most people had for their lunch in the ancient world, and this was eaten around midday after which, in the summer, the heat became too oppressive for any serious work.

As for the medical theories about lunch examined at the beginning of this chapter, these can only have been aimed at the upper classes of society. It is unlikely that slaves in the country or the urban plebs would have paid any attention to them, even if they had known about these theories. Celsus stated that people who did not engage in manual labour and exercised infrequently, such as scholars, should observe a strict diet as their constitution was delicate and easily upset. So the lunches enjoyed by Galen and Seneca were in accord with medical theories, the former because of his profession, the latter because of his desire to lead a frugal life. Bread was regarded as a simple food and the one least active in promoting any change. Both Hippocrates and Galen made extensive use of bread in various diets designed to cure diseases, the bread being eaten on its own or broken up in water, honey and water *(hydromel)* or vinegar and water *(oxymel)*. Telephus the grammar teacher reversed lunch and dinner, eating bread at dinner, and fish, meat and vegetables at lunch; thus the diet remained balanced. But whilst symmetry of diet and the humours was the aim of doctors in the ancient world, most people of course just wanted to fill their stomachs at lunch.

SOFT BREAD

Hapalos Artos

*'Amongst the Greeks is a bread called "soft" which is made with a
little milk and sufficient olive oil and salt. The dough must be
made supple. This bread is called "Cappadocian" since for the most
part "soft" bread is made in Cappadocia. The Syrians call such
bread* lakhma *and in Syria this bread is delicious through being
eaten warm.'*

[*Athenaeus* The Partying Professors]

I tend to use dried yeast for my bread, because although fresh yeast
is reasonably easy to find in shops, the age of the specimens on the
shelves is not always clear, with the annoying result that success in
baking can be a hit and miss affair. At least with dried yeast the
leavening effect is consistent, whilst the difference in taste is negligible.
The purist must turn a blind eye to the use of sugar to reactivate the
yeast in this and some of the recipes that follow; in Roman times
sugar was known solely as a cane to be chewed for medicinal
purposes. Dried yeast is also available in sachets mixed with react-
ivating and proving agents; sugar is then not required, but the added
ingredients similarly detract from total authenticity.

400 g/14 oz strong white flour
125 ml/^{1}/$_{4}$ pint warm water
1 ^{1}/$_{2}$ tsp dried yeast
1 tsp sugar
60 ml/2 fl oz olive oil
75 ml/3 fl oz warm milk
^{1}/$_{2}$ tsp sea salt

Dissolve the dried yeast in the warm water, adding a teaspoon of
sugar to help the process of reactivisation, and leave for 15 minutes
until frothy. Put the flour in a large bowl, mix with the salt, form a
well in the centre and fill with the yeasty water, olive oil and milk.
Combine the flour and liquids to make a dough, kneading firmly for
five minutes. Add a little more flour or water if required to achieve
the desired consistency. Smear a 1 lb baking tin with oil and dust

with flour. Press the dough into the bottom of the tin. Cover the tin with cling film and allow to stand in a warm place for an hour. Set the oven at 200°C/400°F/gas mark 6 and bake the bread for about 40 minutes. The loaf will have a pale crust and a deliciously soft crumb.

MUSHROOM BREAD

Boletinos Artos

'What is known as boletinos *bread is shaped like a mushroom. The kneading-bowl on which the dough is placed is greased and sprinkled with poppy seeds, so that the dough does not stick during rising. When it is put in the oven, some groats are sprinkled over the earthenware pan. Then the loaf is put on top and takes on a very beautiful colour like that of smoked cheese.'*
[*Athenaeus* The Partying Professors]

White flour is necessary for this bread because brown flour will not give the necessary smoky colour after baking. The use of white flour would have made this bread something of a luxury.

450 g/1 lb strong white flour
400 ml/14 fl oz warm water
1¹/₂ tsp dried yeast
1 tsp sugar
1 beaten egg-white
4 tbsp poppy seeds
1 tbsp wheat flakes
1 tbsp olive oil
1 tsp sea salt

Dissolve the sugar in 150 ml/¹/₄ pint of the warm water. Sprinkle with the dried yeast, stir and leave to froth for 15 minutes. Then combine the flour, yeast, olive oil, salt and the rest of the water in a mixing bowl and knead until you have a supple dough. Oil a round cake tin with a diameter of 14 cm/5½ inches. Sprinkle the poppy seeds over the oiled sides of the tin so that they are evenly spread. Press the dough into the bottom of the tin, cover the tin loosely with a plastic bag (I use an old shopping bag for this purpose), and leave in a warm place to rise. After 2 hours or so the dough will rise until it flows over the top of the tin, thus creating a mushroom shape. Remove the plastic bag, brush the top of the loaf with the egg-white and sprinkle on the wheat flakes. Bake the loaf for 40 minutes in an oven set at 200°C/400°F/gas mark 6.

PLAITED BREAD

Streptikios Artos

'Twisted bread is made with a little milk, and there is added pepper and a small amount of olive oil; or if not olive oil, then lard.'
[*Athenaeus* The Partying Professors]

There are many contemporary plaited breads. I have chosen a simple plait for this bread, as we do not know what sort of pattern was used in this Roman version and it seems needless to elaborate. The pepper, of course, makes this very much a savoury bread, although it is also tasty when spread with honey. Substituting lard for olive oil stresses the uncertain nature of food supplies before the modern era. In his book on Sardinian bread, Paolo Piquereddu recalls that breads on the island were made according to recipes that suited the tastes of different families, the time of year and the availability of seasonings like olives, tomatoes, cheese, potatoes, onions and meat. There are two reasons for the use of goat's milk in this and other recipes: the first is the predominance of goats over cows in Roman times, particularly in the lands around the Mediterranean; the second is flavour, the sharpness of this milk adding a necessary piquancy to the dough.

600 g/1 lb 3 oz wholemeal flour
150 ml/5 fl oz warm water
1 ¹/2 tsp dried yeast
1 tsp sugar
200 ml/7 fl oz goat's milk
60 ml/2 fl oz olive oil
1 tsp ground pepper
1 egg-white

Dissolve the sugar in the warm water. Sprinkle on the dried yeast and whisk. Cover with cling film and leave to reactivate in a warm place for 15 minutes. Combine all the ingredients together in a large mixing bowl. Knead for 5 minutes until you have a supple dough. Cover the mixing bowl with cling film and allow the dough to rise for 2 hours. Then knead again and divide the dough into three equal portions. Using your hands, roll out the portions into 30 cm/12 inch lengths. Make a plait, pressing gently at the centre and fusing the ends to prevent the loaf from falling apart. Place the loaf on an oiled baking tray, cover loosely with a plastic bag so that there is room for the dough to expand and allow to rise again. After an hour glaze the loaf with the beaten egg-white and bake for 40 minutes at 200°C/400°F/gas mark 6. Serve with a savoury dip.

SPONGE BREAD

Nanos

'Nanos: *a loaf of bread with the consistency of cake prepared with cheese and olive oil.*'
[*Athenaeus* The Partying Professors]

I make two versions of this bread, both in their own ways resembling cake, but with very different characteristics. The first recipe produces a large marbled loaf with a stretchy crumb, whilst the second is like a modern Italian *focaccia*.

VERSION I

300 g/10 oz strong white flour
200 ml/7 fl oz warm water
1 1/2 tsp dried yeast
1 tsp sugar
100 g/3 oz Cheddar cheese (see pp.27-8)
60 ml/2 fl oz olive oil
1/2 tsp sea salt

Dissolve the sugar in the water, sprinkle on the dried yeast and whisk. Cover with cling film and leave to reactivate for 15 minutes in a warm place. Sift the flour with the salt and combine with the yeast mixture and olive oil. Knead until supple, slapping the dough occasionally against the work surface to give the bread a more stretchy consistency. Cover with cling film and allow to rise for 2 hours. After kneading again, divide the dough into three equal portions. Grate the cheese and divide it into three equal mounds. Press the first portion of dough into an oiled 1 lb bread tin. Arrange a layer of cheese on top of the dough, taking care to leave the edges of the dough free from cheese. Then press the next portion of dough on top of the cheese and repeat the process. Reserve the last mound of cheese. Place the tin in a plastic bag and allow the loaf to rise for 1 hour. Bake in an oven at 200°C/400°F/gas mark 6 for 30 minutes, then sprinkle with the reserved cheese and return to the oven for a further 10 minutes.

VERSION II

400 g/14 oz spelt flour
250 ml/9 fl oz warm water
1 1/2 tsp dried yeast
1 tsp sugar
1 tsp sea salt
60 ml/2 fl oz olive oil
60 g/2 oz goat's cheese

Dissolve the sugar in the water, sprinkle on the dried yeast and whisk. Cover with cling film and leave to reactivate for 15 minutes in a warm place. Sift the flour with the salt, combine with the yeast mixture and olive oil. Knead until you have a supple dough. Cover with cling film and allow to rise for 2 hours. Oil two round baking trays about 22 cm/9 inches in diameter. Knead the dough again, divide into two balls of equal size and, on a floured surface, work these into thin discs. Place these disks in the baking trays and allow to rise again, covering the dough with a plastic bag, for 1 hour. Dice the cheese and make hollows in the dough with your index finger, almost pressing through to the tin. Place a piece of cheese in each hollow and put the breads in an oven pre-heated to 200°C/400°F/ gas mark 6 for 25 minutes.

PASTRY BALLS

Globi

'Pastry balls should be made like this. Mix cheese with spelt flour in the same way. From this you can make as many pastry balls as you like. Put some fat in a bronze pot. Cook one or two pastry balls at a time, turning them frequently with two spatulas, remove when cooked, coat with honey, sprinkle with poppy seeds and so serve.'

[*Cato* On Agriculture]

These pastry balls with their hard shells and slightly sweet taste make excellent accompaniments to a glass of wine or beer. It is not difficult to imagine them displayed on the counter of a Roman bar for clerks and businessmen to nibble at midday.

200 g/7 oz Cheddar cheese (see pp.27-8)
100 g/3 oz spelt flour
1 egg
Olive oil for frying
60 g/2 oz clear honey
1 tbsp poppy seeds

Grate the cheese and work it into the flour with your finger tips. When the mixture resembles breadcrumbs in texture, add the egg and work into a dough. Break off small pieces and roll each of these in your hands, forming balls about 2 cm/1 inch in diameter. Heat the olive oil in a heavy pan. You will need a depth of at least 2 cm/1 inch of olive oil. When the oil is hot, but not smoking, gently lower in the pastry balls on a perforated spoon. The pastry balls take about 5 minutes to cook and will be golden brown on the outside when done. Drain the pastry balls on kitchen paper. Now heat the honey in a frying pan until it is very runny. Pour the poppy seeds onto a plate, roll the balls in the honey until thoroughly coated, then transfer to the plate and coat with poppy seeds. Serve warm or cold with a drink.

SESAME BISCUITS

Itrion

'Itrion: *a thin biscuit made with sesame seeds and honey. Anacreon records it: "I had lunch, breaking off a small piece of itrion and drinking a flask of wine."*'
[*Athenaeus* The Partying Professors]

Nowadays we can buy sesame biscuits in supermarkets, but a glance at the list of ingredients, including glucose syrup and invert starch, will confirm the artificial nature of the age in which we live. Conversely, this ancient recipe contains just three natural ingredients.

100 g/3 oz sesame seeds
60 g/2 oz clear honey
Olive oil

Pour the honey into a pan, bring to the boil and simmer for 10 minutes. Add the sesame seeds and simmer for another 5 minutes, stirring frequently. Spread the mixture as thinly as possible on a plate that has been previously greased with olive oil. Flatten out with a spatula – wetting the spatula from time to time will help the process. Allow to stand for a couple of hours, then cut into wedges and serve as a sweetmeat.

CHEESEBREAD

Libum

'Libum *should be made like this. Thoroughly mash two pounds of cheese in a mortar. When it is properly mashed, add one pound of ordinary wheat flour or, if you want the bread to be softer, half a pound of fine wheat flour, and mix well with the cheese. Add one egg and mix together well. Then form a loaf, place on leaves and bake gently under an earthenware dome in a hot oven.'*

[*Cato* On Agriculture]

Kinta Beevor describes the making of *focaccette* in the Italy of the 1960s by a process which seems remarkably similar to that of *libum*. First a large fire was lit, then terracotta discs (presumably with raised edges) called *testi* were placed in the heart of the flames. As soon as these *testi* were hot they were removed with tongs, filled with unleavened dough and covered with the other hot *testi*. Then, as the *testi* cooled, the bread was cooked. In Roman times this bread was served as a birthday cake or presented as a humble offering to the gods.

500 g / 18 oz Cheddar cheese (see pp.27–8)
1 egg
250 g / 9 oz wholemeal flour
15-20 bay leaves

Grate the cheese. Beat the egg. Knead the grated cheese with the flour and beaten egg. This is hard work, but has to be done by hand, as a food-processor merely swirls the ingredients round and does not combine them. Use your fingertips to mix the cheese and flour together into the consistency of breadcrumbs, then gradually knead the small lumps into a larger mass, until you have made the required dough. Flatten the dough with a rolling pin until it is roughly ½ cm/ ⅓ inch thick. Make 15-20 rounds with a pastry cutter. Lay each disc on a bay leaf, place on an oiled baking tray and cover the tray tightly with silver foil to retain the moisture. Bake in an oven at 190°C/380°F/gas mark 5 for 40 minutes. Serve warm.

CHEESEBREAD WITH HONEY

Savillum

'Savillum *is made like this. Half a pound of ordinary flour, two and a half pounds of cheese, and mix together as for* libum. *Add a quarter of a pound of honey and one egg. Grease an earthenware dish with olive oil. When you have mixed all the ingredients together well, put into the dish, and cover the dish with an earthenware dome. Make sure that you properly bake the middle, where it is deepest. When it is cooked, remove the dish from the oven, paint with honey, sprinkle with poppy seeds, put back under the earthenware dome for a short time and then take it out of the oven. Serve in the dish with a spoon.'*

[*Cato* On Agriculture]

This, as Cato states, is another variation on the cheesy bread theme. I happen to prefer the basic *libum* recipe, yet the sweetness of *savillum* is also appealing.

475 g/15 oz Cheddar cheese (see pp.27–8)
100 g/3 oz spelt flour
1 egg
60 g/2 oz honey
1 tsp olive oil
2 tsp poppy seeds

Grate the cheese. Add the flour and work it into the cheese with the tips of your fingers, gradually combining the two so that they form a mixture like breadcrumbs. Beat the egg and add it and all but a tablespoon of honey to the flour and cheese. Knead into a dough. Use the olive oil to grease a casserole. Press the dough into the bottom of the casserole and cover it with a lid. Bake in the oven at 180°C/350°F/gas mark 4 for 45 minutes. Remove the casserole from the oven, spread the remaining honey over the top of the bread, sprinkle with sesame seeds and replace the lidded casserole in the oven for a further 10 minutes. Serve hot as a pudding.

SESAME SHORTBREAD

Elaphos

'A flat cake in the shape of a deer served at the festival of Elaphebolia made from spelt dough, honey and sesame seeds.'
[*Athenaeus* The Partying Professors]

The sesame seeds in this recipe provide enough oiliness to avoid a wholly dry biscuit. It is not impossible that cheese was used as a binding agent, but I prefer to use water as a variation on the cheese and honey combination.

100 g/3 oz spelt flour
100 g/3 oz sesame seeds
100 ml/3 fl oz water
60 g/2 oz honey
Olive oil

Put the ingredients except the olive oil into a large mixing bowl and knead together thoroughly until you have a smooth dough. Roll the dough out thinly on a floured board. Then, using either a sharp knife or a pastry cutter, make deer-shaped cakes and place them on an oiled baking tray. Bake in the oven for 40 minutes at 180°C/350°F/gas mark 4. Serve as a biscuit with puréed fruit.

PANCAKES

Tagenitai

*'Pancakes are prepared with just olive oil; the olive oil is put into a
frying pan which is placed over a smokeless fire, and onto the heated
olive oil is poured the meal with a lot of water; then as it is briskly
fried in the olive oil it sets and thickens like fresh cheese; at which
point those who are preparing it turn it over at once, causing the
upper surface to be bottom so that it is in contact with the frying
pan, and what was formerly at the bottom, when it is sufficiently
cooked, they raise up so that it is at the top; and when the part that
is underneath has set, they turn the pancake over again perhaps two
or three times, until it seems to them to be cooked evenly ... Some
people mix with it some honey, and there are those who mix in some
sea salt too; this is in fact a sort of flat cake, just like the other such
sorts of flat cake which people in the country and the poor in the
city make in a rough and ready fashion.'*

[*Galen, quoted in Oribasius* Medical Compilations]

If you try to make a pancake with just flour and water, the results are
either a heavy cake with a tendency to burn or a thin friable wafer
that is too greasy to be edible. What is called for is a leavening agent,
either egg, as in the French *crêpe*, or yeast, as in the Italian *pizza al
tegame*. Oribasius would surely have mentioned eggs in his recipe as
they are a distinct ingredient, whilst the yeast could be in the form
of a nugget of sour dough that would hardly require mention in a
description of bread. I specify yeast, on the assumption that it is
easier to use. These pancakes are still quite oily, but they are quite
light and tasty.

200 g/7 oz wholemeal flour
1/2 litre/1 pint warm water
1/2 tsp dried yeast
1 tsp sugar
1 tsp salt
Olive oil for frying

Dissolve the sugar in 100 ml/3 fl oz of water. Add the dried yeast and leave for 15 minutes to reactivate. Combine the yeast mixture with the flour, salt and the rest of the water and stir until you have a smooth batter, then cover with cling film and allow to bubble for one hour. Heat the oil in a frying pan. Gradually pour a ladle of batter into the pan, starting from the centre and working outwards. Fry until firm enough to flip over. Repeat until both sides are golden brown. Continue until all the batter has been exhausted and eat with vegetables or a stew.

BARLEY CAKE

Maza

'Melitoutta *is found in Trophonios meaning a cake, and similarly* hygieia, *for* hygieia *is a type of barley cake. People make the following barley cakes, the names of which are flower cake, lettuce cake, puff cake, wine cake, sacrificial cake ... Barley cakes are kneaded with sifted barley meal, barley biscuits with parched barley meal.'*

[*Pollux* Dictionary]

Milk and barley meal were the basic ingredients for this cake which was the alternative to bread in classical Greece. It was carefully distinguished by ancient writers from leavened barley breads. Flavourings such as wine, herbs or lettuce could be added to this simple recipe. My recipe uses honey and olive oil.

200 g/7 oz barley flour
100 ml/3 fl oz water
3 tbsp clear honey
2 tbsp olive oil

Combine all the ingredients in a mixing bowl and knead thoroughly. The result should be a firm and supple dough – roll this out as thinly as possible on a floured board. Oil a baking tray and, using a 10 cm/ 4 inch diameter pastry cutter, cut out rounds of dough and place these on the baking tray. Bake for 15 minutes in an oven pre-heated to 200°C/400°F/gas mark 6. Cool on a wire rack and serve with one of the vegetable purées (see pp.101-4).

CHEESE DISCS

Phthois

'Phthois *is made like this: break off some cheese, grate it, put it in a bronze sieve and work it through. Then add honey and half a cup of the finest wheat flour and knead it into a soft ball.'*
[*Athenaeus* The Partying Professors]

Athenaeus adds elsewhere that these discs resembled flat plates with raised centres. It is unusual to have descriptions for the appearance of foods, most ancient authors giving merely a basic list of the ingredients. It may be that some recipe books were illustrated, as at one point Apicius refers to a picture of the sort of frying pan required for that particular dish, in which case elaborate descriptions would have been unnecessary.

200 g/6 oz Cheddar cheese (see pp.27-8)
100 g/3 oz white flour
60 g/2 oz clear honey
Olive oil

Grate the cheese. Using your fingertips, work the cheese into the flour to make a soft dough. Add the honey and knead this thoroughly into the dough. Roll the dough into a ball and place in a plastic bag to stand for an hour. Then roll out thinly on a lightly floured surface. Use a 5 cm/2 inch pastry cutter to form discs. Place these on an oiled baking tray and cook in an oven at 180°C/350°F/gas mark 4 for 15 minutes or until golden brown. Serve with a vegetable purée.

FRIED PASTA

Lagana

'Laganon: *a type of small cake, dry, made from the finest wheat flour and fried in a frying pan in olive oil.*'
[*Hesychius* Dictionary]

Lagana (*laganon* in the singular) is the ancient equivalent of pasta, described by Athenaeus as 'both thin and light'. I often chuckle at the statement by the cookery writers Enrica and Vernon Jarratt that the fondness of the first-century BC orator Cicero for *lagana* was the only interesting thing about 'that self-righteous old windbag'. I share some of their aversion to Cicero: he was never a favourite of mine at school, and my students seem to be no fonder of him. On the other hand, his personal letters offer a fascinating glimpse into life among politicians and the intelligentsia in ancient Rome.

The Jarratts add that even now in southern Italy *tagliatelle* is named *laganono* or *lasanon* after its Roman precursor. The difference between the ancient Roman and modern Italian versions lies in the method of cooking: not until the Middle Ages was pasta dough cooked directly in water or soup. The poet Horace writes of eating leeks and chick-peas with *lagana*. As the Romans rarely used cutlery at the table, the *lagana* must have been used to scoop up whatever they were being served with.

125 g/ 4 oz wholemeal flour
100 ml/ 3 fl oz water
Olive oil for frying

Measure the flour into a bowl and add the water. Knead into a stiff dough, adding a touch more flour or water if necessary, and form into a ball. Flour a board and roll the ball out, turning the dough frequently to avoid sticking. When the dough is almost paper thin, cut into pieces about 2 cm/1 inch wide and 3 cm/1$^{1}/_{2}$ inches long. Pour some olive oil into a frying pan, heat and add the dough. Fry so that both sides are golden and crisp. Serve with soup or casseroles, either in true Roman fashion as an aid to eating, or in modern style as a tasty garnish.

FRIED SAVOURY PASTA

Artolagana

'To what is called artolaganon *there is added a little weak wine,
pepper, milk, and some olive oil or fat.'*
[*Athenaeus* The Partying Professors]

The Greek word *artuo* means 'I season' and these fried noodles are
just a more elaborate version of the basic *lagana*.

150 g/5 oz wholemeal flour
1 tbsp olive oil
60 ml/2 fl oz red wine
60 ml/2 fl oz goat's milk
1 tsp crushed peppercorns

The peppercorns should be crushed, not ground, so as to provide
little explosions of fire when the biscuit is being eaten. A very short
burst in an electric coffee-grinder will do the trick, but otherwise a
pestle and mortar can be used, although I find that peppercorns have
the annoying tendency to fly out of the mortar during pounding.
Combine all the ingredients in a mixing bowl and knead until you
have a smooth dough. Roll out thinly on a floured board, as with
lagana. Cut into strips and fry until golden and crisp. Serve in the
same way as *lagana*.

SEASONED FRITTERS

Catillus Ornatus

'What the Romans call catillus ornatus *is made like this: wash
and mash some lettuce, pour wine into a mortar and purée the
lettuce. Then squeeze off the juice, knead fine wheat flour into it,
let it rest for a while, then pound it vigorously. Add a little pork*

fat and pepper, pound it once again, draw it out thinly, cut it into pieces, put the pieces into a strainer and fry in the hottest olive oil.'

[*Athenaeus* The Partying Professors]

This is another ancestor of pasta, similar to the *lagana* described on p.65; a modern descendant called *uruq khass* which hails from Iraq consists of lettuce, onions, parsley, flour, eggs, cumin and pepper. It makes an excellent accompaniment to vegetable purées.

1 lettuce or large endive
150 ml/5 fl oz red wine
30 g/1 oz lard or vegetable fat
300 g/10 oz spelt flour
Black pepper
Olive oil for frying

Purée the lettuce in a blender with the red wine and vegetable fat. Ancient lettuces were more pungent in flavour than the rather bland varieties sold in supermarkets today, so an endive can be used to give a more pronounced green background to this dish. When the lettuce or endive is a pulp, add the spelt flour and process until a soft dough has been formed. Season with plenty of black pepper. Working on a floured board, pat the dough flat until it is as thin as possible. The dough should not need a rolling pin. Dust the top of the dough with flour. Use a pastry cutter to make the individual fritters; this gives a neater and therefore more appetising appearance to the fritters than the strips mentioned in the original text. Heat three tablespoons of olive oil in a frying pan and fry the fritters, turning once so they are brown on both sides. Drain the fritters on kitchen paper when cooked. More olive oil will be required as each batch is fried. Grind a generous amount of pepper over the fritters before serving.

PEA SOUP

Etnos

'Thick soup from peas is less flatulence-inducing than that made from broad beans and is easier to digest.'
[*Dieuches, quoted in Oribasius* Medical Compilations]

This soup could be seasoned with olive oil, dill, leeks, pennyroyal, mint, hyssop or pepper. I have chosen just four seasonings for my version, but there is room for further experiment. The fifth-century BC playwright Aristophanes writes of a slave girl preparing for Hercules a banquet comprising gallons of pea soup, loaves of bread, barbecued ox, roast chicken, fish and sweet wine, the joke being the juxtaposition of grand dishes fitting for the great hero such as ox and fish with this humble soup accompanied by bread.

150 g/5 oz dried peas
1 leek
1 tbsp olive oil
1 tsp dried dill tops
Sea salt

Soak the dried peas overnight. Drain, rinse and return them to the pan. Finely slice the leek. Add the olive oil, chopped leek and 2 pints of water to the peas. Bring to the boil and simmer for about an hour, or until the peas are tender. Season with the sea salt and dill. Put in a blender and process until smooth. Warm gently in the pan before serving with bread or *lagana* (see p.65).

LENTIL AND BARLEY SOUP

Phakoptisana

'There is an excellent dish which is called lentil and barley soup, where barley and lentils are added not in equal quantities, but rather less barley, since barley would thicken the cooking and also gain a great deal in weight; lentils, on the other hand, when boiled swell up by but a small amount. The seasoning is of course the same for this food as for pearl barley, except that when savory or penny-royal have been put in as an addition it becomes more pleasant and easier to digest, whilst pearl barley is unsuitable with these season-ings, and suffices with just dill and leeks.'

[*Galen, quoted in Oribasius* Medical Compilations]

Roman soups were generally thick. There are no surviving recipes with quantities specified to give us this information, but the nature of the Roman table provides the proof. Food had to be eaten with the fingers. Anything fluid was scooped up with bread, cutlery never being used for this purpose at the table, so a watery soup would therefore have been more than awkward. Similarly, lifting a bowl of soup to the lips would have been considered bad manners, at least in polite company, and even people eating on their own at home would have employed bread or fried noodles.

60 g/2 oz pearl barley
100 g/3 oz red lentils
1 leek
A bunch of fresh dill
A bunch of fresh savory
Sea salt

Put the barley and lentils in a large casserole and add 3 pints of water. Leave to soak for 6 hours or overnight. Slice a leek, finely chop the dill and savory and put these together with the salt into the casserole. Simmer the soup gently for an hour with the lid on. Taste just before serving, and add more salt if required. Serve with *lagana* (see p.65) as a substantial dish.

BARLEY SOUP

Ptisana

'Pearl barley is suitably prepared when it has swelled to its fullest extent during boiling, then after this put on a gentle flame until it has wholly converted into juice. There is mixed with it vinegar at that precise moment when it has completely swelled; when it is carefully boiling one must add fine salt, but not too much, for edibility; and if you should wish to add olive oil at once from the start, you will not harm the cooking; it is not necessary to mix in anything else except a little leek and dill, and these right from the beginning.'

[*Galen, quoted in Oribasius* Medical Compilations]

This was a very famous soup in antiquity because of its many applications, both at the table and in dietary repertoire, so much so that in the second century AD Galen wrote a whole treatise devoted to its medicinal properties.

150 g/5 oz pearl barley
1 leek
1 tsp dried dill tops
60 ml/2 fl oz olive oil
2 tbsp white wine vinegar
Sea salt

Soak the barley overnight. Drain. Slice the leek. Place all the ingredients in a heavy pan together with 2 pints of water. Bring to the boil and then simmer gently for an hour. Stir occasionally and check that there is sufficient water. This soup is supposed to be very thick, so add water a little at a time. Before serving, check that the soup is suitably seasoned with salt.

GOAT'S MILK SAUCE

Bucellae cum Lacte Caprino

'This is prepared with round stones that are heated in the fire until glowing and then plunged into the milk without any fire. When the milk boils, remove the stones and put into the milk pieces of finely chopped white bread that has been baked and well leavened. Let this cook slowly on the stove, but in an earthenware rather than a bronze pot. When this has been boiled after the bread has been added, let it be eaten with a spoon. For it is better eaten like this, since the dish gives nourishment; but if plain milk is drunk, it passes straight through and lingers hardly at all in the body.'

[*Anthimus* On Foods]

This dish has a sharp tang that complements vegetables like celery or carrots. It could also be described as a bread sauce. The cooking method has parallels in the medieval and later use of red hot irons for warming mulled wine.

250 ml/9 fl oz goat's milk
100 g/3 oz white bread

Pour the milk into a saucepan. Cut the bread into small pieces, having first removed the crust, and boil the milk and bread together for about 40 minutes or until the mixture begins to thicken to the consistency of double cream. Transfer the resulting mixture to a food-processor and blend until smooth. Decant the blended mixture into small bowls and refrigerate for about an hour. Serve chilled as a dip for vegetable dishes.

GARLIC AND HERB PÂTÉ

Moretum

'Then, with his mind focused on such a thought, he entered the garden. First he pulled up four garlic bulbs with their densely packed cloves, gently digging up the soil with his fingers. Next he plucked delicate celery leaves and stiff rue and coriander trembling on its thin stalk. When he had gathered these, he sat down by the cheerful fire and shouted loudly to his slave for a mortar. Then he stripped each head of garlic of its matted body, removed the outer skin and throwing to the ground discarded here and there whatever he did not want. The cloves he dipped in water and put into a hollow circle of stone. He sprinkled over some grains of salt, and when the salt had been mixed in, hard cheese was added. He heaped the herbs he had gathered on top. He balanced the mortar with his left hand in his rough lap, and with his right hand he first crushed the pungent garlic and he then puréed everything so that the juice was evenly blended. His hand traced a circle: gradually each ingredient lost its individual characteristics and there was one colour produced out of the many, not completely green, because the milky bits stood out, nor yet shining like milk, because it was coloured by so many herbs. Often the sharp savour shot through this man's flaring nostrils, and with his face turned up he showed his dislike for the meal, and often with the back of his hand he wiped his tearful eyes, swearing angrily at the pungency. The work kept going on, but now no longer jerkily, as before, but rather the pestle slid round more slowly in heavy circles. So he poured on some drops of olive oil and added for flavour a little vinegar, and again stirred and pounded the ingredients together. Then finally with two fingers he wiped round the whole mortar and rolled the bits into one ball, and so was made a moretum as excellent in appearance as it was in name.'

[*'Pseudo Virgil'* Moretum]

This recipe is unusual in that it makes use of garlic, an extremely rare ingredient in other ancient recipes since it was considered, at least among cultivated people, unpleasant to have garlic on the breath. So the writer of this poem seems to look at his peasant character through refined eyes, stressing the unpleasantness of the garlic which, in the real world, was a normal part of the everyday diet. The effect is not unlike *salade mechouia*, a Tunisian dish made of mixed roasted vegetables that are puréed to form an accompaniment to bread, although the Roman dish is far more pungent. *Aillade Gasconne* is a French equivalent that derives from *'la très ancienne aillée telle qu'elle était vendue à la criée dans les rues des cités, dès le Moyen Age'*. In common with all peasant dishes, only those ingredients that are locally grown are used. For this version I have suggested grilling the garlic to lessen the tears, although those of an alliaceous temperament could blend the garlic raw. Rue is a medicinal herb and reportedly an abortifacient; whilst I have not encountered any problems when using it, those who are unsure about eating it should omit it from the recipe and perhaps substitute a few fennel leaves.

4 bulbs of garlic
200 g / 7 oz feta cheese
3 celery stalks
A large bunch of fresh coriander leaves
A small bunch of fresh rue leaves
2 tbsp olive oil
4 tbsp white wine vinegar
Sea salt

Break the bulbs of garlic up into cloves, spread these out on a baking tray and cook under a hot grill for 5 minutes, turning the cloves over two or three times to avoid burning. Leave to cool for a couple of minutes and then squeeze out the garlic flesh from the skins. Roughly chop the celery, cheese and herbs and put them in a food-processor with the grilled garlic and blend until smooth. Add the wine vinegar and the olive oil and blend again briefly. Transfer to a bowl and serve as a spread for bread, *lagana* (see p.65) or *catillus ornatus* (see p.66).

OLIVE AND CELERY PÂTÉ

Conditurae Olivarum

'Yet most people finely chop leeks, rue and mint, together with young celery, and mix these with crushed olives. Then they add a little peppered vinegar and a little more honey or honeyed wine, drizzle with green olive oil, and so cover with a bunch of green celery.'

[*Columella* On Agriculture]

This creamy relish contrasts sharply with the herb purées that rely on coriander and cheese for their base (see pp.101-4). You may wish to add more mint; I prefer a delicate hint of this herb rather than anything more overpowering. Use whole olives bottled in brine, as briney olives are called for in the original recipe, and salt is necessary for the flavour of this dish. Whole olives may take some time to stone, but their taste is far superior to olives that have been industrially pitted.

1 leek
A sprig of rue
3 mint leaves
3 celery sticks
2 tbsp white wine vinegar
1 tbsp honey
60 ml/2 fl oz olive oil
150 g/5 oz whole green olives
Pepper

Trim, wash and slice the leek. Parboil it for 5 minutes. Raw leek does not, I think, titillate the palate even when pulverised. Put all the ingredients except for the olives in a blender and process until you have a smooth paste. First stone and then roughly chop the olives with a knife and stir into the purée. Pour the relish into a bowl and store in the fridge until ready to be served with bread or *lagana* (see p.65).

OLIVES WITH HERBS

Epityrum Varium

'You should make an epityrum *of green, black and speckled olives like this. Press out the stones from green, black and speckled olives. Season as follows. Chop the olives, add olive oil, vinegar, coriander, cumin, fennel, rue, mint. Put in an earthenware pot. There should be olive oil on top. Serve like this.'*

[*Cato* On Agriculture]

This is a colourful relish that can be eaten with bread as a starter or as an accompaniment to rice and barley.

100 g/3 oz whole green olives
100 g/3 oz whole black olives
1 tsp cumin
¹/₂ tsp fennel seeds
A bunch of fresh coriander leaves
A sprig of rue (see p.73)
2 or 3 mint leaves
2 tbsp olive oil
3 tbsp white wine vinegar

Grind the cumin and fennel seeds to a fine powder in an electric coffee-grinder. Finely chop the coriander, rue and mint. Stone and then roughly chop the olives. Combine all the ingredients in a bowl, stir and taste. Add a drop more vinegar if required.

TURNIPS WITH MUSTARD

Ius ad Rapa Condienda

'Carefully pick through and sieve some mustard seed. Next wash it in cold water, and when it is properly washed, leave it in the

water for two hours. Then take it out, squeeze it in your hands, and put into a new or a thoroughly scrubbed mortar and pound it with a pestle. When it has been pounded, arrange the purée in the middle of the mortar and flatten it with the palm of your hand. Then, when you have pressed it, score lines in it, place on it a few pieces of hot charcoal, then pour over some water mixed with sodium bicarbonate in order to remove all its bitterness and paleness. Then immediately tip the mortar up, so that all the liquid is drained off. After this add sharp white wine vinegar, mix together with the pestle and strain. This liquid is excellent for preserving turnips.'

[*Columella* On Agriculture]

This recipe makes rather fiery pickled turnips for eating with bread as a sort of *meze.*

2 large turnips (about 250 g/ 1/2 lb)
60 g/2 oz white mustard seeds
1 tsp bicarbonate of soda

You will need three or four sterilised jam jars in which to store the pickled turnips. Place the mustard seeds in a bowl, cover with 300 ml/ 10 fl oz of water and leave to soak for 2 hours. Then drain off and reserve the water. Put the softened seeds in a food-processor and blend for a few seconds to make a coarse mash. Tip this mash into a baking tray and place under a hot grill for 10 minutes, turning the mash occasionally to prevent burning. This will bring out the flavour of the mustard. Peel and chop the turnips into chunks roughly 2 cm/ 1 inch long and 1 cm/ 1/2 inch wide. Gently steam the turnip chunks for 5 minutes. Spoon a little mustard mash into a jar, then a few turnip chunks, then some more mustard mash and so on until the jar is full. When you have dealt with all the mustard and turnips, pour the reserved water into a pan, add the bicarbonate of soda and bring to the boil. Then fill the jars to the top with the water, screw on the lids and leave to cool. The turnips will store for several months.

PICKLED CHEESE

Tyros eis Halmen

'About the making of cheese, from a recipe by Berutios. Many people make cheese, which at the outset some people call whey, but most farmers name the same thing junket. It is better made from kid's milk. And parched salt curdles milk, as does fig juice, and the young twigs of fig trees or their leaves, and the fur that grow in the heads of artichokes that are unfit for eating, and pepper, and the gizzard of any domestic bird which has been laid up in some dung within the intestine as a sort of husk. Animals that have been pastured on hound's berry will produce rather good milk, but they will make far better milk after grazing on clover. The milk lasts for three days, if the day before transporting you pour it into a pan, boil it and then transfer it from one pot to another, stirring it with giant fennel or a reed until it cools, and then you sprinkle over it a little salt. Soft cheese keeps for longer if it is made up with thistle seed and a little warm water, or even added to warm honey. Cheese keeps after being washed in fresh water and dried in the sun, then put in an earthenware jar together with savory or thyme, each cheese separated from the other according to its strength, with the addition of sweet wine vinegar or a mixture of vinegar and honey, until the liquid rises above the cheese and herbs. Some people preserve the cheese by putting it in sea water. Cheese stays white after being put in salt; it stays firm and sharp hung over smoke. All cheese if dipped in pulses, and especially chickling or peas, seems to last longer. But if it is hard or bitter through age, you should mash it with bruised barley meal (that is the bruised meal that comes from unparched barley), put the cheese in water and then remove whatever floats to the surface.'

[*Bassus* Country Matters]

Without refrigeration cheese would obviously grow mouldy quickly unless preventive measures were taken. Salt was the obvious one since it required no special packaging, but pickling was also used, as in this recipe.

200 g/7 oz feta cheese
A handful of fresh thyme
200 ml/7 fl oz white wine vinegar
1 tsp clear honey

Wash and dry the feta cheese and cut it into 1 cm/^{1}/$_2$ inch cubes. Sterilise a 1 lb glass jar. Put in a layer of cubed cheese, then some thyme, then another layer of cubed cheese, and so on until the jar is full. Dissolve the honey in the vinegar and pour over the cheese until the jar is full. Screw on the cap and leave to marinate for a day. Serve with fresh bread.

DRIED FIG CAKES

Palathai

'Palathai *are cakes made of figs. And cakes of* palasiai, *that is of dried figs that have been squashed.'*
[The Suda Lexicon]

Fig cakes are still made in Turkey today, and these provide the inspiration for the completion of this dish, for the ancient description as it stands is surely incomplete, since figs squashed together on their own are sticky and awkward to store. The softer the dried figs, the more palatable the cakes, since the pips of old dried figs can be unpleasantly crunchy.

400 g/14 oz dried figs
1 tsp ground coriander seeds
1 tsp white flour

After removing their stalks, put the figs in a blender and process to a paste. Remove the paste from the blender, flatten and shape it with your hands into an oval cake. Mix together the flour and ground coriander seeds. Dust the outside of the fig cake with the flour and coriander mixture. Cut into small wedges for serving as a dessert.

CHEESE WITH FIGS

Caseus cum Recenti Fico

'A recent idea has been to eat a fresh fig instead of salt with cheese.'
[*Pliny* Natural History]

This suggestion by Pliny works particularly well with a white cheese such as Cheshire or Lancashire, the slight chewiness of the figs contrasting pleasantly with the friable cheese.

500 g/1 lb white cheese (Cheshire or Lancashire)
6 fresh figs

Cut the cheese into small cubes and arrange in a pile in the centre of a plate. Slice the figs into wedges and place round the edge of the cheese. The proportion of figs to cheese is simply a suggestion based on my experience of people's usual preference for cheese over figs and the availability of the fresh fruit. Adjust the ratio to suit the tastes of your own guests.

CURDS WITH HONEY

Hypotyrides

'Curds are made like this: pour honey into some milk, squeeze it out, put in a bowl and leave it to thicken. If you have a fine sieve to hand, turn the bowl into this, and allow the whey to run off. And when you think that it has thickened, take away the bowl and place the curds on a silver dish, and the pattern of the sieve will be on top. But if you do not have any sieves, use new fans, with which the fire is fanned; for they do the same job.'
[*Athenaeus* The Partying Professors]

The text is obviously garbled at this point, for the instructions about making curds are missing. Nevertheless, this recipe as it stands works excellently with Greek yoghurt or crème fraîche, especially if you use a fine aromatic honey. The following recipe gives an authentic version of curds.

400 g/14 oz Greek yoghurt or crème fraîche
4 tbsp honey

Arrange the yoghurt or crème fraîche on four small plates for individual portions. Use a spoon to create small mounds and a knife to score a hatched pattern on the surface. Pour a spoonful of honey over each mound and serve.

CURDS

Melca

'The best method for making what are known as curds is to pour sharp vinegar into new earthenware pots and then to put these pots on a slow fire. When the vinegar begins to boil, take it off the flame so it does not bubble over and pour milk into the pots. Place the pots in a store or some other place where they will not be disturbed. The next day you will have curds that are much better than those which are made with a great deal of fuss.'

[*Bassus* Country Matters]

These curds resemble cream cheese and were no doubt a familiar sight in Roman shops, for they will keep fresh far longer than milk, the sale of which must have always caused farmers difficulties. It is hardly surprising, therefore, that there are instructions in farming manuals on how to disguise the taste of sour milk.

2 litres/4 pints milk
225 ml/8 fl oz white wine vinegar

Bring the vinegar to the boil in a large pan, take it off the heat and add the milk. Cover and leave for two hours. Strain off the whey and serve the curds as in the previous recipe.

BARLEY WATER

Kykeon

'Kykeon: *a drink mixed from wine and honey and water and barley groats.'*
[*Hesychius* Dictionary]

Homer describes an eighth-century BC version of barley water in *The Iliad*, listing barley meal, wine and cheese as the ingredients. In *The Classical Cookbook* Sally Grainger interprets this as a type of soup or porridge. Hesychius, writing probably in the fifth century AD, records its evolution into a drink. My recipe leans on the extensive researches in the early 1930s of Ernst Darmstaedter into barley and its culinary uses in ancient times to produce a Roman equivalent of barley water.

60 g/2 oz pearl barley
125 ml/¼ pint sweet white wine
2 tbsp honey

Simmer the barley in 2 pints of water in a covered pan for an hour and a half. Strain off the juice into a jug or bottle and discard the barley. Mix the juice with the wine and honey and add more water so that you have 2 pints of drink. Refrigerate before serving.

FRUIT WINE

Oinos Dia Melon

'Put the sweetest smelling quinces into an earthenware jar and pour over some wine. Then, having poured over the wine, leave for three days, and use on the fourth.'
[*Bassus* Country Matters]

Quinces have a most attractive scent when ripening on the tree. For this drink you really need freshly picked quinces, as those bought in shops have already lost that heady aroma. This capturing of the perfume of a fruit recalls an Italian dessert described by Elizabeth David which consists merely of placing a peeled and sliced peach in a glass of wine. Quinces, however, have too much tannin in them for this, and I think they impart a finer flavour if left whole in the wine.

1 bottle sweet white wine
3 fresh quinces

Wash the quinces in cold water. Decant the wine into a glass jar with a lid. Place the quinces in the wine, seal the jar and leave for three days. The wine will have a strong bouquet of quinces for serving with a dessert.

HONEY WATER

Hydromel

'Chop up 32 of the finest apples, removing the core with a reed, mix in 8 pints of the best honey and leave for 8 months. Mix in 12 pints of old rainwater and warm in the sun in the heat of the Dog-Star, guarding against rain and dew. Some people make a superior version by preparing the honey water in the following way: the finest ripe apples are chopped up and have their juice extracted; 4 pints of juice and 8 pints of the finest honey, mixed with 12 pints of rain water, and after being warmed in the sun, a fire is used to simmer it gently. People use a double copper pan so that it is boiled over water rather than directly over the fire, as in Beroia.'

[*Bassus* Country Matters]

This seems to be a non-alcoholic version of *mulsum*, the Roman wine and honey aperitif that was said to promote the digestion and aid longevity. The emperor Augustus once asked a centenarian how he had achieved the feat of longevity, to which the reply was the application of olive oil to the outside and *mulsum* to the inside.

200 ml/7 fl oz apple juice
400 ml/14 fl oz clear honey
600 ml/21 fl oz water

Mix all the ingredients together in a pan. Bring to the boil and then simmer for 30 minutes. Leave to cool, strain into a jug and refrigerate before serving as an aperitif.

DINNER AT
THE BAR

The Athenians of the fifth century BC loved their bars, to judge from the literary evidence which extols their warm welcome to all classes of society, although the symposium in a private house was held to be a culturally superior occasion. Wine could be drunk at the bar, accompanied by pastries and cakes and discussion of the latest political issues. Not long ago a classical bar was excavated close to the gate in the city walls that guarded the road to Eleusis. Amphorae imported from all over the Aegean were found here, together with the bones of hundreds of fish, one of the most highly prized delicacies of the Greek world.

Rome was very different. Although the number of bars and restaurants mirrored what we might expect to find in a similar modern city, the general literary assessment of these establishments was not favourable, and the archaeological evidence appears to confirm this verdict. An examination of Pompeii has shown that the entrances to the houses of the wealthy were rarely situated near a bar, for bars were the haunt of prostitutes and distinguished guests and visitors would not want to compromise their reputation by being seen in what could be construed as a sleazy situation. In literature the Roman bar sinks deep in opprobrium, but its physical remains are ubiquitous, so at first sight it appears as something of an enigma. Why attack what most people obviously enjoyed? One needs to remember that those who set down their disapproval on paper were satirists like Juvenal or politicians like Cicero, both of whom had strong points to make. The link between the opponents of the bar must be humour. When Cicero upbraids Piso, the consul who had helped to engineer the orator's exile, a sense of farce accompanies the suggestion that the object of the attack preferred bars to cities, particularly when his inebriated condition is likened more to a pallid corpse than a distinguished general. Similarly, when Juvenal launches his tirade against a provincial governor, he places him in a bar with a selection of seedy characters ranging from sailors to runaway slaves, and once again the comic hyperbole is crowned, this time with the outrageous picture of a priest who is not only dead drunk but castrated to boot.

A poem attributed to Virgil probably provides the answer to this dichotomy. The author is young and carefree; the bar has a garden that is rich in sexual imagery, from the sensual heat and the redness of the roses to the suppleness of the girls and the statuette of an erect Priapus. He can curse those who fret about tomorrow, rolling his dice while drinking neat wine, simply because he does not have any responsibilities; in Roman terms he is not a *paterfamilias*, in modern terms he is a student. Add this to the liberal character of Micio from the play called *The Brothers* by Terence: he argues that allowing his son a free rein in his youth will help towards sobriety in later years, so he pays for his girlfriends and parties and wild nights at the bar. If the bar had an aura of licence, if it was a magnet for young men and those from the plebeian class, then the derogatory remarks made about it hold rather more subtlety than has hitherto been acknowledged. A contemporary parallel might be locating a middle-aged politician at a rave: there would be a clash of generation, culture and expected behaviour. Yet there are middle-aged ravers who, in their ordinariness, attract as much bad press as the characters drinking their wine at a Roman bar. Music might brand a person today; in antiquity food and drink were seen as revealing the inner self.

The bars of Rome were usually open for business between the

fourth and twelfth hours, that is between lunch at midday and sunset, although many served food and drink late into the night. Bars were almost indiscriminately called *tabernae, popinae, thermopolia* or *tabernae vinariae*. Some *cauponae* not only offered food but also a bed for the night, and in this capacity were named *tabernae, deversoriae* and *tabernae deversoriae*. Situated all the way along the great roads of Italy, they were speculative buildings put up by neighbouring landowners and either let or managed by slaves. They usually included a stable for horses. Cicero, in his *On Invention*, describes a couple of travellers on a road:

> Now let us begin with the conjectural issue (or issue of fact), and let the following be taken as an example. On a road a traveller met someone who was on a business trip and had on him a considerable sum of money. As is natural, they struck up a conversation as they went along, and the result was that they were ready to make the trip together as friends. So on stopping at the same inn, they planned to dine together and sleep in the same place. After dinner they went to bed in the same room.

A rollicking account of a night at a roadside inn occurs in *The Golden Ass* by Apuleius. Amidst the nocturnal scenes of witchcraft and necromancy are workaday details of bedroom furniture, stables off the central courtyard, the grumpy landlord and the locking of the outside gate from sunset to daybreak. Such establishments were to be found throughout the Roman world, in certain ways resembling the great Elizabethan coaching inns, some of which are still found in the high streets of English towns.

Examples of *cauponae* can be seen in Pompeii, Herculaneum and Ostia. They can be recognised easily, not only by their characteristic counter occupying the whole of the shop-front, but also by the fixtures necessary for pouring out beverages and for storing amphorae, as well as by the rooms at the back intended to accommodate and attract customers. For often the bar did not supply just drink, but was also a restaurant, gambling den and a brothel. Archaeologists have found lively sketches and graffiti left by locals and travellers who, having come to the bar on business, stayed on for a drink and a night with a prostitute. For the wealthy, dinner could be a prelude to sex, just as in classical Greek times with flute girls after a symposium. Cicero writes of Mark Antony dining with his mistress Cytheris, yet not only women, but also slaves and attractive boys could find themselves fancied. Although all this could be classed as depravity, and therefore draw the disapproval of more sober people, it did at least preserve a veil of respectability through being behind the closed doors of private houses. The bar, on the other hand, was too low and public for a discreet gentleman. Juvenal complains of the powerful Lateranus sinking to the same depths as his common friends by holding a party at a bar. In law, a barmaid was considered a prostitute, even if reality might have been otherwise, yet there was no need for such a woman to register with the local town council, as the main source of her income was not from serving men but drinks. Some graffiti from Pompeii chronicle the rivalry of two men for a barmaid called Iris: Successus the weaver wanted to go out with Iris, but Severus had stepped in, claiming that he was far sexier and better looking, and that Iris preferred him to Successus. What these words highlight are the respective statuses of bar clients (plebs, not magistrates) and barmaids (women of easy virtue, not matrons). In another bar an advertisement, not unlike the calling cards in a modern telephone box, prices the oral services of a girl named Fortunata at two bronze asses, the price of half a litre of olive oil or two litres of ordinary wine. Next to the door of another pub is a lament by a man frustrated in love. Interestingly, it is in verse, thereby suggesting an educated and consequently upper-class Roman; conversely, its lyrics are evocative of a contemporary pop song and point a finger at an adolescent for whom love was once such an easy game to play. Horace, journeying across Italy in 36 BC, recounts his frustration at lying in bed awake until midnight in such an inn, expecting the appearance of a prostitute with whom he had earlier arranged an appointment. Charinus, a young man in *The Businessman* by Plautus, relates what the audience would have liked to have experienced: namely being invited by an old friend to dinner and to a night of passion with a girl. Aeschinus in *The Brothers* by Terence goes off to a party with friends; the father at the beginning of the play announces that he did not come home that night. The leather bikini discovered in London in a first-century AD well may well have been the outfit for a dancer at a Roman bar.

Sometimes the innkeeper worked out his day's takings or a patron's credit on the wall, and since he wanted to maintain some semblance of standards, there would be written for all to see the rules of behaviour which drinkers were supposed to observe. Seneca recalls the restaurant that lurched into bankruptcy through serving a special paella of mussels, oysters, sea urchins and mullet which, although a moralising example on the evils of luxury, none the less strikes a chord in Pliny's rebuke of Septicius Clarus for preferring an extravagant meal elsewhere rather than a modest repast with him.

The inn at Pompeii at the corner of Mercury Street, mentioned earlier for its paintings of cheeses and sausages, was equipped with a marble-topped counter on which wines and other refreshments were served to customers. Behind the counter there were two small rooms and a larger room where regular customers could eat. Some paintings in an inn belonging to a certain Salvius refer to incidents that could happen in any pub today: an innkeeper is depicted as trying to separate two customers fighting over a game of dice. Remains have also been found of marble tables for serving food and mosaic pavements advertising the sale of wines.

The *cauponae* seem to have specialised in fried foods and cheap wine, Horace describing one such establishment as 'oily' and Cicero taunting an opponent about his alcoholic breath after emerging from another. Ausonius remarks on pike being chosen for frying in greasy inns, adding that nobody would present this fish at a dinner party. Varro relates how chicken was a popular dish at inns. In addition to fish and fowl, eggs, black olives and bread were on offer for the hungry diner.

Fast food in the Roman world meant bread, so a meal at the bar would certainly have been based around this staple food and an accompaniment. Bread would have been delivered to the landlord by slaves from the local bakery. Every bakery consisted of a large courtyard for grinding the flour, an area for kneading the dough and the oven for baking the finished products. At least twenty bakeries have been excavated in Pompeii. An important source of information about the life of a typical baker is contained in the sculptured frieze on the tomb of the baker Eurysaces in Rome. Here the assistants are shown mixing the dough, forming loaves and preparing the ovens for baking. At Pompeii the mills were made of the local tufa, but elsewhere in the empire other coarse stones were employed. The lower stone was shaped like a cone and was fixed into a base with a raised edge for catching the flour; the upper stone was fitted over this cone and was turned either by hand or by blindfolded donkeys. There has been some debate about the speed at which flour could be ground. It has been argued that Pompeii possessed a large number of bakeries because that was the only way the population could be fed using such slow equipment. Recent research, however, suggests that the population was larger than previously believed and also that the mills were fairly efficient at processing grain. Flours ranging from coarse wholemeal to fine white were produced through a combination of milling and sieving.

To bake the bread it was necessary to make a fire in the oven and to let this burn until the required temperature was reached. Then the ashes were raked out, the loaves put in using a spade with a long handle and the oven door closed to retain the heat. During excavations at Pompeii, 81 loaves were found in the oven of Modestus' bakery on the Street of the Augustali, carbonised by the pyroclastic flow during the eruption of Vesuvius in AD 79. The loaves were scored into eight wedges and the name of the baker stamped on each loaf. These loaves of bread are found depicted on wall paintings all round Pompeii, although their pedigree may be much more ancient. For the Greek poet Hesiod in the eighth century BC seems to describe the shape of these loaves in his *Works and Days* when he writes of 'dining off bread scored four ways and consisting of eight pieces', although most modern commentators appear puzzled by this line.

As for the composition of classical bread, there are many difficulties, caused in the main by the sheer brevity of the references. There was once a widespread view that it was unleavened, yet, judging by the carbonised loaves and the puffy shape of their segments, yeast, or at least some other rising agent, must have been used. Pliny explains that leaven was made by kneading fine wheat bran with must and then drying the resulting dough in the sun. When it came to panification, the dried blocks of bran were soaked in water, cooked with fine flour and then mixed into the flour being used for the loaves. The medical writer Celsus believed that leavened bread was alien to the stomach, although he confessed that it was excellent at relieving constipation. There were many different types of bread, some, such as oyster bread, called after the dishes eaten with them, others, such as oven bread, named after the method of baking. Small tins were used to give a special shape to cakes and pastries: at Pompeii archaeologists have found some carbonised cakes that look like doughnuts and others that resemble miniature bread loaves with a central pattern. Pliny records that bread was imported from the Parthian Empire with a thin spongy consistency full of holes. It may be that this was some sort of matzo, for the bread would have to have kept well to have survived the long journey to Rome from what is now Iran and Iraq. Other ingredients could be added to the dough for variety of flavour, for example eggs, milk and cheese.

From Martial we learn that *cauponae* were equipped with stools just like a modern Italian bar. They seem, as has already been noted, to have been frequented not only by the poorer people, but also by rather disreputable characters, although we must beware of taking our literary evidence too literally. For example, to be accused of eating in a *caupona* or *popina* was a stock invective in the law court. When the historian Sallust wrote that Pompey had an honest face but a dishonest character, a freedman of Pompey called Lenaeus accused Sallust of being a drunk, a spendthrift and an habitué of the *popinae*. A character in *The Weevil* by Plautus suggests that Greeks wandered round with books in their hands uttering intellectual remarks, but as soon as they managed to pilfer some money they went and spent it in the *popinae*. At Asellina's *thermopolium* in Pompeii a bronze heater was discovered whose purpose was to warm the wine for serving to customers. The Greeks and Romans often enjoyed their drinks hot. The wine was often blended with herbs, spices and salt when it was transferred into amphorae, but it seems too that customers at a *popina* or *caupona* could add hot or cold water to their wine according to taste.

Martial tells us that beet was eaten at midday by workmen and that cooks tried to liven up the insipid flavour of this vegetable with wine and pepper. Dates were cheap, for poor clients gave them as gifts to their wealthy patrons as a New Year present. Juvenal complains that in his day the most wretched navvy was nostalgic for the whiff of tripe in some hot and crowded *caupona*. It appears to have been a common form of invective for satirists to picture *cauponae* as dubious and unsavoury. The same satirist pictures corrupt army officers wasting their time in *popinae* instead of hardening themselves for the defence of the empire, whilst a character in a play by Plautus suggests that bartenders in *cauponae* were gay. Yet evidence apart from satire seems to argue for some luxury and style to these establishments. The emperor Tiberius proposed a series of sumptuary restrictions on *popinae* that included the banning of pastries for sale and Nero tried to limit the menus in *popinae* to simple vegetable dishes. The assumption behind these proposals was that *cauponae* and *popinae* did in fact have an extensive range of foods on offer, as the recipes will show, and thus were far more sophisticated than the wit of Juvenal and fellow writers would ever admit.

Not long ago an invitation to dinner dating from the second century AD was discovered in the dry sands of Egypt. 'Diogenes invites you to dinner for the first birthday of his daughter at the temple of Serapis tomorrow, which is 26th Pachon, from the eighth hour onwards.' This slip of papyrus illustrates the hour when dinner was generally served (from about five o'clock onwards), for Diogenes did not hold any important political posts in the town of Oxyrhynchus and so there is nothing extraordinary about the note. This timing, coupled with the considerable amount of information concerning what was eaten at a small dinner party or at a dinner with the family, perhaps affords a glimpse of what was really eaten at the bar and when, rather than what the lurid tales of satirists and politicians would have us believe. A farmer described by Horace relates that most evenings he ate no more than vegetables and slices of smoked ham, but if a friend came to visit him he would serve chicken or kid. His dessert consisted of raisins, nuts and figs. Then came the drinking. Martial also describes a modest supper: lettuce, leeks, tuna with eggs, sausage with porridge, cabbage and white beans with pink bacon; raisins, pears, chestnuts and wine for dessert, and for a savoury, if an edge to the appetite still persisted, olives, lupins and chick-peas.

Horace elsewhere speaks of a slightly more elaborate meal: wild boar with turnips, lettuces, radishes and fish sauce, accompanied by Caecuban wine; then cheesebread, game bird, oysters and lamprey with shrimps. It is likely that such foods were on offer at the bar, depending on the time of year and their availability, and that they were spiced, although a cook in *The Liar* by Plautus inveighs against too heavy a hand with the seasoning. In the *cauponae* and *popinae* the food seems to have been remarkably similar to that eaten in the southern Mediterranean today, in an Italian *trattoria*, a Turkish *lokanta* or a Greek *taverna*. Go into a modern *trattoria* in the backstreets of Naples or Palermo: there are wooden tables and benches and on the walls in place of the frescoes of antiquity small framed paintings. Ignore the tomato pizzas and the boiled pasta, and there on the menu, which is sometimes written on a large board just as the menus of a caupona were painted on a wall, will appear chicken, kid, sausages, fish, cheeses, fruit and vegetables. This is what the ordinary Roman ate; it was only the Neros and Elagabali and their courtiers who indulged in dormice, steamed jellyfish and ostrich, and they were an extremely small minority.

STUFFED VINE LEAVES

Thrion Demou

'Ordinary thrion: *an Athenian dish into which go pig and kid lard, flour, milk and the yolk of an egg to bind it. Wrapped in fig leaves, it makes a most delicious food according to Didymus.'*

[*Ancient commentator on Aristophanes* Acharnians]

The several variants on these recipes for stuffed vine leaves prove, of course, the origin of the modern Greek *dolmades*. As with the modern version, there are vegetarian and omnivorous varieties. I use vine leaves as a substitute for fig leaves, because the former can be readily bought in convenient jars or sachets from supermarkets, whilst fig leaves, at least in Britain, tend to be too tough and fibrous for presentable cooking.

200 g/6 oz flour
100 ml/3 fl oz milk
1 egg

25 g/1 oz lard
25-30 vine leaves
Salt
Garum *or* liquamen *(pp.29-32)*

Melt the lard, beat the egg and stir both into the milk. Put the flour in a large mixing bowl, add the milk mixture and salt and work into a soft dough. Break off enough dough to make a cylinder approximately 7 cm/3 inches long and 1 cm/¹/₂ inch in diameter. It is helpful to flour your hands when making these. Lay each cylinder on the bottom third of a vine leaf. Bring the bottom part of the leaf over the ball, fold the sides of the leaf over and then roll the ball up to the top of the leaf to form a neat parcel. Repeat the process until all the dough has been wrapped. Gently steam the parcels for 1 hour. Sprinkle with whichever *garum* or *liquamen* you prefer and serve warm.

SMOKED FISH IN VINE LEAVES
Thrion Tarikhous

'*Smoked fish* thrion: *smoked fish* thrion *is the name given to another recipe consisting of brain and smoked fish seasoned with fish sauce and cheese, wrapped in a fig leaf and baked.*'
[*Ancient commentator on Aristophanes* Acharnians]

Animal brains have been banned from sale in Britain because of the risks they pose to the health, although years ago my grandmother used regularly to serve scambled brains on toast. I have therefore simplified this recipe. In any case, brains were never one of my favourite foods.

250 g/¹/₂ lb smoked mackerel
250 g/¹/₂ lb feta cheese
20-25 vine leaves

1 fish stock cube
2 tbsp garum *(see p.29) or sea salt to taste*

Skin the mackerel, remove its bones and, using a fork, mash the mackerel flesh with the feta cheese. Then take a tablespoon of the mackerel and cheese mixture and lay it on the bottom third of a vine leaf. Bring the bottom part of the leaf over the mixture, fold the sides of the leaf over and then roll the mixture up to the top of the leaf to form a neat parcel. Repeat the process until all the mixture has been wrapped and arrange the parcels in a heavy casserole so that they are packed together tightly. Dissolve the stock cube in 100 ml/ 3 fl oz of boiling water, season the stock with *garum* or sea salt and pour over the parcels. Put the casserole in the oven at 170°C/330°F/ gas mark 3 and cook the parcels for one hour. Serve hot with bread and vegetables.

GOAT'S CHEESE AND RICE IN VINE LEAVES

Thrion ex Oryza

'Thrion *is wheat groats or rice or finest wheat flour boiled in sufficient quantities. Then pour off the water and knead the mixture with soft cheese and a few eggs. Then it is enclosed with fig leaves and tied up with hemp or papyrus or flax and placed in a stock of boiled meat until it has been sufficiently cooked. Then take out, remove the leaves, put in a new frying pan with fresh honey and cook. Turn it until it is properly done and is brown. Remove and serve with honey poured around it, either from the boiled honey or another lot of honey. It is called* thrion *because of the fig leaves which are called by the same name.'*

[*Ancient commentator on Aristophanes* Knights]

Somewhat surprisingly, rice is only mentioned once by Apicius, although the context in which it appears suggests that it was a familiar ingredient, for the water in which it has been boiled is suggested for thickening a sauce, as if a pot of cooked rice was a typical accompaniment to other dishes. In the early fourth century AD cleaned rice cost twice as much by weight as barley and lentils, but the same as spelt grits. When one remembers the extent to which rice swells up during cooking, so that in terms of dried volume it will go further than a less expandable grain like barley, it cannot have been a particularly luxurious item.

100 g / 3 oz basmati rice
1 tbsp olive oil
1 beef stock cube
100 g / 3 oz goat's cheese
20-25 vine leaves
1 egg
60 ml / 2 fl oz honey
Sea salt

Fry the rice in olive oil for two minutes in a heavy pan, stirring frequently. Add 1 pint of boiling water, season with salt, turn down the heat and simmer gently with the lid on until the rice is expanded and soft and the water all absorbed into the rice. Remove the pan from the flame. Finely dice the cheese and beat the egg and combine them with the rice. Take a heaped tablespoon of the rice mixture and lay it on the bottom third of a vine leaf. Bring the bottom part of the leaf over the rice mixture, fold the sides of the leaf over and then roll the rice mixture up to the top of the leaf to form a neat parcel. Repeat the process until all the rice has been used. Place the parcels in a casserole. Dissolve the stock cube in half a pint of boiling water and pour over the rice parcels. Put the covered casserole in the oven at 170°C/330°F/gas mark 3 for an hour. Pour the honey into a large frying pan. Heat the honey and gently transfer the parcels from the casserole to the frying pan. Turn several times until the parcels are coated with honey. Remove the parcels and serve with a spicy accompaniment, honey being a popular adjunct of peppery foods in ancient times.

SAVOURY BARLEY

Mystron

'Nicander of Colophon is the author who employs the word mystron *when describing the use of the word barley groats in the first of his two books* On Farming. *He writes: "But when you are making a dish of fresh kid or lamb or capon, put some barley groats in a mortar, pound them well, then stir in some ripe olive oil. When the stock is boiling hard, pour it over the pounded groats, put the lid on the pot and steam it; for when it is cooked in this way, the heavy meal swells up. Serve it when lukewarm in hollow* mystra.*"'*

[*Athenaeus* The Partying Professors]

Barley has a pleasant flavour but can be slightly dry. This recipe imparts a savour and softness to the barley that must surely have dispelled any qualms ancient cooks had about using this grain. Pliny says that the Roman army commissariat had, by his day, modernised the military rations from barley to wheat, and whilst transportation dockets survive from Roman Egypt listing shiploads of barley, the supposition is that fodder rather than *haute cuisine* is being recorded.

100 g / 3 oz pearl barley
1 litre / 2 pints water
60 ml / 2 fl oz olive oil
1 chicken stock cube
Sea salt

Put all the ingredients in a pan, cover and bring to the boil. Then simmer for one hour or until tender, stirring occasionally. This dish can be served as an accompaniment to vegetables or stews or else spooned into hot pitta bread that has been cut widthways and opened up like a bowl.

HONEY AND SESAME PIZZA

Staititai

'Staititai: *A type of cake made with spelt dough and honey.
Epikharmos mentions it in his* Marriage of Hebe. *The moist
dough is spread on a frying pan, and on it are poured honey, sesame
seeds and cheese, according to Iatrokles.'*
[*Athenaeus* The Partying Professors]

Provided that these cakes are cooked carefully, they provide an
ancient equivalent of pizza, to be eaten as a snack or as part of a
larger meal.

*250 g/9 oz spelt flour
1 tsp dried yeast
1 tsp sugar
150 ml/5 fl oz warm water
Olive oil for frying
200 g/7 oz feta cheese
2 tbsp sesame seeds
2 tbsp clear honey
Sea salt*

Dissolve the sugar in the warm water. Spoon in the dried yeast and
leave to stand for 15 minutes to reactivate. Add the yeast mixture to
the flour and knead into a supple dough – you may need to add a
touch more flour or water. Put in a bowl, cover with cling film and
allow to rise for one hour. Then divide the dough into two equal
balls. Roll the balls out on a lightly floured surface until you have rounds
25 cm/10 inches in diameter. Place these in separate plastic bags and
leave for 30 minutes. Heat the oil in a large frying pan. Slide a disc
into the pan and fry very gently, turning over from time to time until
golden brown on both sides. Repeat with the other disc. Mash the
feta cheese and spread it over both discs. Drizzle with honey and
sprinkle with sesame seeds. Flash under a hot grill to melt the
cheese, cut into wedges and serve.

BROAD BEANS

Faba Integra

*'Whole broad beans when properly cooked both in stock and in oil
are better with seasoning or salt than chopped beans, because the
latter burden the stomach.'*

[*Anthimus* On Foods]

I am not particularly keen on broad beans, probably because of their
rather earthy taste and starchy texture, but this recipe always has me
delving in the pan for second helpings.

300 g/10 oz fresh broad beans
1 vegetable or beef stock cube
1 tbsp olive oil
Sea salt

Heat 1 pint of water in a pan. When boiling, dissolve the stock cube
in it. Add the beans and the olive oil. Reduce the heat and simmer
the beans with the lid on for 20 minutes or until they are tender.
This dish likes to stand: when the beans are almost cooked, turn off
the heat and leave the beans to marinate for an hour in the stock and
olive oil. Bring to the boil again just before serving. Use as an
accompaniment to any main dish.

DICE BREAD

Kyboi

*'How would you know that dice – not the sort that you always
play with – are loaves in the shape of a cube, seasoned with dill and
cheese and olive oil, as Heracleides says in his* Art of Cooking*?'*

[*Athenaeus* The Partying Professors]

The dill lends to this bread an unusual acidity that makes it an ideal accompaniment to savoury dishes, particularly vegetable purées. The crisp cheese topping has a beautiful golden colour and a delicious flavour. Games of dice were popular in Roman bars, but fascination with the game extended even to the imperial family, the emperor Claudius publishing a treatise on the subject.

400 g/14 oz wholemeal flour
300 ml/10 fl oz warm water
1 tsp dried yeast
1 tsp sugar
60 ml/2 fl oz olive oil
2 tsp dried dill tops
30 g/1 oz grated Cheddar cheese (see pp.27-8)
Sea salt

Dissolve the sugar in a measuring jug with half of the warm water. Stir in the dried yeast, whisk and cover the jug for 10 minutes to allow the yeast to reactivate. Put the flour in a mixing bowl, stir in the dried dill tops and some salt for seasoning. Add the yeast mixture, olive oil and the rest of the warm water to a well made in the flour. Mix together with your hands and knead for 5 minutes. Then cover the bowl with cling film and put in a warm place for the dough to rise. When the dough has doubled in size − after about 2 hours − knock down and knead again for 5 minutes. Oil and flour a 6 inch/16 cm square baking tin. Divide the dough into three equal portions and press the first portion into the bottom of the tin. Sprinkle the dough with a third of the grated cheese. Press the next portion of dough down on top of the cheese, sprinkle this with a third of the grated cheese and then press the last portion of dough down on top of this layer of cheese. Put the tin in a plastic bag and leave the loaf to rise in a warm place. After 1 hour it should have doubled in size. Bake in an oven pre-heated to 200°C/400°F/gas mark 6 for 35 minutes. Take out, sprinkle the top with the remaining cheese and bake for a further 10 minutes.

EGGS POACHED IN WINE

Oa Pnikta

'Better than boiled and baked eggs are those called poached. The recipe for them is as follows: pour some olive oil, fish sauce and a little wine over the eggs, put hot water into a large basin in which is placed the pot containing the eggs, then cover everything with a lid. Put the basin over a flame until the eggs are of a moderately firm consistency. If they become too firm, they turn out like boiled and baked eggs, but if they are only just firm they are better digested than hard eggs and furnish the body with superior nourishment.'

[*Galen* On the Powers in Foods]

The Romans enjoyed many different kinds of eggs, chicken and pheasant eggs generally being considered the best, followed closely by goose and ostrich eggs. My adaptation of Galen's simple recipe – using an oven instead of the top of the stove – allows for a gentle and uniform cooking that produces a delicious result.

6 eggs
3 tbsp garum *(see p.29)*
6 tbsp dry white wine
6 tbsp olive oil

Grease six ramekins with a tablespoon of olive oil, then crack an egg into each and put them in a *bain-marie* filled with boiling water. Drizzle each egg with a tablespoon of wine and half a teaspoon of *garum*. Cover the *bain-marie* tightly either with a lid or with silver foil and place it in an oven pre-heated to 190°C/380°F/gas mark 5 for 15 minutes. Serve hot with bread and vegetables.

HERB PURÉE WITH CHEESE

Mixtura cum Caseo

'Put into a mortar savory, mint, rue, coriander, parsley, leeks (or, if leeks are unobtainable, green onion), lettuce leaves, rocket leaves, green thyme or catnip, and also green pennyroyal and fresh and salted cheese. Pound all these together and blend in a little peppered vinegar. When this mixture has been arranged in a bowl, pour olive oil over it.'

[*Columella* On Agriculture]

There are several recipes for puréed herbs and cheese with nuts or sesame seeds. They make excellent dips for vegetables or spreads for bread. Of all the recipes in this book, they are perhaps among the most accessible for the modern reader, being not far removed from the herb pâtés on supermarket shelves today. Do not be afraid to adjust the quantities, which are in any case fairly vague as it is. If you cannot procure one of the herbs, do not worry: the overall flavour will be much the same.

1 leek
100 g/3 oz feta cheese
100 g/3 oz Cheddar cheese (see pp.27-8)
2 or 3 mint leaves
1 small lettuce
A handful of rocket leaves
A handful of fresh coriander leaves
A handful of fresh parsley
A sprig each of savory, rue, thyme and pennyroyal
1/2 tsp ground black pepper
2 tbsp white wine vinegar
2 tbsp olive oil

Finely slice the leek, steam it until tender and put it in a food-processor. Wash the lettuce and add to the leek, together with the herbs, cheese, pepper and vinegar. Process until you have a fine paste. Taste, and add more vinegar if required. Pour the olive oil over the purée before serving with bread.

HERB PURÉE WITH WALNUTS

Mixtura cum Nucibus

'When you have pounded the green herbs which are listed above, pound with them as many walnuts which have been hulled as seems sufficient, blend in a little peppered vinegar and pour olive oil on top.'

[*Columella* On Agriculture]

Follow the instructions for the previous recipe, but substitute 200 g/7 oz of walnuts for the cheese. Blend in a food-processor, add more vinegar if required and serve after pouring olive oil over it.

HERB PURÉE WITH SESAME SEEDS

Mixtura cum Sesamis

'Pound with the green herbs detailed above some sesame that has been lightly toasted. Blend in a little peppered vinegar. Then pour olive oil on top.'

[*Columella* On Agriculture]

Follow the instructions for the previous recipe, but substitute 200 g/7 oz of tahini (sesame-seed purée) for the cheese or walnuts. Blend in a food-processor, add more vinegar if required and serve after pouring olive oil over it.

HERB PURÉE WITH PINE KERNELS

Mixtura cum Nucleis Pineis

'Chop into small pieces Gallic cheese, or any other well-known cheese you like. Pound it. Take pine kernels, if you have a lot of them, but if not, hazelnuts toasted after their shells have been removed, or almonds, and mix them in equal quantity with the seasonings detailed above. Add a small amount of peppered vinegar and blend. Pour some olive oil over the mixture. If there are no green seasonings, pound dry pennyroyal or thyme or oregano or dry savory with the cheese, and add peppered vinegar and olive oil. But, if the other herbs have no pungency, each of these herbs can be mixed when dry with the cheese.'

[*Columella* On Agriculture]

This is a delicious pâté, and surely the origin of modern Italian *pesto*, although there is no basil. Basil was rarely employed by Roman cooks, but is frequently found in ancient medicine. Superstition had it that the herb attracted scorpions, so this may have discouraged its use in the kitchen, whilst doctors considered it awkward to digest because of its juices. The pine kernels lend a creamy texture and an aromatic savour that invariably provokes questions at the dinner table as to the exact nature of the recipe. The pâté is still good with hazelnuts, but its origins are more likely to be betrayed by the recognisable flavour of this ingredient.

100 g/3 oz pine kernels or hazelnuts
A handful of fresh parsley
80 ml/3 fl oz olive oil
80 ml/3 fl oz red wine vinegar
1/2 tsp ground black pepper
125 g/4 oz feta cheese
A handful of fresh coriander leaves
2 or 3 mint leaves
A sprig each of savory, rue and thyme
Sea salt

Put all the ingredients in a food-processor. Purée until you have a smooth consistency and serve with bread. If you are using hazelnuts, roast them first under a hot grill for 5 minutes to release their nuttiness, turning them frequently to avoid burning.

CHEESE AND PASTRY PIE

Placenta

'Make pastry pie like this: 2 pounds of wheat flour for the crust, 4 pounds of prime groats for the pastry. Soak the groats in water and when they have softened pour into a clean bowl, drain well and knead by hand. When they are properly kneaded, gradually work in 4 pounds of flour. From this dough make the strips of pastry. Spread the strips of pastry on a wickerwork basket where they can dry. When they are dry, arrange carefully. Prepare each strip of pastry as follows: when you have kneaded them, wipe them with a cloth soaked in olive oil, using a circular movement and coating them. When the strips of pastry are ready, heat the oven thoroughly where you are going to bake, and the dome too. Then add water to 2 pounds of flour, knead it and make a thin lower crust. Soak 14 pounds of sweet fresh sheep's cheese in water. Change the water three times as you mash the cheese. Take out a small quantity at a time, thoroughly squeeze the water out with your hands, and when it is dry place it in a bowl.

When you have dried out the cheese completely, knead it in a clean bowl with your hands, and make it as smooth as possible. Then take a clean flour sifter and force the cheese through it into the bowl. Add four and a half pounds of good quality honey and mix it carefully with the cheese. Place the crust on a clean board that is one foot in width, putting underneath bay leaves brushed with olive oil, and make the pie as follows: place a first layer of pastry strips over the whole crust, cover it with the mixture from the bowl, add the pastry strips one by one, covering each layer until you have used up all the cheese and honey. Place a single strip of

pastry on the top, then fold over the crust and prepare the oven.
Then put the pie in the oven, cover with a dome and pile the hot
ashes on top and around. Ensure that it bakes thoroughly and
slowly by uncovering it two or three times to examine it. When it
is done, remove and spread with honey. This will make a pie of
half a modius *in weight.'*

[*Cato* On Agriculture]

The complicated instructions are most disconcerting, whilst the
closing sentence about a pie over 6 lb in weight is probably enough
to discourage most modern cooks. Yet if the recipe is looked at
again, an ancient form of *tyropitakia* or Greek cheese pastries
emerges. Individual pies are more presentable and will cook more
easily.

FOR THE SHELL:

200 g/7 oz wholemeal flour
2 tbsp olive oil
100 ml/3 fl oz water

FOR THE PASTRY STRIPS:

200 g/7 oz white flour
1 tbsp olive oil
120 ml/4 fl oz water

FOR THE FILLING:

400 g/14 oz feta cheese
4 tbsp honey
1 tsp sea salt

FOR BRUSHING:

60 ml/2 fl oz olive oil

To make the shell, work together the wholemeal flour, olive oil and
water to make the dough for the crust. You may need to use a little
more flour or water to achieve a pliable dough. Put in a plastic bag
and allow to rest in the fridge for 1 hour.

Then work together the white flour, olive oil and water for the
pastry strips. Again, you may need to add further water or flour to

achieve a smooth dough. Roll this dough out as thinly as possible on a floured board and cut into 10 cm/4 inch squares and leave to dry on a floured surface for 30 minutes.

Make the filling by mashing the feta cheese, honey and salt together.

Now divide the wholemeal dough into four similarly sized balls. Roll a ball out as thinly as possible (a type of filo pastry is the goal) until you have a disc about 25 cm/10 inches in diameter. Brush a pastry strip with olive oil and lay it in the centre of the wholemeal disc. Top with a thin layer of cheese and honey. Repeat the process until the stack of pastry and cheese is about 4 cm/1½ inches high, finishing with a pastry strip. Fold the wholemeal crust around the stack of pastry and cheese, leaving an opening at the top so that the pie resembles a rose bud about to open. Dab the folds with water if they do not stick properly. Brush the outside of the wholemeal crust with olive oil. When you have finished all four pies, place them on an oiled baking tray and put in the oven at 190°C/380°F/gas mark 5 for 40 minutes, or until golden brown on the outside. Serve as a main course.

POPPY SEED BISCUITS

Laterculi

'*They are nothing but* laterculi: *sesame seeds, poppy seeds, wheat flour and chopped nuts.*'
[*Plautus* The Little Carthaginian]

FOR THE SHELLS:
200 g/7 oz wholemeal flour
2 tbsp olive oil
100 ml/3 fl oz water
1 egg-white

FOR THE FILLING:

50 g/2 oz sesame seeds
25 g/1 oz poppy seeds
250 g/¹/₂ lb ground mixed nuts
50 g/2 oz honey

Make the pastry shells by combining the wholemeal flour, olive oil and water and knead into a supple dough. Gather into a ball and place in a plastic bag for an hour. Mix together all the ingredients for the filling. Roll out the pastry as thinly as you can. It is easier if you work with a portion of the pastry at a time. Use a round pastry cutter about 6 cm/2½ inches in diameter to form the individual shells. Place a dessertspoon of the mixture in the centre of each shell, wet the edges of the shell with water, then bring the edges of the shell together to seal in the filling. Beat the egg-white and glaze the shells. Place the shells on an oiled baking tray and put in the oven at 180°C/350°F/gas mark 4 for 20 minutes. Serve as a sweet with puréed fruit.

SWEET WINE CAKES

Glykinai

'Glykinai: *the cakes from Crete made with sweet wine and olive oil, so Seleukos says in his* Glossary.'
[*Athenaeus* The Partying Professors]

Eastern European pastry often lacks the crumbliness that those of us from the northern parts of the continent associate with recipes involving large quantities of butter. Ancient pastry entails a similar shock, which is reinforced by the absence of sugar. Although these cakes might be dubbed sweet, or *glykus* in Greek, to the modern palate it is a very subtle sweetness derived from the grape juice, which I use in preference to wine for this very reason. The dryness of these biscuits demands an accompanying drink, and a glass of wine will complement their sweetness.

200 g/7 oz light white flour
60 ml/2 fl oz olive oil
80 ml/3 fl oz white grape juice or very sweet white wine
1 egg-white

Combine the flour and olive oil with your fingers so that they form a crumble-like consistency. Add the grape juice or wine and knead into a smooth dough. You may need a little more flour, grape juice or wine to achieve this smoothness. Gather the dough into a ball and place in a plastic bag to rest in the fridge for an hour. Oil a baking tray. Roll the dough out thinly and use a pastry cutter about 2 cm/ 1 inch in diameter to form the biscuits – a cutter in the shape of a flower produces attractive biscuits. Arrange the biscuits on the oiled baking tray. Brush each biscuit with beaten egg-white to glaze. Bake in the oven for 25 minutes at 190°C/380°F/gas mark 5. Cool on a wire rack and serve.

HONEY BISCUITS

Enkrides

'Enkrides: *small biscuits fried in olive oil and drenched with honey. Stesichorus mentions them in these verses: "Groats and* enkrides *and other biscuits and fresh honey".*'
[*Athenaeus* The Partying Professors]

Modern Greek cooks make a fried biscuit called *diples* that resembles a bow. That it too is soaked in honey shows the age of the technique, but does not shed any light on the ancient biscuit. Thus my version is very much a reconstruction, although firmly based on the other pastries and biscuits for which we have more information.

200 g/7 oz light white flour
3 tbsp olive oil
1 egg

80 ml/3 fl oz honey
2 tbsp white grape juice
1/2 tsp pepper
1/2 tsp sea salt

Beat the egg. Mix the olive oil, egg, salt and pepper into the flour so that a mixture with the consistency of breadcrumbs is formed. Add the grape juice and knead to a smooth dough. You may need to add a little more grape juice or flour to achieve this smoothness. Form a ball with the dough and put it in a plastic bag to rest in the fridge for one hour. Then roll out thinly on a floured board. Cut into rounds with a pastry cutter about 3 cm/1 inch in diameter. Shallow-fry in plenty of olive oil until puffed up and golden on both sides. Heat the honey in a pan until it bubbles. One at a time, drop the biscuits into the honey for a few seconds. Serve with a dessert wine at the close of a meal or as a snack on their own.

MUST CAKES

Mustacei

'Make must cakes like this. Sprinkle one modius *of wheat flour with must. Add together aniseed, cumin, two pounds of fat, one pound of cheese and the bark of a bay twig. After you have shaped this into cakes, put bay leaves underneath, as you are cooking them.'*

[*Cato* On Agriculture]

I use grape juice rather than must. The use of the initial flowings from a wine kit might, I suspect, provide a more authentic equivalent of must, but I have not attempted such an experiment. Sally Grainger in *The Classical Cookbook* suggests the use of yeast, on the grounds that the must would have acted as leaven, and this seems a commendable idea. Cheddar cheese may seem peculiar in an ancient dish, but it cooks well and has a pleasing flavour. When I worked as a cook, surplus milk was sometimes offered to the staff at a low price, and this allowed me to experiment with Roman cheese-making, using upturned cake tins and bricks in place of moulds and presses. Although fig sap could be employed as a curdling agent, and salt was often packed round the outside to assist with storage, the results were not unlike many modern hard cheeses. A Roman cook in Britain would have used a local cheese, so it is not necessary to buy an Italian variety. In fact a monk, writing probably in Wales in the sixth century AD in the dim twilight of the Roman world, refers to 'British cheese' almost as if this were a recognised type like Cheddar. These cakes were designed to be cheap: Cato was using them to feed his farm workers rather than his aristocratic friends, another reason for using economical ingredients. A *modius* of wheat flour weighed approximately 9 lb and cost 30 *as*, the price of two tunics in first century AD Pompeii. The flour-to-fat ratio is therefore about one to five.

200 ml/7 fl oz white grape juice
1/2 tsp dried yeast
50 g/2 oz Cheddar cheese (see pp.27-8)
400 g/14 oz wholemeal flour
3 tsp ground cumin
1/2 tsp ground aniseed
50 g/2 oz lard or hard vegetable fat
Olive oil
Bay leaves, preferably fresh

Pour the grape juice into a pan and warm it to body temperature. Dissolve the dried yeast in the grape juice and leave to froth for a few minutes. The grape juice, of course, contains enough sugars to activate the yeast, so there is no need to add anything to the juice. Grate the cheese. Put the flour into a mixing bowl and stir in the cumin and aniseed. Add the grated cheese and vegetable fat. Work the cheese and fat into the flour until it is the consistency of bread crumbs. Pour on the grape juice and yeast mixture. Knead for 5 minutes until you have a supple dough and roll into a ball, adding a little more flour if the dough seems too sticky. Cover the bowl with a damp tea towel. Now smear a baking tray with olive oil and position the bay leaves on it at 2 inch intervals. Flour a board. Place the ball of dough on the board and, using a rolling pin, roll out the ball until it is 1 cm/1/2 inch thick. A pastry cutter about 5 cm/2 inches in diameter can be used to make the individual cakes. Place each cake on a bay leaf. Bake the cakes in the oven at 180°C/350°F/gas mark 4 for 40 minutes. Serve warm with a vegetable purée.

HONEYED QUINCES

Kydonion syn Meliti

'The quince is not completely ruined if you follow these instruct-ions: boil it with honey and a little wine, after peeling off the skin; or remove the core and steep in honey, mould dough made from spelt around the whole quince, place in the embers and let the dough burn away completely; then this burnt layer is removed, and so the whole quince is cooked and all the honey absorbed.'
[*Rufus, quoted in Oribasius* Medical Compilations]

Quinces are an exquisite fruit. One of my favourite sweets when I was small was quince paste prepared in the Hungarian way. Tangy and sweet, fleshy and smooth, it was a paradise of sensual explor-ation. The Roman dish is more basic, yet combined with a good sweet wine it still has the power to thrill. Fortunately, quinces now make a brief appearance on supermarket shelves in the autumn, so shopping for this recipe should not pose undue problems.

10 quinces
100 ml/3 fl oz honey
250 ml/9 fl oz sweet white wine

Peel, core and dice the quinces; put them in a pan. Pour the wine and honey over the diced quinces and simmer gently with the lid on for 30 minutes or until soft. Transfer the quinces to a blender and purée. Spoon the quince purée into individual glass bowls for serving. You can chill the purée in the fridge. This dish goes well with sesame biscuits and cream. A Roman living in northern Europe would have been quite happy eating fruit with cream, something that a tradi-tionalist from the Mediterranean would have considered barbaric.

BAKED QUINCES

Kydonion en Staiti

The baking method as detailed above by Rufus is, I think, less effective, but still worth trying. Quinces have a slightly gritty texture which the blender can help to avoid. Eating quinces whole therefore leaves one vulnerable to the full nature of the fruit. The pastry has a slight sweetening effect and imparts a distinct wheaten taste to the fruit.

6 quinces
300 g/10 oz spelt flour
150 ml/5 fl oz water
6 tbsp honey

Peel the quinces, cut them into quarters and remove the woody core. Put the spelt flour and the water in a bowl and stir and then knead into a dough, adding more water or flour if needed to make a firm dough. Divide the dough into six balls of equal size. Roll each ball out thinly. Put 1 tablespoon of honey in the hollow where the core was in each quince. Then remake the quinces and encase each one in dough, making sure that there are no gaps or cracks. Place the quinces on an oiled baking tray and leave in the oven at 180°C/350°F/gas mark 4 for 1 hour. Serve the balls whole, but warn your guests to eat only the quinces and to discard the pastry cases.

PEAR JELLY

Pira Pulmentari Vicem

*'Cooked in wine and water they take the place of a jelly, which no
other fruit does apart from the quince and the sparrow apple.'*
[*Pliny* Natural History]

A simple recipe that furnishes a calm end to a spicy dinner. Served
with cream in the style of the northern provinces of the Roman
empire, it is a rich and satisfying dish.

*1 kg/2 lb pears
300 ml/10 fl oz sweet wine*

Use either one of the sweet white dessert wines from Germany or
the heavy sweet red wine from Greece called Mavrodaphne,
depending on the chromatic effect you wish to achieve. In my
opinion, red wine tends to make the dessert look better, whilst
white wine gives a more powerful sweetness. Peel, core and dice the
pears. Put them in a heavy pan and add the wine. Simmer very
gently with the lid on for 30 minutes or until soft. Purée in a
blender and pour into individual bowls. Cool in the fridge before
serving with cream and biscuits.

BRAISED PEARS

Pira Conditiva in Sapa

*'Plant or graft giant pears, pears named after Anicius that ripen
in late autumn (these will be good preserved in* sapa*), pears from
Tarentum, must pears, melon pears, and so on for as many other
varieties as possible.'*
[*Cato* On Agriculture]

Lucius Anicius Gallus was consul in 160 BC. Presumably he was the first to grow this particular variety of pear. My version of pears in *sapa* is inspired by the classic French dish of pears braised in spiced red wine, and is designed for the table rather than the store cupboard.

4 pears
60 ml/2 fl oz sapa *(see p.33)*

Peel and cut the pears in half. Remove the stalks and core. Steam gently for 20 minutes or until soft. Place in a serving dish, pour over the *sapa*, and allow to marinate for at least an hour, spooning the *sapa* onto the pears from time to time. Serve with a cake or biscuits.

DINNER IN THE DINING ROOM

It would be an understatement to regard the study of what the Romans ate for dinner as a complex matter, for whereas breakfast and lunch were generally simple affairs, dinner was often elaborate and eaten by all layers of Roman society. In addition, the literary sources are almost overwhelming in their detail, and selecting rather than searching for material is required, in contrast to the study of other meals. That it took place towards the close of the day is not disputed: numerous papyri have been discovered in Egypt which record invitations to birthday and religious dinners at the eighth or ninth hours, that is at about five o'clock in the afternoon or later, depending on the season. It has been pointed out that the Roman courtyard house, especially planned for the morning ritual of visits from clients and the evening ritual of dinner, was dominated by men at the beginning and end of the day, but was a woman's domain during the rest of the day. For an important citizen, the evening meal was a grand finale, the conclusion of a day spent in professional duties. Even an ordinary Roman held the evening meal in the same high regard; indeed, this meal might be the only one of any substance for those whose resources could not stretch to breakfast and lunch. Cicero, in fact, records Plato's disapproval, no doubt on moral rather than dietary grounds, of the habit at Syracuse of filling one's stomach twice a day. For one group of Romans, this structure was frequently amended: soldiers on sentry duty for the first watch of the night had to postpone their dinner until they were relieved at the start of the second watch, the rationale behind this being that an early dinner would cause laziness and insubordination. Soldiers rounding up barbarians who had crossed the frontier illegally also had to disrupt their dinner: the best time for ambush was deemed to be when the barbarians had settled down for their evening meal and were tired from lugging their sacks of Roman loot.

Before dinner it was customary to go to the baths, and in fact it was at the baths that many people received invitations to dinner. A chapter of *The Satyricon*, the picaresque first-century AD novel by Petronius that centres on the dinner given by the hugely wealthy Trimalchio, begins with a surreal scene at the baths and the handing out of invitations. The philosopher Seneca and other moralists who wrote diatribes against the perversities of an extravagant lifestyle have not rendered service to the history of Roman dining. They might make titillating reading – who is not intrigued by the notion of slaves tickling the throats of their masters to induce such vomiting as to allow for the eating of yet more courses? – but reality was, as is invariably the case, rather more prosaic.

Aulus Gellius, writing in the second century AD, reminisces about a dinner of Egyptian lentils served with diced cucumbers and olive oil that he enjoyed at Athens with the philosopher Taurus, and ʹso about being entertained by the poet Julius Paulus in the Vatican district of Rome on vegetables and fruit. Pliny details to an acquaintance called Septicius Clarus his dinner which allowed for each guest a lettuce, three snails, two eggs, a barley cake, chilled wine sweetened with honey, olives, beetroots, cucumbers and bulbs, the Romans being partial to baked gladiolus and asphodel. This, he adds, is a refined meal which, interestingly enough, resembles in many way a dinner menu from Egypt that lists liver, oysters, lettuce, small loaves of bread and a water fowl. These are certainly not extravagant spreads, but at the same time they show variety and balance. Yet it must be remembered that literary evidence can be misleading, for the writers were from the upper echelons of society, cushioned from food shortages and the emergency substitutions of strange roots and berries.

Archaeology can afford a glimpse at the effect of inadequate diet, although it cannot usually describe exactly what comprised that diet. A study of the Roman graveyard at Poundbury outside Dorchester revealed lesions on the skulls of children buried there, indicative of iron deficiency caused either by malnutrition or a high level of parasitic infection. The remains also show a comparative reduction in the cortical thickness of the long bones, a feature of a shortage of calcium through lack of iron or vitamin D or the inhibition of calcium absorption because of a predominantly cereal diet. These observations are not a vagary of the province of Britain, for the same problems appear elsewhere: of a sample of twelve inhumations at the necropolis of the Sicilian town of Selinunte, all the children and two young adults exhibited the furrows in the eye sockets indicative of a lack of iron. The reason for this may have been the Roman practice of feeding children on barley soup rather than milk, but food short-ages may have been equally to blame. Recent excavations along the ancient waterfront at Herculaneum uncovered hundreds of skele-tons, many of which had been scorched black by the surge that overwhelmed the town when Vesuvius erupted. Analysing the bones poses some fascinating questions. For example, a girl in her teens was found holding a baby, but this was not mother and daughter, for the baby was wearing expensive jewelry and the girl had both dark indentations in her teeth and also muscle lesions to her arm bones. It was concluded that the girl was a slave who, when younger, had been exposed to severe malnutrition and excessive manual labour.

At a private dinner it was strongly recommended that guests happy in each other's company should be invited; this theme crops up again and again in Roman writers. Perhaps some people were using dinners as a means of social advancement, as is often the case today, or those who had suffered as a result put their complaint into stressing the importance of guests over food. After all, as the poet Martial argued, friendships bought with meals are not genuine. Pliny deprecates the action of a recent host who had served food graded according to the status of a particular guest: the best dishes were set before a select few, whilst the rest had to make do with the left-overs. At a Greek banquet, at least in classical Athens, democratic ideals resulted in equality in the dining room. However whilst there might be no distinction drawn between those from different stations in life, there was a sharp division according to sex: the only women at a Greek banquet were the ubiquitous flute girls. At Rome, on the other hand, women attended dinners from the second century BC, although some conservative men would still raise their eyebrows at women dining with those outside their immediate family circle. Sempronia, the mother of the Brutus who assassinated Julius Caesar, was such a woman. The historian Sallust suggests as much with his references to her dancing more skilfully than was proper and chatting up men rather than letting men court her, something that could only happen at a mixed event like a dinner. Later in the Roman Empire dinners were once again same-sex events, following the strictures of the early Christians who pursued such a practice so as to avoid any hints of prostitution or debauchery. But returning to social ranking, it must be remembered that Roman society was structured along the lines of wealthy patrons supporting a mass of clients in return for reciprocal favours, so it was normal for guests to be distinguished by the food they ate. The emperor Augustus may, on occasion, have dined with freedmen like the slave dealer Toranius Flaccus, but his usual habit was to hold formal dinners with strict attention paid to social rank, freedmen being excluded from the society of free citizens.

The location of the dinner party was carefully considered. Varro, writing in the first century BC, suggests separate dining rooms for winter and summer, each equipped with the appropriate types of doors and windows for the different seasons. A winter dining room had to be light and warm; a summer dining room cool and airy, perhaps following Pliny's description of an impressive construction on the east coast of Italy with a panoramic view over the sea. Archaeology has shown the variety of space given over to entertainment: at Pompeii the Villa of the Mysteries seems to have had four seasonally adjusted dining rooms, but lesser houses were also richly equipped. In the cities many dining rooms were found cheek by jowl with neighbouring houses, and were thus in the shade and required artificial lighting. With as many as six oil lamps suspended in a sort of chandelier above the table, a warm light could be created, an ideal atmosphere for the telling of stories or the playful touching of lovers. A Greek and Latin phrasebook from the fourth century AD known as *The Monaco Conversations* shows that the dining room was sometimes perfumed with flowers and incense, while Plutarch suggested an infusion of vervain and maidenhair for sweetness of smell at a banquet.

Some culinary occasions were highlighted by the pomp that surrounded their being served. The emperor Domitian tried to impress by quantity, his banquets sometimes comprising a thousand wealthy Romans with him as a remote and mysterious figure on a distant dais. Seneca is perhaps referring to such gatherings when he remarks on dining halls large enough to hold a crowd. Similarly a structure designated by archaeologists as a large imperial Roman dining pavilion was excavated north of the prytaneion at Eleia in Greece. These extravaganzas might terminate only in the small hours, as illustrated by the story of Cornelius Fronto: bidding leave of his host as the sun was rising, he headed in his evening wear straight to an early court session and greeted everyone with a 'Good evening' rather than a 'Good morning'. Cicero similarly expresses amazement at how long some dinners could drag on. These pictures illustrate just how easy it is to settle into gawping at one Roman outdoing another in terms of size, splendour and expense. Yet as Seneca says, it is not accoutrements of the table and the attendant slaves that matter; rather it is the food itself that is important. An apophthegm of Socrates that was current under the Roman empire was that one should eat and drink in order to live, rather that live in order to eat and drink.

The key to Roman cooking is its pronounced seasoning, a contrast with the Greek kitchen. However even in the fifth century BC tastes were changing and Socrates argued that a multiplicity of dishes and a variety of sauces was both extravagant and ruinous. Plautus in the second century BC was already describing a cosmo-politan cuisine at Rome, the product of wars of conquest and the Roman interest in assimilating and adapting all that was considered fine in other cultures, from architecture to religion. At York the Roman sewers have yielded the remains of blackberries and raspberries, Winterton villa in Lincolnshire has evidence of figs, cereals and horsebeans and Frenchgate at Doncaster has left hazelnuts, sloes,

apples and wheat. Wild and cultivated celery has been found, probably used more for the aromatic seeds than for the stems, at Alcester
and Berinsfield in Oxfordshire and Droitwich in Cheshire. Just as
potatoes and rice often provide the comfort of something starchy in
today's cooking, so bread, beans and porridge did the same in the
Roman world. Seneca believed that he could compete in happiness
with Jupiter himself as long as he had water and polenta. Lentils too
could serve the same function. Their cheapness made them particularly attractive to poor people, which resulted in the proverb
'perfume on lentils' or wasting what was valuable on something that
was worthless. At a dinner given by Nomentanus and described by
Horace, the aptly named Porcius swallowed whole cheese pastries in
one mouthful and so caused much merriment among his fellow
guests.

The Monaco Conversations sums up a Roman dinner most compactly: there were cabbages, leeks, beets, mallows, eggs, asparagus,
nuts, beans, plums, pears, lupins, bulbs, radishes, turnips, salted fish
and meat, rice, peas, fresh fish and meat, pork and apples. Pepper,
asafoetida, cumin and salt are listed individually, and silver pots, of
which examples have been discovered at Cahors in Gaul and
Corfinium in Italy, are known to have been used as cruets. These,
according to Varro, should be beautifully shaped by an artist so as to
satisfy not just the basic instinct for nutrition but also the human
need for refinement. Already at the beginning of the second century
AD the Roman army was eating a wide variety of foods: a letter from
the northern frontier of Britain details beans, chickens, apples, eggs,
fish sauce and olives. It can only be wondered at what delicacies the
army ate when the emperor Severus relaxed the previous austerity of
the military diet at the turn of the second century AD.

As an accompaniment to a civilised dinner, a book might be read
aloud by a slave, or by a younger member of the household. Aulus
Gellius enjoyed such a diversion at the house of the philosopher
Favorinus. If the family was sufficiently wealthy, special clothes,
loose fitting and less cumbersome than the toga, were worn at
dinner. Some people may have felt that they had reached the peak of
their ambition if the mullet in their fish ponds fed out of their
hands, but true pleasure for many Romans lay in moderation, excess
only causing ulcers, gout, indigestion and heart palpitations. And if,

when relaxing among friends over beans and bread, a sense of space and well-being is generated, that is no more than a reflection of Plutarch's conundrum of the second century AD: the question he posed concerned the apparent squash on the dining couches at the start of the meal and the comfort that ensued at the close of the evening. He suggests that diners lay flat to allow for the right hand to reach forward to the table, all food being eaten with the fingers, but that later everyone turned on their sides and thus occupied less room. Perhaps another answer would have been that the diners were relaxed and no one minded being so close to their neighbour, with the result that any concern over squeezing was gently dissipated in the aroma and savour of fine wines and cooking. This was the difference between imperial banquets, the stuff of sensation, and the *convivium* or dinner party of pleasant company, community of life and mental relaxation.

BEEF CASSEROLE

Carnes Vaccinae

'Beef that has been steamed can be used both roasted in a dish and also braised in a sauce, provided that, as soon as it begins to give off a smell, you put the meat in some water. Boil it in as much fresh water as suits the size of the portion of meat; you should not have to add any more water during the boiling. When the meat is cooked, put about half a cup of sharp vinegar, some leeks and a little pennyroyal, some celery and fennel in a casserole and let these simmer for one hour. Then add half the quantity of honey to vinegar, or as much honey as you wish for sweetness. Cook over a low heat, shaking the pot frequently with one's hands so that the sauce coats the meat sufficiently. Then grind the following: 50 peppercorns, half a solidus coin by weight each of costmary and spikenard and one tremissis coin by weight of cloves. Carefully grind all these spices together in an earthenware mortar with the addition of a little wine. When well ground, add them to the casse-

role and stir well, so that before they are taken from the heat, they may warm up and release their flavour into the sauce. Whenever you have a choice of honey or must reduced either by a third or two-thirds, add one of these as detailed above. Do not use a bronze pan, because the sauce tastes better cooked in an earthenware casserole.'

[*Anthimus* On Foods]

This is, in effect, an early example of a *daube*. Bear in mind that the recipe originated in northern France not long after the collapse of the Roman empire in this area; the Franks had taken over the reins of power and trade had all but been strangled in the upheavals of war, yet here are pepper from India and cloves from Indonesia, for although cloves are today cultivated principally in Zanzibar, they are in fact native to eastern Indonesia. Such is and was the power of the market and of the appetite.

Coins were employed as weights in ancient Greece, their comparative regularity being ideal for measuring herbs, spices and drugs. Abbreviated to s, the memory of the *solidus* was maintained in Britain until the decimalisation of the currency. The taste of the dish is not wholly Roman – although there is the classic juxtaposition of sweet and sour – for there is a hint of the medieval kitchen with the employment of cloves.

Pennyroyal can be obtained without difficulty in health food shops and garden centres. Spikenard and costmary, however, will have to be grown in the garden or on a window ledge, but their aromas, sweet and slightly bitter respectively, can be substituted by a couple of bay leaves and a few mint leaves without radically altering the overall flavour of the stew.

1 kg/2 lb beef
1 tsp olive oil
1 leek
2 stalks celery
Half a head of fennel (about 175 g/6 oz)
125 ml/4 fl oz red wine vinegar
1 tbsp honey
4 or 5 spikenard leaves
4 or 5 costmary leaves

2 cloves
1 tsp peppercorns
80 ml/3 fl oz red wine
A pinch of pennyroyal, fresh or dried
1 tbsp sapa (see p.33)
Salt

You will need a heavy casserole for this stew. Cut the beef into 1 inch cubes and fry it gently in the olive oil until brown. Remove the casserole from the heat. Coarsely chop the celery, leek and fennel and add them to the beef together with the vinegar and wine. Pour on enough water to cover the ingredients. Put the lid on the casserole and place it in an oven pre-heated to 170°C/330°F/gas mark 3 for 2 hours. Grind the peppercorns and cloves in a coffee-grinder and finely chop the spikenard, costmary and pennyroyal. Add these with the honey, salt and *sapa* to the stew. Stir and leave to marinate for six hours. Re-heat for 30 minutes in an oven pre-heated to 200°C/400°F/gas mark 6 before serving with bread and vegetables.

HARE IN A SWEET SAUCE

Lepores

'If they are young, hares too may be eaten, in a sweet sauce with pepper, a little cumin and ginger, costmary and spikenard or bay leaves.'

[*Anthimus* On Foods]

This is a characteristically Roman sauce that could have stepped from the pages of Apicius. Hot and spicy, it conjures up echoes of Indian cooking. Wild rabbit has a superior flavour and texture to its farmed cousin and if possible should be used for this recipe.

1 hare or wild rabbit
2 tsp peppercorns

1 tsp cumin seeds or ground cumin
1 tsp ground ginger
3 or 4 costmary leaves
1 bay leaf
¼ litre/ ½ pint sweet white wine
Olive oil
Sea salt

You need the sweetest dessert wine you can find to give this dish the sweet and sour flavour of which the Romans were so fond. If you reduce the peppercorns and cumin seeds to a fine powder in a coffee-grinder you will enjoy a finer flavour, but cumin in pre-powdered form is perfectly acceptable. Finely chop the costmary leaves; if you cannot find costmary, you can use mint. Mix the pepper, cumin, costmary, ginger and bay leaf with the wine, season with salt, put the hare or rabbit in a casserole and pour over the marinade. Cover and leave to marinate overnight or for 12 hours. Remove the hare or rabbit from the marinade and dry with a paper towel. Heat 3 tablespoons of olive oil in a frying pan and brown the meat all over to seal in the flavour. Return to the casserole, spoon the sauce over the hare or rabbit and roast in an oven pre-heated to 180°C/350°F/gas mark 4 for an hour and a half.

HAM IN A RED WINE AND FENNEL SAUCE

Krea Tareikhera

'Cured meat or slices of ham, similarly raw meat: first the cured meat is boiled a little just to take away its saltiness. Then put all these ingredients into a pan: four parts of wine, two parts of grape syrup, one part of wine vinegar, dry coriander, thyme, dill, fennel. Fry, after putting everything in together at the start, then boil. Half-way through the cooking some people add honey and ground cumin, others pepper, and after putting the sauce into a warmed

pot they add little pieces of hot loin and bread.'
[Heidelberg Papyrus]

A criticism sometimes levelled at Roman cooking is that browns and greens predominate, the reds and yellows of modern cooking being absent without tomatoes and peppers. This sauce therefore provides a welcome shade of plum to the main course and serves as an excellent accompaniment to thin slices of ham. I use dried herbs for their convenience and concentrated flavour, and fennel bulb because in this recipe I think its flavour works better than that of the seeds. You could, however, substitute a teaspoon of ground fennel seeds for the bulb.

1/4 litre/1/2 pint red wine
120 ml/4 fl oz sapa (see p.33)
60 ml/2 fl oz red wine vinegar
1 tsp dried dill tops
1 tsp dried thyme
2 tsp ground coriander
1 tbsp honey
Half a head of fennel (about 175 g/6 oz)
1 tsp ground pepper
1 large slice wholemeal bread
Sea salt
Sliced ham

Finely chop the fennel. Combine all the ingredients except the bread in a pan and braise the chopped fennel in the sauce until tender. Meanwhile cut the crust off the slice of bread. Pour the fennel and wine sauce into a blender and liquidise together with the bread until smooth. Return the sauce to the pan and heat gently before serving, stirring occasionally to prevent sticking. The sauce should have a spicy sweet and sour flavour. Serve hot or cold with slices of ham.

PORK IN A PIQUANT SAUCE

Psoai

'Loin and pieces of meat: mix together in sufficient quantity with salt, coriander and fig sap. Cook until it has thickened. Make a hot sauce in a pan: wine vinegar, one part of olive oil to two parts of sweet wine, a pinch of salt. When it has boiled, add a handful of oregano, skim off the froth and sprinkle on some green stuff.'

[Heidelberg Papyrus]

This recipe comes from a papyrus fragment of a cookery book that was found in Egypt and first published in 1921. Interestingly, a recipe in a satirical poem about ancient foodies by Horace has echoes of this sauce in its oiliness. I use lemon juice as a substitute for fig sap: the flavour is obviously not the same but, as fig sap was employed for its acidity, it does not seem too heinous to suggest an ingredient that can be procured more easily. In the ancient world vinegar was usually made from wine, but as there are references to vinegars made from fruit juices and because there could be confusion with the modern use of acetic acid, it seems sensible to specify the type of vinegar.

1 kg / 2 lb pork
120 ml / 4 fl oz olive oil
Juice of half a lemon
1/4 litre / 1/2 pint sweet white wine
5 dried figs
2 tsp coriander seeds
2 tsp dried oregano
3 tbsp white wine vinegar
A handful of fresh parsley
Sea salt

Cut the pork into 1 inch cubes, place them in a casserole and fry in a little olive oil until brown. Powder the coriander seeds in an electric coffee-grinder. Then toss the pork in the salt, lemon juice and ground coriander. Chop the figs and boil them in another saucepan for 5 minutes in a couple of wine glasses of water. Strain off the resulting fig stock and reserve. The figs themselves can be discarded as their seeds make the sauce unpleasantly gritty. Add the wine, oregano, vinegar and fig stock to the pork. Cook the casserole for an hour and a half in an oven pre-heated to 180°C/350°F/gas mark 4. Just before serving, sprinkle the finely chopped parsley over the pork. Bread or barley accompany this dish well.

FRIED LIVER

Ficatum Porcinum

'Cut it up carefully, place on a metal gridiron with broad rods and baste either with olive oil or with fat. It is grilled like this over fine charcoal so that it is cooked, and people eat it while still hot, but underdone, with olive oil, salt and chopped coriander sprinkled on top.'
[*Anthimus* On Foods]

Ficatum refers to a liver fattened on figs. Athletes in the ancient world used figs as a way of gaining muscle, so it is not surprising that this fruit was fed to animals to help them put on weight. Calf's and lamb's liver are less coarse than pig's liver and, as they are more easily found, are given as a more acceptable substitute. As a further variation on the original recipe, I prefer frying rather than grilling the liver as the meat tends to stay more succulent that way – the use of flour is the classic French method of sealing in the juices – but you may prefer to keep to Anthimus' instructions.

6 slices of lamb's or calf's liver (about 250 g/ 1/2 lb)
60 g/2 oz white flour
A handful of fresh coriander
Olive oil
Salt

Purée the coriander leaves in a blender with 2 tablespoons of olive oil and a pinch of salt until you have a smooth paste. Pour another couple of tablespoons of olive oil into a frying pan. Pat the slices of liver in the flour and sauté over a high heat for 2 minutes on each side. Serve each slice of liver with a spoonful of the coriander purée. If you do decide to follow Anthimus, brush the slices of liver all over with olive oil, place under a grill for 3 minutes on each side and serve with the coriander paste as above.

BAKED PLAICE

Myma

'Epaenetus says as follows in his Art of Cookery: *a myma of every kind of meat, and also bird, should be made by finely chopping the soft bits of flesh, adding mashed offal and intestines and blood and seasoning with vinegar, baked cheese, asafoetida, cumin, fresh or dried thyme, savory, fresh or dried coriander, horn onion, toasted onion that has been peeled or poppy seeds and raisins or honey and the seeds of bitter pomegranate. One can have the same myma with fish.'*
[*Athenaeus* The Partying Professors]

Plaice works wonderfully with the rich flavours that make up this dish, although in the process it loses its own identity, a typical feature of Roman cooking in which the disguising of a main ingredient was held to be a consummate art. A less delicate fish such as cod or haddock could be substituted, although plaice provides the dish with great succulence. Using fish avoids the inclusion of mashed offal, intestines and blood which the meat and poultry versions demand. Barley or lentils set this dish off nicely.

4 fillets of plaice
1 onion
1 tbsp olive oil

100 g/3 oz feta cheese
150 ml/5 fl oz dry white wine
30 g/1 oz seedless raisins
2 tbsp white wine vinegar
2 tsp coriander seeds
1 tsp cumin seeds
A sprig each of fresh thyme and savory
1/2 tsp asafoetida
Sea salt

Finely slice the onion and fry it gently in olive oil until it is translucent. Arrange the onion slices at the bottom of a casserole dish and place the fish fillets on top of them. Grind the coriander and cumin seeds in a blender, mix with the asafoetida and raisins and sprinkle over the fish. Place the sprigs of thyme and savory on top. Mix together the wine and vinegar and a little salt and pour over the fish. Thinly slice the feta cheese and arrange the slices to cover the fish. With the lid on the casserole dish, bake the fish in an oven preheated to 150°C/300°F/gas mark 2 for 1 hour.

FISH IN FRESH HERB SAUCE

Glaukos

'I take two particularly large pieces of grey fish with the heads removed, put them in a large casserole and add sparingly some green herbs, cumin, salt, water and olive oil.'
[*Sotades* The Keyless Girls, *quoted in Athenaeus*
The Partying Professors]

In his *Glossary of Greek Fishes* D'Arcy Thompson held that the *glaukos* was impossible to identify for certain, although he cites tentative suggestions by other scholars ranging from the blue shark to a type of horse mackerel. I suggest using cod.

4 cod steaks
60 ml/2 fl oz olive oil
3 tsp ground cumin
A handful each of fresh parsley, lovage, savory, thyme and oregano
Sea salt

Finely chop the fresh herbs and put them, half a wineglass of water, olive oil, sea salt and ground cumin in a casserole, stir to combine and then add the cod steaks. Cook in the oven at 150°C/300°F/gas mark 2 for 1 hour. Serve with bread.

FISH IN VINE LEAVES

Amia

'I took without using any sauce a tuna fish, an exceedingly fine specimen, poured plenty of olive oil over it, wrapped it like a baby in fig leaves, sprinkled it with marjoram and buried it like a firebrand in the hot ashes.'
[*Athenaeus* The Partying Professors]

Many ancient dishes were very oily, as are a number of their modern Greek counterparts, and a fragrant olive oil is to be savoured. Feta cheese, for example, is nowadays sometimes served swimming in a pool of olive oil. Bread serves as an effective counterbalance to any cloying tendency, as do lentils or barley. This recipe works with any oily fish. I have specified herring or mackerel as they should be easier to obtain fresh than tuna, and are much cheaper.

4 herring or mackerel, gutted and filleted
20–25 vine leaves
A handful of fresh marjoram
Olive oil
Salt

Wash the fish and finely chop the marjoram. You will need four pieces of tin foil each large enough to form a parcel for the fish. Overlap the vine leaves in a row on the tin foil. Place the fish fillets on top of the vine leaves. Pour 3 tablespoons of olive oil over the fish, sprinkle with marjoram and salt and wrap around with the vine leaves. You may need to use more leaves to cover the top of the fish. Close the parcels, place on a baking tray and cook for 1 hour in an oven pre-heated to 150°C/300°F/gas mark 2. Remove the tin foil and serve the fish wrapped in the vine leaves.

BUTTER BEANS IN HERB SAUCE

Zomos

'Put wheat groats, coriander, leeks, onion, dill, basil and a little aniseed into a mortar. Boil on the stove and moisten with water, wine, garum and wine vinegar all mixed together. When it has boiled and you are about to take it off the heat, sprinkle on some ground pepper. Some people make it slightly sharp with wine vinegar by pouring over a little, and then remove it from the fire; but others boil everything when the wine vinegar has been added, and by adding green herbs they make it ready to serve.'

[Heidelberg Papyrus]

Although in the original recipe there is no mention of what this sauce should accompany, it is particularly delicious with butter beans.

6 oz/175 g dried butter beans
1 onion
2 tbsp olive oil
1 leek
60 ml/2 fl oz white wine
3 tbsp wheat flakes
1 tbsp garum (see p.29)
A handful of coriander leaves

½ tsp dried dill tops
½ tsp dried basil
500 ml/1 pint water
1 tbsp white wine vinegar
A pinch of aniseed
Sea salt
A handful of fresh parsley (optional)

After soaking the butter beans overnight, boil them in salted water
for 30 minutes. Then take a heavy casserole and fry the onion in the
olive oil until it is soft, then finely slice the leek and put it in the
casserole together with all the other ingredients except for the parsley.
Bring to the boil and then simmer on a very low heat for an hour.
The wheat flakes will thicken the sauce, as will the beans. If you
wish, chop the parsley and sprinkle it over the sauce just before
serving.

NINE TIMES SAUCE

Dodra

*'"I am called Nine Times Sauce." "Why is that?" "I have nine
ingredients." "What are they?" "Stock, water, honey, wine, bread,
pepper, herbs, olive oil, salt."'*
[*Ausonius* Poems]

Although this sauce is used as part of the soufflé which follows, it
could also be served with vegetables.

Half a vegetable stock cube
1 tbsp white wine
1 tbsp olive oil
1 tbsp clear honey
A handful each of fresh parsley, thyme and oregano
75 g/2 ½ oz white bread
A pinch of salt

Boil 150 ml/5 fl oz of water and dissolve the stock cube in it. Finely chop the fresh herbs – I suggest a handful of parsley and a few sprigs each of thyme and oregano, but other combinations can be tried. Cut the crust off the bread. Now put all the ingredients in a food-processor and blend until smooth. The sauce is ready to serve. For the soufflé, I would suggest omitting the salt as the *garum* will be salty enough.

SOUFFLÉ

Spumeum

'What is called in Greek afrutum *and in Latin* spumeum *is made from chicken and egg-white. Lots of egg-white must be used so that the* afrutum *becomes foamy. It should be arranged in a mound on a shallow casserole with a previously prepared gravy and diluted liquamen underneath. Then the casserole is set over the heat and the* afrutum *is cooked in the steam of the sauce. The casserole is then placed in the middle of a serving dish and a little wine and honey poured over it. It is eaten with a spoon or a small ladle. I often add to this recipe some good fish or even some scallops, because they are extremely tasty and are particularly plentiful where I live.'*
[*Anthimus* On Foods]

Nine Times Sauce goes extremely well with this soufflé. In the original version there is merely the mention of some sort of gravy and the inclusion of chicken, but Anthimus does not say what sort of sauce this should be nor how the chicken should be incorporated. I have taken the liberty of combining the sauce with the egg-whites, rather than resting the whites on the sauce, thus following the pattern of a modern soufflé.

6 egg-whites
1 tbsp garum *(see p.29)*
1 tbsp water

— 133 —

1 tsp olive oil
Nine Times Sauce (see above)

Grease a casserole with the olive oil. Separate the eggs and beat the whites until they stand in peaks. Mix the *garum* and water together and add to the Nine Times Sauce. Pour the sauce into the casserole. Gently fold the egg-whites into the sauce. Bake for 25 minutes in an oven pre-heated to 190°C/380°F/gas mark 5. Serve immediately with vegetables (perhaps French beans or asparagus) and bread. If you wish to include chicken with this recipe, I suggest mincing 60 g/2oz of cooked chicken and stirring this into the sauce before folding in the egg-whites.

TANGY SALAD DRESSING

Oxyporium

'One *uncia of lovage, one* sextans *of skinned raisins, one* sextans *of dried mint, one* quadrans *of white or black pepper. To avoid any more expense, these ingredients can be mixed with honey and stored like this.'*

[*Columella* On Agriculture]

There are several recipes for digestive dressings, so called because certain vegetables like lettuce were thought to cause flatulence and which therefore required measures to render them safe for polite company. These dressings were generally diluted with vinegar.

30 g/1 oz lovage or celery leaves
1/2 tsp raisins
1/2 tsp dried mint
1 tsp ground white pepper
2 tbsp clear honey
1 tbsp red wine vinegar
Sea salt (optional)

Finely chop the lovage leaves and raisins, then combine in a small bowl with the other ingredients. If you wish, salt can be added to taste, but with its sharpness the sauce can stand on its own without salt. Stir and serve with a green salad.

BRAISED CUCUMBERS

Cucumeres

'When scraped and cooked in olive oil, vinegar and honey, cucumbers are without doubt more delicious.'
[*Pliny* Natural History]

When cooked, this vegetable belies the old saw 'as cool as a cucumber' and comes as something of a surprise to anyone who has only eaten cucumber as a salad ingredient. This is a surprisingly good recipe that enlivens the sometimes watery cucumber specimens that inhabit supermarket shelves.

1 large cucumber
3 tbsp white wine vinegar
3 tbsp olive oil
1 tbsp clear honey
Sea salt (optional)

Peel and cut the cucumber into thick slices. Pour the white wine vinegar, olive oil and honey into a heavy pan and cook the slices of cucumber gently in the sauce until they are tender, shaking the pan occasionally to redistribute the cucumber slices and ensure even cooking. Serve hot as a side dish.

FRIED SQUASH

Kolokynthe Teganistheisa

'When baked or fried they lose a considerable part of their special moistness, and what remains does not acquire any strong power, something which does not happen when they are prepared in a simple sauce. Naturally oregano accompanies gourds well because of the watery quality that is innate in them; for everything of this nature demands to be mixed with bitter, sharp, astringent or salty flavours, if the intention is for them to be eaten without unpleasantness and without causing nausea.'

[*Galen* On the Powers in Foods]

This recipe is delicious made with any type of squash, the combination of salt and olive oil certainly supporting Galen's closing statement. My favourite is the butternut squash because of its lovely creamy texture.

1 butternut squash (about 600 g/1 lb 5 oz)
90 ml/3 fl oz olive oil
2 tsp oregano
Salt or garum (see p.29)

Peel the squash, cut into large chunks and steam for 10 minutes until cooked but still firm. Heat the oil in a frying pan. Add the chunks of squash and the oregano. Fry the squash until it begins to brown on the outside, but do not worry if it begins to disintegrate as you cook it, for the taste is still excellent. Sprinkle generously with salt or drizzle with *garum* before serving.

LENTIL STEW

Laganophake

'*Break a well baked lentil cake into chicken stock and boil. Or pound dried dill and cumin in wine, water and aniseed, but boil the lentils separately. Chop onions, add cumin, vinegar, olive oil, fresh herbs, and boil. Then combine both of these when boiled well, add good olive oil and leave to simmer on the stove until thickened.*'

[Heidelberg Papyrus]

I have used the alternative version for this recipe, as the first sentence of the instructions on the papyrus, with its reference to an unidentified lentil cake, is too vague to construct a coherent set of instructions for the modern kitchen. My version ignores the demand to boil the lentils separately as being too pernickety and of no apparent benefit to the final taste.

100 g/3 oz Puy lentils
1 onion
125 ml/4 fl oz red wine
1 tsp cumin seeds
1 tsp dried dill tops
A sprig each of fresh thyme and oregano
A handful of fresh parsley
1 tbsp olive oil
A pinch of aniseed
Sea salt

Thinly slice an onion and fry it gently in the olive oil until soft and just beginning to turn brown. Then add 1 pint of water, the red wine and the lentils. Grind the cumin and aniseed in a coffee-grinder and stir these into the liquid together with the dill. Bring to the boil, then turn down the heat and simmer, covered, for about 45 minutes or until the lentils are tender. The dish should be quite dry to allow eating with the fingers or scoops of bread. Just before serving, stir in the thyme and oregano after chopping them finely. Garnish with coarsely chopped parsley. These lentils can be eaten with bread as a substantial meal in themselves or as an accompaniment to other dishes.

SPICY LENTILS

Lenticula

'Lentils are good when washed and carefully boiled in fresh water. Make sure that the first lot of water is poured away, and a second lot of hot water added as required, but not too much, and then boil the lentils slowly on the stove. When they are cooked, add for seasoning a little vinegar, together with the addition of that spice which is called Syrian sumach. Sprinkle a spoonful of this spice over the lentils while they are still on the fire and stir in well. Take the lentils off the fire and serve. You can add for flavouring a good spoonful of oil from unripe olives to the second lot of water while the lentils are still cooking, as well as one or two spoonfuls of coriander including the roots – not ground but whole – and a pinch of salt for seasoning.'

[*Anthimus* On Foods]

This dish has a clean fresh taste that takes the lentils away from their sometimes rather dreary image. The description in Roman times of sumach as Syrian merely indicates the spice's supposed place of origin. Its sharp lemony taste means that, as here, a lemon can be substituted, although of course the only citrus fruit that the Romans knew was the citron. Citrons have a thick skin, a substantial pith and are more than twice the size of lemons; they are still grown in the southern Mediterranean today for candying. If you can find sumach, you will be rewarded with not just a lemony taste, but also a hint of incense in this most aromatic of spices. To make the dish more presentable, I suggest using ground coriander seeds and fresh coriander leaves rather than the roots and all approach adopted by Anthimus.

200 g/6 oz Puy lentils
1 tbsp red wine vinegar
Juice of half a lemon or *2 tsp sumach*
1 slice of lemon
1 tbsp olive oil
2 tsp ground coriander seeds

A handful of fresh coriander leaves
Sea salt

Boil the lentils in 1 pint of water for about 30 minutes or until tender. Then drain off the water, add the vinegar, lemon juice, slice of lemon, olive oil, half a wineglass of water and the ground coriander seeds. Season with salt and simmer gently with the lid on for 20 minutes. Just before serving, chop the coriander leaves finely and sprinkle over the lentils.

LENTILS WITH BEET

Teutlophake

'*I sometimes serve a dish of beet and lentils. Heracleides of Tarentum often used to give it without any complications both to those in good health and to those who were poorly. First I put in plenty of beet, then after seasoning it I either add a little more salt or some sweet fish sauce, because then it is more laxative.*'
[*Galen* On the Powers in Foods]

I offer two very different versions of this recipe, both of which furnish taste enough to lend further weight to Galen's argument that a good doctor should also be a good cook. Both the leaves and the root of the beet were eaten by the Romans, but as beet is rarely sold today with the leaves fresh enough for eating, I suggest using spinach leaves in the second version. Red lentils are used in the first version to ensure a vibrant addition to the culinary palette. Brown lentils work well in the second not only because they blend attractively with the spinach, but also because, in keeping their shape when cooked, they provide a pleasing texture alongside the slight chewiness of the spinach.

VERSION I

100 g/4 oz red lentils
3 or 4 beetroots (about 250 g/8 oz)
Olive oil
Garum (see p.29)
Salt

Peel and finely chop the beetroots. Put the chopped beetroots and lentils in a pan with 1 pint of water and simmer gently for 20 minutes. Pour the mixture into a blender and process until it becomes a smooth purée. Return the purée to the pan and season with a good quantity of salt. When serving, pour generous quantities of olive oil and *garum* over the top of the individual portions of purée.

VERSION II

100 g/4 oz brown lentils
Two handfuls of fresh spinach leaves (about 100 g/3 oz)
2 tbsp olive oil
1 tbsp garum (see p.29)
Salt

Put the lentils in 1 pint of water, bring to the boil and then cook gently for 20 minutes. Meanwhile, after trimming off their gritty stems, shred the spinach leaves. Add the spinach, olive oil and *garum* to the lentils and simmer for a further 10 minutes or until the lentils are tender. Serve as a side dish.

ADRIATIC BREAD

Panis Picens

'There still remains a sense of pride in Picenum over the local recipe for bread made with groats. Soaked for nine days, then kneaded on the tenth day with raisin juice to look like pastry, it is

afterwards put in earthenware pots and baked in the oven where the pots should crack open. It is not served unless it has been softened, usually in milk or honeyed wine.'

[*Pliny* Natural History]

This is an unusual bread which is well worth trying. Picenum in the Latin title refers to the area around modern Ancona on the east coast of Italy, but I have brought Adriatic into the title as it has greater resonance today. Soaking the grains for nine days causes fermentation and, when successful, imparts a pleasant sourness to the bread. If, however, the fermentation does not work, the grains rot and smell foul. I have therefore modified both the method of preparation and the principal ingredient, firstly to obviate any culinary disasters and secondly to avoid the sort of lengthy wait which sits uneasily in a modern kitchen. The malted flour that I have specified is much easier to obtain than groats, while the malt approximates to the fermented taste of the original recipe and the whole grains give the necessary coarse texture. The recipe is included in this chapter because it appeared at a banquet attended by Julius Caesar, although it does not have the makings of a luxurious dish and could be served at breakfast.

300 g/10 oz malted brown flour with wheat flakes
180 ml/6 fl oz red grape juice
5 tbsp milk or red wine
1 tbsp clear honey

Mix the flour with the grape juice, work into a dough and knead for a couple of minutes. Place the dough in a plastic bag and leave to rest for an hour. Then roll the dough out thinly on a floured surface, hatch the top with a knife and cut into rectangles about 3 cm / 1 inch wide and 7 cm / 3 inches long. Place these on a floured baking tray, cover with tin foil and bake for 40 minutes in an oven pre-heated to 200°C/400°F/gas mark 6. When cooked, allow to cool on a wire rack. Meanwhile warm the milk or wine in a pan and stir in the honey until it is completely dissolved. Steep the bread in the honeyed milk or wine for 5 minutes before serving with vegetables or meat.

ASPARAGUS

Asparagus

'*Do not boil asparagus for too long, for it will lose its power and flavour unless it is strong. Eat with salt and olive oil.*'

[*Anthimus* On Foods]

I love asparagus, the king of vegetables when plump and tender. French noblemen under the *ancien régime* used to eat asparagus to ensure that their making water was as sweet as their manners. This recipe is very much on the French lines of tossing in butter, but then Anthimus did write in northern France not long after the collapse of the Roman Empire there. Whilst I prefer to keep salt to a minimum in cooking, asparagus are an exception in demanding a salty tang.

500 g/1 lb asparagus
1 tbsp olive oil
1 tsp sea salt

Scape any stringy bark off the asparagus and tail the ends. Steam the asparagus until tender. Then heat the olive oil in a frying pan, add the salt and toss the asparagus briefly before serving with the oil, salt and the juices from the frying.

CABBAGE SALAD

Krambe

'*You should cut up cabbages with a very sharp knife, then wash them and allow the water to drain off; cut up together with the cabbage a sufficient quantity of coriander and rue; then sprinkle with honeyed vinegar and grate on top a small quantity of asafoetida.*'

[*Mnesitheus of Cyzicus, quoted in Oribasius* Medical Compilations]

This recipe affords one of the few instances where the omission of a flavouring really matters, and unfortunately the ingredient in question is something not available in supermarkets. Rue used to be a popular herb, yet its English use dwindled into nothing during the Tudor period. It can, however, be bought as a plant at most garden centres and its seeds germinate easily, so there should be no problem over growing it in the window-sill or in the garden. Asafoetida can be purchased from Indian and health food shops.

1 white cabbage
2 tbsp white wine vinegar
2 tbsp clear honey
A bunch of fresh coriander leaves
A sprig of fresh rue (see p.73)
1 tsp asafoetida powder
Sea salt (optional)

Thinly slice the cabbage as for a coleslaw and arrange in a salad bowl. Combine the vinegar with the honey in a cup. Finely chop the coriander and rue and add to the honeyed vinegar. Season with salt if you wish, although the dressing is strong enough not to need it. Stir the asafoetida into the dressing and pour over the cabbage. Toss before serving.

CELERY WITH RAISIN SAUCE

Olusatra

'Carefully clean the alexanders so that it does not have any soil on it. Put it in vinegar and salt. After thirty days take out and peel off and throw away the skin. Chop up the inner part and put into a glass jar or a new earthenware pot and add a liquid, which should be made as detailed below. Take mint, raisins and a small dried onion. Purée these with some parched meal and a little honey. When these have been properly puréed, combine with one

part of sapa *or* defrutum *to one part of vinegar. Pour this into the
jar and seal with a lid.'*
[*Columella* On Agriculture]

Alexanders is an umbelliferous plant growing up to five feet high
whose original habitat was the Mediterranean, although it is now
found all over Europe on wasteland and by the sea. It resembles
celery in both appearance and taste. Since alexanders is not available
in supermarkets, I use celery in this recipe. The accompanying sauce
is excellent not only with vegetables other than celery, such as carrots
or peas, but also with slices of a cheese like Cheddar or Caerphilly.

*1 head of celery
100 g/3 oz raisins
60 ml/2 fl oz red wine vinegar
60 ml/2 fl oz* sapa *(see p.33)
1 tbsp clear honey
2 tsp dried onion flakes
1 tsp spelt flour
Sea salt (optional)*

Wash and chop the celery and then steam gently until it is tender.
Serve it hot with a sauce which you make by soaking the raisins in
the *sapa* and vinegar for 1 hour and then adding the other ingredients and puréeing them in a blender until very smooth.

FRENCH BEANS

Fasiola

'French beans are good, even when dried, provided they are
cooked well.'
[*Anthimus* On Foods]

I am perhaps taking liberties in quoting this as a recipe, but French
beans are still served as the mainstay of the meals in the monaster-

ies on Mount Athos, where the pattern of life has continued much as in the days of the Byzantine Empire, thus providing a link with the Roman past. In the refectory at Vatopedi there are horseshoe marble tables embraced by stone benches in larger horseshoes. Although built during the reign of the emperor Alexius in the twelfth century, the design is much older, reflecting the move in late antiquity from the traditional three couches set before a round table to a semicircular couch embracing a semicircular table. The French beans there are served in salt and olive oil and eaten with rough bread and olives, and this has been the source of my recipe.

There is some doubt about the meaning of the Latin word *fasiolum.* I have translated it here as French bean, because of its availability and connection with Mount Athos, although alternatively it could refer to the green pods of the Celtic bean. It might be thought strange that French beans should be dried, yet many green foods were dried either to preserve them for use during the winter or to concentrate their powers. A modern example of the latter can be observed in the case of dried wild lettuces, which herbalists say have a sedative and narcotic effect.

French beans
Olive oil
Sea salt

Boil as many beans as you need in a small amount of water. When they are cooked, drain off the water, pour over the olive oil and salt and toss on a high flame. Use a good olive oil, and be generous with it. Incidentally, frozen beans are much improved by this recipe.

FRIED CARROTS

Pastinacae

'Parsnips and carrots are good when boiled well and mixed in other dishes. They are also diuretic. If they are eaten fried, parboil them first in water.'
[*Anthimus* On Foods]

In Roman times carrots had a rather woody centre. The paler core in modern carrots furnishes a record of this horticultural history. The Roman carrot was also white, which is why it is bracketed with parsnips in this and other recipes.

> *500 g/1 lb carrots*
> *Olive oil for frying*
> *Sea salt (optional)*

Wash and peel the carrots, cut them into strips and steam gently for 10 minutes. Heat the oil in a frying pan and fry the carrots until they begin to turn brown. Serve hot, sprinkled with salt if you wish.

MUSHROOMS IN HONEY

Mykai

'For which reason mushrooms should in particular be prepared with vinegar, or a mixture of honey and vinegar, or honey and salt alone.'
[*Diphilus, quoted in Athenaeus* The Partying Professors]

Mushrooms were often regarded with suspicion in the ancient world. The dour Pliny records the deaths of whole dining rooms of revellers through fungi poisoning and the emperor Claudius was supposedly murdered with a dish of doctored mushrooms. Not surprisingly, ancient mushroom recipes are few and far between.

25 g/1 oz dried porcini mushrooms
2 tbsp red wine vinegar
1 tbsp clear honey
Sea salt (optional)

Cover the mushrooms with boiling water and soak for half an hour. Then add the vinegar and honey and simmer, covered, for half an hour. Season with salt if you wish. Serve hot.

CELERY IN VINEGAR

Tybaris

'And they used to call this "seasoning". They used to dub salad "green purées". The side dish the Dorians called tybaris, *namely celery in vinegar.'*
[*Pollux* Dictionary]

This is a piquant dish, not unlike sauerkraut. Doris is a town a few miles north of Delphi in central Greece, and this recipe may hail from there, but it is more likely that Pollux is referring to the area of southern Greece which spoke the Dorian dialect, for these people had a name for a simple lifestyle and this is certainly a straight-forward dish. I suggest reducing the acidity by using equal portions of wine and vinegar, on the grounds that in antiquity the term vinegar could be applied to a rough beverage as well as the familiar condiment. None the less, the sharp flavour necessitates serving the celery in modest portions as a relish.

1 head of celery
125 ml/4 fl oz white wine
125 ml/4 fl oz white wine vinegar

Wash and chop the celery and simmer it gently with the wine and vinegar until tender. You may wish to add some salt to taste, although this may not be necessary with the sharpness of the dish. Serve either hot or cold.

CHICK-PEAS WITH CHEESE

Erebinthoi syn Xeroi Tyroi

'Chick-peas boiled in water are customarily eaten by many people, some serving them plain, others seasoning them with a little salt. Those who live where I do make a sort of flour out of dried cheese and sprinkle the chick-peas with this.'

[*Galen* On the Powers in Foods]

The cheese in this recipe sticks the chick-peas together and allows for them to be eaten easily with the fingers. Parmesan and pecorino cheese are ideal as they grate finely and impart a robust flavour to the dish.

200 g/6 oz chick-peas
100 g/3 oz Parmesan or pecorino cheese
Sea salt

Soak the chick-peas overnight, boil them in salted water for 40 minutes or until tender and then drain. Finely grate the cheese and stir it into the chick-peas. Serve while still warm. The cheese will coat the chick-peas and add a glistening effect.

CHICK-PEAS IN SAFFRON

Erebinthoi Knakosymmigeis

'And then chick-peas marinated in saffron, plump in their tender youth.'
[*Philoxenus* The Dinner, *quoted in Athenaeus*
The Partying Professors]

I particularly like this dish – the colour is exquisite and the taste very subtle. It recalls the ideal of a Roman dining room, a place of rich colours and symbolic decoration.

200 g / 6 oz dried chick-peas
A generous pinch of saffron
Sea salt

Soak the chick-peas overnight. Drain them and put them in a heavy pan with 2 pints of water and salt. Bring to the boil, add the saffron, stir and simmer, covered, very gently for at least an hour. Taste to check on its saltiness. Serve warm.

CHEESE WITH HONEY

Tyros Dia Koskinou

'Break off a piece of cheese, put it in a bowl, then turn a bronze sieve over the top, and work the cheese through. Whenever you are about to serve, pour sufficient honey over it.'
[*Athenaeus* The Partying Professors]

If this recipe is intact – and there is no reason why this should not be the case – then it comprises simply grated cheese with honey.

200 g / 7 oz feta cheese
4 tbsp clear honey

Grate the feta cheese and arrange in a pile on a plate. Pour the honey over and serve immediately as a dessert with biscuits. Other cheeses can also be used, from Cheddar to goat's. Ring the changes until you find your favourite combination.

HONEY CAKE

Enkhytoi

'Menander makes mention of the flat cakes called "moulded" in his Heracles the Imposter: *"It is not possible to make those Lydian recipes nor the sort of dishes you usually beat into one mass – honey, fine flour, eggs."'*
[*Menander, quoted in Athenaeus* The Partying Professors]

This precursor of a sponge cake comes from Lydia in what is now western Turkey, which enjoyed a reputation for culture and refinement. Traditionally, Heracles (or Hercules as he was known to the Romans) liked to eat well, so he appears frequently in comic burlesques involving food.

3 eggs
200 g / 7 oz clear honey
50 g / 2 oz white flour

Beat the eggs until stiff, gradually adding the honey as you do so. Fold in the sifted flour, pour into an oiled casserole dish and place in an oven pre-heated to 170°C/330°F/gas mark 3 for 1 hour. Serve warm with honey.

NUT CAKE

Gastris

'In Crete, says Chrysippus, they make a small cake called gastris.
*It is made as follows: walnuts, hazelnuts, almonds and also some
poppy seeds. Roast, keeping a close eye on them, and pound
carefully in a clean mortar. Mix in fruit softened with boiled
honey, add plenty of pepper and soften. It becomes dark with poppy
seeds. Flatten it out and make into a square. Next purée some
white sesame seeds, soften them with boiled honey and draw out
into two thin slabs. Place one slab underneath and the other on
top, so that the dark slab is in the middle, and shape it properly.
This is what the wise* pâtissier *Chrysippus says.'*
[*Athenaeus* The Partying Professors]

This is a particular favourite of mine, partly because of its rich
flavours, but also because it is a rare survivor from what was an
extensive branch of ancient cooking. Few of the other extant recipes
for cakes would have warranted the force of Roman law in trying to
have them banned on the grounds of excessive extravagance, yet this
melange of honey, fruits and nuts possesses the necessary sumptuous-
ness. In many ways it resembles Italian *panforte*, whose origins date
back at least to the Middle Ages.

100 g/3 oz poppy seeds
100 g/3 oz ground walnuts
100 g/3 oz ground hazelnuts
100 g/3 oz ground almonds
100 g/3 oz dried and stoned dates
100 g/3 oz dried figs
150 g/5 oz sesame seeds
75 g/2 1/2 oz clear honey
1/2 tsp ground black pepper
Flour

Put the poppy seeds and ground nuts on a baking tray and place
under a hot grill for 5 minutes, turning them over with a spoon from

time to time to prevent them from burning. The grilling brings out the full flavour of the nuts. Put the sesame seeds in another bowl. Purée the figs and dates in a blender; the softer the dried fruits, the better they will mash. Add the nut mixture and pepper to the dried fruits and blend until they are the consistency of a sticky dough. The pepper complements the honey which is to be added later, both ingredients bringing a certain fire to the back of the throat. Pour the honey into a pan and bring to the boil. Boil for 3 minutes or until the honey begins to darken. The boiling will harden the honey when it cools and thus bind the cake together. Then blend one-third of the honey into the dried fruit and nut mixture and stir the rest into the sesame seeds. Divide the sesame seed mixture into two balls of equal size. Flour your hands and flatten one of the sesame seed balls into a disc about 25 cm/10 inches in diameter and put this onto a flat plate. You could use rice paper as a base for ease of serving, although the sesame seeds should not stick too much and rice paper would be an anachronism. Place the nut mixture on top of the sesame seeds and flatten with your hands until the sesame seeds are completely covered. Flatten the remaining sesame seed ball with floured hands and position this on top of the cake. Use a metal spatula to ensure a smooth finish. Leave for an hour to allow the honey to set and serve at the close of a meal or as a snack during the day.

WALNUT AND FIG CAKES

Basyniai

'Semus, in the second book of his History of Delos, states: "On the island of Hecate the people of Delos offer to Iris what are called basyniai. These consist of dough made from wheat flour cooked with honey and the so-called kokkora, namely a dried fig and three walnuts." '

[*Athenaeus* The Partying Professors]

It is not clear exactly what the dried fig and three walnuts are doing in this recipe. Are they there to merely flavour the honey? Or are they added to the cake itself? The numbers suggest a religious symbolism, which my prosaic interpretation has rendered as a proportion rather than an exact number. Iris was the rainbow goddess and these cakes are indeed colourful with their golden exterior and dark filling.

FOR THE PASTRY:

200 g/7 oz light white flour
60 ml/2 fl oz olive oil
80 ml/3 fl oz water

FOR THE FILLING:

75 g/3 oz walnuts
25 g/1 oz dried figs

FOR FRYING:

80 ml/3 fl oz olive oil

FOR COATING:

80 ml/3 fl oz clear honey

Combine the flour, olive oil and water in a large mixing bowl. Knead until you have a smooth dough, adding a touch more water or flour if needed. Gather up into a ball and place in a plastic bag for an hour. Finely grind the walnuts and figs in a blender. Roll the pastry out as thinly as possible on a floured surface. Using a cutter with a 6 cm/2½ inches diameter, cut the pastry into rounds. Place a teaspoon of the walnut and fig mixture on one round. Paint water around the edge of another round with a brush and gently pinch the edges of the two together. Repeat until you have used up all the pastry. Heat the olive oil in a large frying pan and fry the pastries until they are crisp and golden on both sides. Drain. Simmer the honey in a pan and, as it bubbles, toss in the pastries so that they are coated. Serve warm.

RICE PUDDING

Oriza

'Rice is boiled in fresh water. When it is properly cooked, the water is drained off and goat's milk is added. The pot is put on the flame and cooked slowly until it becomes a solid mass. It is eaten like this hot, not cold, but without any salt or oil.'
[*Anthimus* On the Observance of Foods]

Is this a pudding? Anthimus does not say, but if served with honey it provides a substantial end to a meal.

100 g/3 oz pudding rice
300 ml/10 fl oz goat's milk

Using a heavy casserole with a lid, boil the rice in water until soft. Drain off the water and add the goat's milk. Place in an oven at 170°C/330°F/gas mark 3 for 1 hour or until a solid pudding is formed. Serve hot, perhaps with Rose Honey (see p.43) or Spiced Sauce (see p.31).

SESAME WAFERS

Sesamides

'Round biscuits from honey and toasted sesame seeds and olive oil.'
[*Athenaeus* The Partying Professors]

These nutty and crumbly cakes are among my favourites in the ancient biscuit repertoire.

100 g/3 oz sesame seeds
50 g/2 oz spelt flour
1 tbsp olive oil
2 tbsp honey
3 tbsp water

Spread the sesame seeds on a baking tray and toast them under the grill for 3 minutes, shaking frequently until golden. The seeds will pop and jump under the heat, growing in flavour as they do so. Combine all the ingredients together in a large mixing bowl and work into a tough pastry. You may have to add a drop more water, but ensure that it is no more than that, otherwise the cakes will become brittle. Gather the pastry into a ball and place in a plastic bag for an hour. This will make the pastry more manageable. Then roll the pastry out thinly on a lightly floured board. Using a 5 cm/ 2 inch pastry cutter, cut out discs and place them on an oiled baking tray. Bake in an oven pre-heated to 190°C/380°F/gas mark 5 for 10 minutes. Cool on a wire rack and serve.

DRIED PEAR PUDDING

Apioi eis Kykliskous

'They slice pears into thin discs which they dry and store away. When food is short during the winter and spring, they cook these discs as a substitute for foods that contain little nourishment.'
[*Galen* On the Powers in Foods]

Accompanied by cream, this recipe makes a pleasant fruit salad. Alternatively it can be served with a dash of Spiced Sauce (see p.31).

250 g/½ lb dried pears

Gently braise the dried pears in a little water until they are plump. Cool and serve with the resulting juice.

ANCIENT AUTHORS

I have presented my own translations of the ancient recipes quoted in this book, but some readers may be interested to explore further the original sources.

Anthimus (c. AD 450-520): A doctor from Constantinople who wrote a medical and culinary treatise in northern France when on a diplomatic mission to King Theuderic of the Franks. English translation and commentary by Mark Grant, *Anthimus: On the Observance of Foods*, Totnes 1996.

Aristophanes (c. 457-385 BC): A playwright in Athens. The popularity of his works later led to commentaries being written to explain his rich vocabulary and political allusions. Some of the comments take the form of recipes. There is no English translation of the Greek text of these commentaries.

Athenaeus (c. AD 170-230): Author of *The Deipnosophists*, which can be translated as *The Partying Professors*. This work uses the literary device of a conversation at an imaginary dinner party to discuss food and related subjects. There is an English translation in the Loeb Classical Library by C.B. Gulick, Cambridge, Massachusetts/London 1927-41.

Bassus (tenth century AD): Supposed author of an agricultural manual known as the *Geoponica* or *Country Matters*, composed of extracts from earlier writers. The Greek text is available in the Teubner (Leipzig) series, but no English translation exists at present.

Cato (234-149 BC): Author of many books, the only one that still survives being his *On Agriculture*. This gives advice on the planting of crops, as well as listing numerous recipes for pickles and simple cakes. The Loeb Classical Library has an English translation by

W.D. Hooper and H.B. Ash, Cambridge, Massachusetts/London 1935. There is also a new translation with a brief commentary by A. Dalby, Totnes 1998.

Columella (first century AD): A Spaniard from Cadiz who owned estates in Italy. He wrote his *On Agriculture* between AD 60 and 65. There is an English translation by E.S. Forster, E. Heffner and H.B. Ash in the Loeb Classical Library, Cambridge, Massachusetts/ London 1941-55.

Galen (c. AD 129-200): Personal physician to the emperor Marcus Aurelius and the prolific writer of medical texts that were to form the basis of western medicine until the beginning of the nineteenth century. English translations of the books that discuss food can be found in P.N. Singer, *Galen: Selected Works*, Oxford 1997 (*The Thinning Diet*) and Mark Grant, *Galen On Food and Diet*, Princeton forthcoming (*On the Powers in Foods, On Barley Soup*).

Heidelberg Papyrus: This fragment of a Greek cookery book was found in the dry sands around the ancient city of Oxyrhynchus in Egypt. The Greek text is included as an appendix to the Teubner edition of Apicius *On the Art of Cooking* by C. Giarratano and F. Vollmer, Leipzig 1922.

Hesychius (fifth century AD): Author of a dictionary of terms used by ancient Greek writers. There is no English translation of this work.

Oribasius (c. AD 320-390): The author of a digest of medical knowledge, based on quotes and paraphrases of earlier writers. The first five books deal with food and drink. There is a French translation of the whole of the Greek text by C. Daremberg and U. Bussemaker, Paris 1851. Books 1 and 4 only have been translated into English by Mark Grant, *Dieting for an Emperor*, Leiden 1997.

Pliny (c. AD 23-79): Served as a senior officer in the Roman army and fleet. Author of the magisterial *Natural History* which encompasses everything from geography to plants and rocks. An English translation is available in the Loeb Classical Library by H. Rackham, W.H.S. Jones and D.E. Eichholz, Cambridge, Massachusetts/London 1938-62.

Pollux (second century AD): Professor of rhetoric at Athens some time after AD 178 and author of a dictionary. The Greek text is available in the Teubner series, but there is no English translation of this work.

The Suda Lexicon: *Suda* means 'fortress'. This encyclopaedia of ancient literature was composed in the tenth century AD. There is a Teubner edition of the Greek text, but no English translation.

REFERENCES

References to ancient authors follow the standard classical conventions with just a few minor changes for the sake of clarity.

INTRODUCTION

9   So I got myself ready: Apul.*Met.* 2.19
      we recall Seneca's dictum: Sen.*Cons.Helv.*10.3

11   '*Kai su teknon*' ('You too, my child'): Suet.*Caes.* 82
     'The temptation to ... ': Jongman, *The Economy*, 16

12   Martial tells of a black kitchen: 1.92.2
     Horace moans about smoke: Hor.*Sat.* 1.5.20
     Seneca often refers: e.g. *Ep.* 90.19, 114.26
     the kitchen caught fire: Hor.*Sat.* 1.5.71-76
     As food was eaten at the table with fingers: Plaut.*Ps.* 884, Alex. *ap.* Ath. 12.516e
     virtually raw eggs: Pliny *HN* 7.183, Ath. 2.58e, Dsc. 2.50

13   Martial remarks that a cook: 14.220
     In fact, the historian Livy: 39.6.9
     Cicero, writing a little earlier: *Rosc.Am.* 49.134
     Seneca, a century later: *Ep.* 88.18
     to hang around in marketplaces: Alex. *ap.* Ath. 4.137c-d, Posidipp. *ap.* Ath. 14.659c-d, Ter.*Eun* 255-259, Macho *ap.* Ath.13.579e
     The cook in the *The Liar* by Plautus: *Ps.* 791-895
     Plato in *The Republic*: 373c
     while in Persia they were exchanged: Xen.*Cyr.* 5.5.39
     took a somewhat more callous view: Hdt. 4.71

14   Fast-food establishments: Col. 8.16.5, Mart. 1.41.9-10, Hor.*Sat.* 2.4.62
     Catullus mentions: 95.7-9

But *popinae* had a reputation: Apul.*Met.* 1.13, 8.1, Col. 1.8.2, Cicero *Phil.* 13.24

Juvenal describes in passing: 8.158

as Horace described them: *Ep.* 1.14.21

Asellina's *thermopolium*: Maiuri, *Pompeii*, 134-7

strings of onions and cheeses hanging from the rafters: ibid., 130

the hovel of a poor elderly couple: Ov.*Met.* 8.647-648

whilst Virgil has a round cheese: [Verg.] *Mor.* 57-58

The Art of Dining ... by Clearchus: Ath. 1.4c

The Banquet by Philoxenus: Ath. 1.5b

Breadmaking by Chrysippus: Ath. 3.113a

Cookery by Simus: Ath. 4.164d

On Cakes by Iatrocles: Ath. 1.4e

15 *The Art of Dining* by Archestratus: Ath. 1.7a-c

He was spending some time at Minturnae: Ath. 1.7a-c

16 Galen actually begins: *Bon.Mal.Suc.* 1.1=6.749K

that otherwise would have been avoided: e.g. bitter vetch, Gal. *ap.* Orib. 1.27.1 and unripe vetch, Gal. *ap.* Orib. 1.34.1

Seneca attacks the fashion: Sen.*Ep.* 110.12-13

castigates the apparent need: Sen.*Ep.* 114.26, cf. 60.2

simple pastry with honey: Sen.*Ep.* 63.6

Peter Garnsey, in his book: Garnsey, *Famine*, 39

Famine could be defined as: ibid., 6

while city dwellers were cushioned: Bisel (*The Secrets of Vesuvius*, 59) concludes from her study of the bones found at Herculaneum that the inhabitants were 'in general ... well nourished'.

17 Thus in Britain and Germany long halls: Percival, *The Roman Villa*, 135-7

in northern Gaul butter and cream: Grant, *Anthimus*, 31-2

butter being eaten by barbarians: Plin.*HN* 28.133

instead of olive oil: Plin. *HN* 11.239

At Canterbury: Arthur, 'Roman Amphorae'

with accolades bandied about: e.g. Ath. 1.27a, 26f, 33a

Massic Wine: Front. *Caes. ad Front.* 4.6.1

the vintage season: Gell. 20.8.1
Sabine wine: Hor.*Od.* 1.9.7-8

18   shards at Marseilles: Bonifray and Piéri, 'Amphores du Vième au VIIième s.'
Especially popular: Grant, *Anthimus*, 26 and Plu.*Mor.* 676b-c
grape pips have been discovered: Williams, 'A Consideration of the Sub-Fossil Remains'
three to one: Plu.*Mor.* 657c and Lissarrague, *The Aesthetics*, 8
dangerous and beneficial: ibid., 5-6
hot or chilled: Sen.*Ep.* 78.23, 122.6, Gell. 19.5.5
insulating layer: Plu.*Mor.* 691c-d

19   Beer and wine are juxtaposed: see Bowman, *Life and Letters*, 115-7 (Tablet 5.2.190)
Some Romans railed: e.g. Sen. *Ep.* 95.25
labels advertising the manufacturer's name: *CIL* 10736: the manufacturer in this instance was one Titus Claudius Atimetus
the Roman dockyards in London: Arthur, 'Roman Amphorae'
When the emperor Severus Alexander: van Minnen and Sosin, 'Imperial Pork'

20   Michael Jameson suggests: Jameson, 'Sacrifice and Animal Husbandry' in Whittaker (ed.), *Pastoral Economics*, 107-12
and adds that: ibid., 87
In Homer's writing: e.g. *Il.* 24.125
Archaeology has furnished: Davies, 'The Roman Military Diet'
Decree on Maximum Prices: see Lewis and Reinhold, *Roman Civilisation*, 463-74
wall paintings are now generally interpreted: Ellis, 'Late-Antique Dining' in Laurence and Wallace-Hadrill (eds), *Domestic Space*, 44

21   the slaves who worked on his farm: Cato *Agr.* 58
Using the evidence: Etienne, *La Vie Quotidienne*, 230-3
Seneca espoused: Sen.*Ep.* 108.22. Interestingly, before 1847 and the founding of the Vegetarian Society, vegetarians called themselves 'Pythagoreans' after the sixth-century BC philosopher who professed this diet on religious

grounds: see Humphreys, 'The Way We Were'.
works on diets devoid of meat: see Dombrowski, *Vegetarianism*
and Clark, 'Animal Rights'

22 substituted by ground walnuts: Apic. 9.13.3
King Nicomedes of Bithynia: Ath. 1.7d-f
Colin Spencer understandably expresses his astonishment:
Spencer, *The Heretic's Feast*, 94
Seneca quickly abandoned his vegetarianism: Griffin, *Seneca*,
40-1
Willem Jongman argues: *The Economy*, 77-85
The emperor Trajan ordered: cf. Plin.*Pan.* 31, *Ox.Pap.* 2958
(2 December AD 99)

23 The Romans made barley into porridge: Gal.*Ptis.*=6.816-831K
made into bread: cf. Gal.*Alim.fac.* 1.10.5=6.506K
the peninsula was named after: Col. 6.pref.7
As Colin Spencer says: *The Heretic's Feast*, 90
Helmut Birkhan: 'Some Remarks on Medieval Cooking' in
Adamson (ed.), *Food in the Middle Ages*, 95

INGREDIENTS

25 Pliny writes that trees: *HN* 12.26-27
Theophrastus describes *peperi*: *HP* 9.20.1
as does Celsus: 2.27
jarring to modern tastes: e.g. Edwards, *The Roman Cookery of
Apicius*, xxi, xxii, xxix

26 some plants have evolved: e.g. Halstead and Jones,
'Agrarian Ecology' and Grant *Anthimus*, 109
Lead pipes were recognised: Vitr. 8.10-11, cf. Plin. *HN*
34.167
high proportion of lead: the Roman-British skeletons found at
Poundbury near Dorchester revealed a 'lifetime accumulation'
of lead and 'it is very likely that some children died as a

result of lead poisoning', Farwell and Molleson (eds), *Excavations at Poundbury*, 185-6.

The ancient world relied: Olson, 'Firewood and Charcoal'

a special savour: see Gray, *Honey from a Weed*, 18-9

27 But for some reason: Pliny *HN* 19.38-45

that it might have survived: Roques ('Médecine et Botanique') argues that Oribasius, writing in the fourth century AD, had personal experience of using silphium, since there are references to the Cyrenaican variety of the spice in his works.

'To which you should': Apic. 2.2.8

'Although cucumbers': Anthim. 57

28 'lioness on a cheesegrater': Ar.*Lys*. 231-2

Decree on Maximum Prices: Lewis and Reinhold, *Roman Civilisation*, 467

29 *Garum*/Fish Sauce: *Gp*. 20.46

30 *Liquamen ex Piris*/Piquant Pear Sauce: Pall. 3.25.12

31 *Garon tou Ioachou*/Spiced Sauce: Gal. *Rem.Par*. 16.346-348K

32 unlikely to be by Galen: The genuine version of Galen's work *On Quick Remedies* seems to have been been lost by the middle of the fourth century AD, so Nutton argues (*Karl Gottlob Kühn*, 24). If this is the case, what is the provenance of this *garum*? Sugar was certainly known from the fourth century BC, but its use was slow to expand (C. Balandier, 'Production et Usages du Miel dans l'Antiquité Gréco-Romaine' in Amouretti and Comet (eds), *Des Hommes et des Plantes*, 93). Seneca (*Ep*. 84.4) considers it a type of honey from reeds, and it was the Arabs who mastered the process of refining it in the early Middle Ages.

33 *Sapa*/Reduced Wine Sauce: Plin.*HN* 14.80

BREAKFAST

36 Homer describes how: *Od.* 16.2, cf. *Il.* 24.123-124, D.H. 3
    hunger caused the body to tremble: Gal.*Trem.* 5=7.601K
    before attending the Assembly: Ar.*Eccl.* 291
    or the Festival of Dionysus: Philochorus *ap.* Ath.11.464f
    The military writer Vegetius: Veg.3.11
    Yet Simulus, the humble farmer: [Verg.] *Mor.*106

37 The Byzantine lexicographer: Phot. s.v. *'acratisasthai'*
    derived from *akratos*: Ath. 1.11c, Plu.*Mor.* 726c, cf. Apul.*Met.*
    9.15
    The Romans similarly derived their word: Fest. 347.26,
    Isid.*Orig.* 20.2.10
    a surviving fragment: quoted in *The Suda* s.v. *'airein'*
    Bread was the other main component of breakfast:
    Aristomenes *ap.* Ath. 1.11c
    boys selling loaves: Mart. 14.223
    but meat and cheese: Mart. 13.31, Apul.*Met.* 1.18
    preserved by the monks: cf. Cassian 4.14 and Fermor, *Roumeli*,
    216
    This was bread that was baked twice: cf. Hsch. s.v. *'dipuroi*
    artoi', Phryn.Com. *ap.* Poll. 7.22
    eaten hot, either on its own: Eub. *ap.* Ath. 3.110a
    with a sliced egg: Alex. *ap.* Ath. 12.516e
    A lexicon of the Byzantine period: *The Suda* s.v. *'paxamas'*
    Patrick Leigh Fermor ... describes how he: *Mani*, 14-5
    Chris Connell, who recorded: *In the Bee-Loud Glade*, 58
    'normally or in the manner of a sodomite': Gild. *Pen.* 1

38 Herodas, writing in the third century BC: 9
    Religious breakfasts: e.g. Apul.*Met.* 11.24, cf. Plaut.*Curc.* 72
    Invitations to breakfast: Afran.Com. *ap.* Non. Marc. 126M
    his guest did not turn up: Mart. 8.67.9-10
    Martial ridiculed Fescennia: Mart. 1.87.1-3
    The gluttonous emperor: Suet.*Vit.* 13.1

39 *Puls Punica*/Carthaginian Porridge: Cato *Agr.* 85
    groats from emmer wheat: T. Braun, 'Barley Cakes and

Emmer Bread' in Wilkins, Harvey and Dobson (eds), *Food in Antiquity*, 37

40 *Granea Triticea*/Creamed Wheat: Cato *Agr.* 8
   Milium in Aqua/Millet Porridge: Anthim. 71

41 the trade routes from the Middle East: Grant, *Anthimus*, 24-7
   J.M. Renfrew suggests: 'The Archaeological Evidence for the Domestication of Plants' in Ucko and Dimbleby (eds), *The Domestication*, 151 and D.M. Dixon, 'A Note on Cereals in Ancient Egypt', ibid., 136
   Polenta de Hordeo/Barley Porridge: Pliny *HN* 18.73

42 *Pyramides*/Pyramid Cakes: Ath. 14.647c

43 *Rhodomeli*/Rose Honey: *Gp* 8.29
   Arto der Haroutunian gives: *Middle Eastern Cookery*, 325-6

LUNCH

44 'That over-eating': Hp.*VM* 10=1.590-592L

45 Hippocrates says as much: *Acut.* 30

46 the body contained blood, phlegm: Hp.*Nat.Hom.* 4
   Galen elaborates on this idea: Gal.*Hum.*=19.491K
   as Hippocrates says: Hp.*Vict.* 1.32=6.511L
   Galen explains: Gal.*Com.Hp.Acut.* 4.79=15.868K
   as Martial says: Mart. 4.8.1
   The emperor Claudius: Suet.*Aug.* 78

47 Galen used to have: Gal.*San.Tu.* 6.7=6.314K
   the doctor Antiochus, a contemporary of Galen: Gal.*San.Tu.* 5.4=6.332K
   The Roman doctor Celsus: Cels. 1.1.2
   What people ate for lunch: the literary sources of course dwell on massive lunches 'merging into dinners lasting until dawn', Sen.*Q.N.* 4.13.6, cf. Cic.*Phil.* 2.101 'what preparation for lunches', *Mur.* 73

Telephus the grammar teacher enjoyed vegetables: cf. on
vegetables, Hor.*Ep.* 1.17.13

Pliny the Younger: Plin.*ep.* 3.5.10

48 Plutarch remarks: Plu.*Mor.* 6.726e

Fronto wrote to Marcus Aurelius: *Front. ad Caes.* 4.6

Martial describes: Mart. 13.30

In the time of Plautus: Plaut.*Poen.* 759, cf. *Bacch.* 716: 'Is it a
cooked lunch?'

the frugal Catus Aelius: Plin.*HN* 33.142

'Do you remember, you foul creature': Cic.*Pis.* 13

workmen had beet: Mart. 13.13

game being eaten for the midday meal: Mart. 1.49.13-14

The sons of Quintus Arrius: Hor.*Sat.* 2.3.243

49 The Greek and Latin phrasebook: *CGL* 3.650, see Dionisotti
'From Ausonius' Schooldays?'

an Epicurean philosopher: Hor.*Sat.* 2.4.21

Galen describes a popular snack: Gal.*Alim.fac.*1.13.19=6.518K

Seneca disapproved of drinking after lunch: Sen. *Ep.* 122.6

as did Cicero: Cic.*Mil.* 56

a few glasses of wine: Tac.*An.* 14.2

the story of the wife: Apul.*Met.* 9.5

Juvenal mocks the preposterous Greek stories: Juv. 10.173-8

had lunch at a farm at Arcanum: Cic.*Att.* 5.1.3

Seneca enjoyed picnics: Sen.*Ep.* 87.2

50 wedding lunches: Cic.*Clu.* 166

lunches to commemorate military victories: Suet.*Caes.* 38.2

Theocritus paints a picture of a little boy: Theoc. 1.47-51

In Babrius there is a tale of a fox: Babr. 86

The goatherd Daphnis: e.g. Longus 1.13.1 and Ricotti, *L'Arte
del Convito*, 47 (fig. 32)

A rustic lunch: Ar.*Pl.* 298

Hermippus said: *ap.* Ath. 1.29e

although for Cicero this was a novel experience: Cic.*Div.*
2.142

Horace enjoyed pottering around the house: Hor.*Sat.*
1.6.127-8

more exciting afternoons: Ov.*Am.* 1.5

'sweet Ipsithilla': Cat. 32
Aristotle recommended a large lunch: Arist.*Pr.* 876a5
Livy tells of the consul Aemilius: Liv. 9.32

51 as the Spartans discovered: Hdt. 6.78, cf. 3.26.3 and Xen.*An.*
    6.5.1
    Martial hints at this: 13.30
    cheeses could weigh up to one thousand pounds: Plin.*HN*
    11.241
    people who did not engage in manual labour: Cels. 1.2.1, cf.
    Paul.Aeg. 1.23 on diet in old age

52 *Hapalos Artos*/Soft Bread: Ath. 3.113b-c

53 *Boletinos Artos*/Mushroom Bread: Ath. 3.113c

54 *Streptikios Artos*/Plaited Bread: Ath. 3.113d

55 *Nanos*/Sponge Bread: Ath. 14.646c

57 *Globi*/Pastry Balls: Cato *Agr.* 79

58 *Itrion*/Sesame Biscuits: Ath. 14.646d and Grant, *Dieting for*
    an Emperor, 316

59 *Libum*/Cheesebread: Cato *Agr.* 75
    the making of *focaccette*: Beevor, *A Tuscan Childhood*, 243-4
    served as a birthday cake: Juv.16.38, Mart. 10.24.4

60 *Savillum*/Cheesebread with Honey: Cato *Agr.* 84

61 *Elaphos*/Sesame Shortbread: Ath. 14.646e

62 *Tagenitai*/Pancakes: Gal.*ap.* Orib. 1.7.1-2
    pizza al tegame: David, *Italian Food*, 150-1

63 *Maza*/Barley Cake: Poll. 6.76 and Grant, *Dieting for an*
    Emperor, 127-8

64 *Phthois*/Cheese Discs: Ath. 14.647d-e
    picture of the sort of frying pan: Apic. 4.2.14

65 *Lagana*/Fried Pasta: Hsch. s.v. '*lagana*'
    'that self-righteous old windbag': Jarratt, *The Complete Book of*
    Pasta, 10
    pasta dough cooked directly: Buonassisi, *The Classic Book of*
    Pasta, 7-8 and Santich, 'The Evolution of Culinary
    Techniques in the Medieval Era' in Adamson (ed.), *Food*

in the Middle Ages, 74-5
eating leeks and chick-peas: Hor.*Sat.* 1.6.115. Similar breads,
but made of barley and resembling chapatis in appearance, are made in Sardinia, see Piquereddu (ed.), *In Nome
del Pane,* 51 and plates 12 and 14

66 *Artolagana*/Fried Savoury Pasta: Ath. 3.113d
Catillus Ornatus/Seasoned Fritters: Ath. 14.647e

67 *uruq khass:* see Jamil-Garbutt, *The Baghdad Kitchen,* 69

68 *Etnos*/Pea Soup: Dieuch. *ap.* Orib. 4.8.14

69 *Phakoptisana*/Lentil and Barley Soup: Gal. *ap.* Orib. 4.1.22-3

70 *Ptisana*/Barley Soup: Gal. *ap.* Orib. 4.1.16-18

71 *Bucellae cum Lacte Caprino*/Goat's Milk Sauce: Anthim. 75

72 *Moretum*/Garlic and Herb Pâté: [Verg.] *Mor.* 85-116
garlic on the breath: Gowers, *The Loaded Table,* 280-310: here
Hor.*Epod.* 3 is discussed, a poem that attacks the evil
effects of garlic. Hippocrates (*Decent.* 15) recommended
that doctors should avoid garlic as being offensive to
their patients.

73 *'la très ancienne aillée':* Couffignal, *La Cuisine des Pays d'Oc,* 148

74 *Conditurae Olivarum*/Olive and Celery Pâté: Col. 12.49.5

75 *Epityrum Varium*/Olives with Herbs: Cato *Agr.* 119
Ius ad Rapa Condienda/Turnips with Mustard: Col. 12.57

77 *Tyros eis Halmen*/Pickled Cheese: *Gp.* 18.19

78 *Palathai*/Dried Fig Cakes: *Suda* s.v. *'palathai'*

79 *Caseus cum Recenti Fico*/Cheese with Figs: Plin.*HN* 15.83
Hypotyrides/Curds with Honey: Ath. 14.647f

80 *Melca*/Curds: Paxamus *ap. Gp.* 18.21

81 *Kykeon*/Barley Water: Hsch. s.v. *'kykeon'*
a type of soup: Dalby and Grainger, *The Classical Cookbook,*
40-1
a Roman equivalent of barley water: Darmstaedter, 'Ptisana:
Ein Beitrag zur Kenntnis der Antiken Diaetetik' and
Grant, *Dieting for an Emperor,* 125

Oinos Dia Melon/Fruit Wine: *Gp.* 8.17

82   recalls an Italian dessert: David, *Italian Food*, 281
Hydromel/Honey Water: *Gp.* 8.7
The emperor Augustus: Plin.*HN* 22.113-4

DINNER AT THE BAR

84   one of the most highly prized: Davidson, *Courtesans and Fishcakes*, 53-60

85   a sleazy situation: Laurence, *Roman Pompeii*, 75
a pallid corpse: Cic.*Pis.* 53
his tirade against a provincial governor: Juv. 8.171-6.
he is a student: [Verg.] *Cop.*, especially 3, 5, 14, 23-4 and 37-8
the liberal character of Micio: Ter.*Ad.* 122-4
a magnet for young men: see Garland, 'Juvenile Delinquency'
in antiquity food and drink: see Grimm, *From Feasting to Fasting*, 56

86   late into the night: Laurence, *Roman Pompeii*, 125
'Now let us begin': Cic.*Inv.* 2.4.14
A rollicking account: Apul.*Met.* 1.6-17
Such establishments: see de la Bédoyère, *The Buildings of Roman Britain*, 111

87   Cicero writes of Mark Antony: *Fam.* 9.26 and Corley, *Private Women, Public Meals*, 34-52
attractive boys could find themselves fancied: Juv. 9.26, cf. J. D'Arms, 'The Roman *Convivium* and Equality' in Murray (ed.), *Sympotica*, 315
In law, a barmaid was considered: Laurence, *Roman Pompeii*, 72
Successus the weaver wanted to go out: *CIL* 8259
two bronze asses: *CIL* 8185
Next to the door: *CIL* 9123
Horace, journeying across Italy: Hor.*Sat.* 1.5.82-5
Charinus, a young man: Plaut.*Merc.* 98

the father at the beginning: Ter.*Ad.* 26
The leather bikini: Marsden, *Roman London*, 65 and Fear, 'The Dancing Girls of Cadiz'

88 Seneca recalls: Sen.*Ep.* 95.26
a modest repast with him: Plin.*Ep.* 1.15.2-3
Some paintings in an inn: Jackson, 'It Was Your Move, Claudius'
Remains have also been found: Girri, *La Taberna*, 6-7,17 and 21
Horace, describing one such establishment: Hor.*Sat.* 1.5.82-5
Cicero taunting an opponent: Cic.*Pis.* 22.53
Ausonius remarks: Aus.*Mos.* 123-4
Varro relates: Var.*R.R.* 3.9.18, reading *genanium* (belonging to a *ganea* or 'pub' rather than *cenantium* or 'diners').
In addition to fish and fowl: Hor.*Sat.* 2.2.44-46

89 There has been some debate: Jasny ('Wheat Prices and Milling Costs in Classical Rome') tackles the problems associated with supplying enough wheat to the Roman people. On the other hand Moritz (*Grain-Mills and Flour*, 216) suggests that the people in the Roman Empire had reached a sufficiently high standard of living that they could eat the grain which they preferred rather than that which nature forced on them. Further ideas about the supply and distribution of wheat are contained in Garnsey and Whittaker (eds), *Trade and Famine*.
Flours ranging from coarse: Grant, *Dieting for an Emperor*, 257-9
During excavation: see Giacosa, *A Taste of Ancient Rome*, plate 7
'dining off bread': Hes.*Op.* 442; see the edition with prolegomena and commentary by M.L. West, Oxford 1978, 270-1 for various other interpretations.
Pliny explains that leaven was made by: Plin.*NH* 18.102
The medical writer Celsus: Cels. 2.25

90 Small tins were used to give a special shape to cakes and pastries: B.J. Mayeske, 'A Pompeian Bakery on the Via dell' Abbondanza' in Curtis (ed.), *Studia Pompeiana*, Vol.1, 154
Pliny records that bread was imported from the Parthian

empire: Plin.*HN* 18.105

Other ingredients could be added: see Cato *Agr.* 75, Ath. 3.113d

From Martial we learn that *cauponae* were equipped: Mart. 5.70.3. For an interesting description of a *caupona* see C.G. Pelegin *et al.*, 'Missione Archeologica Spagnola a Pompei', especially plate 3

When the historian Sallust: Suet.*Gram.* 15

Greeks wandered round with books: Plaut.*Curc.* 288-293

their drinks hot: cf. Pl.*R.* 437e, Plaut.*Rud.* 529, Petr. 41.11

Martial tells us that beet was eaten: Mart. 13.13

Juvenal complains: Juv. 11.80-1

91 corrupt army officers: Juv. 8.172

bartenders in *cauponae* were gay: Plaut.*Poen.* 1298

The emperor Tiberius proposed: Suet.*Tib.* 34, *Ner.* 16

'Diogenes invites': *Ox.Pap.* 2791

A farmer described by Horace: Hor.*Sat.* 2.2.116-122

a modest supper: Mart. 5.78, cf. 11.52 with lettuce, leeks, tuna with eggs and rue, cheese, olives, fish, shellfish, sow's udders and fowl.

a slightly more elaborate meal: Hor.*Sat.* 1.5.71-76, cf. Mart. 7.61.8 where a *popina* is described as 'blackened', presumably from the kitchen fires.

92 although a cook: Plaut.*Ps.*810-825

Thrion Demou/Stuffed Vine Leaves: Sch. *ad.* Ar.*Ach.* 1102

93 *Thrion Tarikhous*/Smoked Fish in Vine Leaves: Sch. *ad.* Ar.*Ach.* 1101

94 *Thrion ex Oryza*/Goat's Cheese and Rice in Vine Leaves: Sch. *ad.* Ar.*Eq.* 954

96 *Mystron*/Savoury Barley: Ath. 3.126b-c

the Roman army commissariat: Gal.*Alim.fac.* 1.11=6.507K. Watson (*The Roman Soldier*, 119) states that as a punishment Roman soldiers could be fed on barley instead of wheat.

transportation dockets: *Ox.Pap.* 4087 (fourth century AD): 'To the men and animals of a Palatine official, travelling

up to the Thebaid, in the public inn at Tacona for 1 day…
90 loaves of bread, 90 pints of wine, 720 pints of barley'.

97 *Staititai*/Honey and Sesame Pizza: Ath. 14.646b

98 *Faba Integra*/Broad Beans: Anthim. 65
Kyboi/Dice Bread: Ath. 3.114a

99 the emperor Claudius publishing: Suet.*Claud.* 33

100 *Oa Pnikta* / Eggs Poached in Wine: Gal.*Alim.fac.*3.21.3=
6.706-7K

101 *Mixtura cum Caseo*/Herb Purée with Cheese: Col. 12.59

102 *Mixtura cum Nucibus*/Herb Purée with Walnuts: Col. 12.59
Mixtura cum Sesamis/Herb Purée with Sesame Seeds: Col.
12.59

103 *Mixtura cum Nucleis Pineis*/Herb Purée with Pine Kernels:
Col. 12.59

104 *Placenta*/Cheese and Pastry Pie: Cato *Agr.* 76

106 *Laterculi*/Poppy Seed Biscuits: Plaut.*Poen.* 329

107 *Glykinai*/Sweet Wine Cakes: Ath. 14.645d

108 *Enkrides*/Honey Biscuits: Ath. 14.645e

109 *Mustacei*/Must Cakes: Cato *Agr.* 121
suggests the use of yeast: Dalby and Grainger, *The Classical
Cookbook*, 109-10

110 In fact a monk: Gildas *Pen.* 1

111 *Kydonion syn Meliti*/Honeyed Quinces: Ruf. *ap.* Orib. 4.2.20
eating fruit with cream: see Grant, *Anthimus*, 31-2

112 *Kydonion en Staiti*/Baked Quinces: Ruf. *ap.* Orib. 4.2.20

113 *Pira Pulmentari Vicem*/Pear Jelly: Plin.*HN* 15.58
Pira Conditiva in Sapa/Braised Pears: Cato *Agr.* 73

DINNER IN THE DINING ROOM

115 That it took place towards: *EM* 262.40-42, Plu.*Mor.* 726c
   numerous papyri: e.g. *Ox.Pap.* 2678, 2791, 3693
   It has been pointed out: Laurence, *Roman Pompeii*, 8, 127 and
   141

116 Plato's disapproval: Cic.*Tusc.* 5.100
   soldiers on sentry duty: Aen.Tact. 16.12
   Before dinner it was customary: Plin.*Ep.* 6.20.2
   surreal scene at the baths: Petr. 26-27
   a dinner of Egyptian lentils: Gell. 17.8.1-3
   entertained by the poet Julius Paulus: Gell. 19.7.1
   Pliny details to an acquaintance: Plin. *Ep.* 1.15.1
   a dinner menu from Egypt: *Ox.Pap.* 738

117 A study of a Roman graveyard: Farwell and Molleson (eds),
   Excavations at Poundbury, 178-9
   the Sicilian town of Selinunte: Wilson, 'Archaeology in Sicily'
   a girl in her teens: Bisel, *The Secrets of Vesuvius*, 54-8
   this theme crops up again and again: e.g. Mart. 11.35,
   Plu.*Mor.* 7.708d
   put their complaint: Mart. 5.78.31-2, 10.48.5-24, Philodemus
   ap. AP 11.44.5, Hor.*Ep.* 1.5.26
   friendships bought with meals: Mart. 9.14, 7.86
   food graded according to the status: Plin.*Ep.* 2.6

118 some conservative men: Corley, *Private Women, Public Meals*,
   22-3 and 25
   dancing more skilfully: Sall.*Cat.* 25
   same-sex events: Corley, *Private Women, Public Meals*, 75-8
   the slave dealer Toranius Flaccus: Macr.*Sat.* 2.4.28
   the society of free citizens: J. D'Arms, 'The Roman
   Convivium and Equality' in Murray (ed.), *Sympotica*, 308
   and 312
   separate dining rooms: Varr.*L.L.* 8.29. See also L. Richardson,
   'A Contribution to the Study of Pompeian Dining-
   rooms' in Irelli (ed.), *Pompeii, Herculaneum, Stabiae*, 61-71
   A winter dining room: Vitr. 6.3.2, Sid.*Ep.* 2.2.11

construction on the east coast: Plin.*Ep.* 2.17.5

the Villa of the Mysteries: Wallace-Hadrill, *Houses and Society*, 52-4

a sort of chandelier: S.P. Ellis, 'Late-Antique Dining' in Laurence and Wallace-Hadrill (eds), *Domestic Space in the Roman World*, 44 and 48

119 the dining room was sometimes perfumed: Dionisotti, 'From Ausonius' Schooldays?'

an infusion of vervain: Plu.*Mor.* 614b

The emperor Domitian tried: J. D'Arms, 'The Roman Convivium and the Idea of Equality' in Murray (ed.), *Sympotica*, 309-10

dining halls large enough: Sen.*Ep.* 115.8

a large imperial Roman dining pavilion: French, 'Archaeology in Greece 1991-2'

the story of Cornelius Fronto: D.C. 69.18

dinners could drag on: Cic.*Att.* 9.13.6

accoutrements of the table: Sen.*Ep.* 119.13

An apophthegm of Socrates: Gell. 19.2.7

Socrates argued: X.*Mem.* 3.14.5-6, cf. Seneca: Sen.*Ep.* 95.15

a cosmopolitan cuisine at Rome: Frangoulidis, 'Food and Politics in Plautus, *Captivi*'

At York ... apples and wheat: Williams, 'A Consideration of the Sub-Fossil Remains of *Vitis vinifera* L.'

120 Wild and cultivated celery: S. Woodiwiss (ed.), *Iron Age and Roman Salt Production*, 105

Seneca believed that he could compete in happiness: Sen.*Ep.* 110.18

'perfume on lentils': Cic.*Att.* 1.19.2

The aptly named Porcius: Hor.*Sat.* 2.8.23-4

Roman dinner most compactly: Dionisotti, 'From Ausonius' Schooldays?'

used as cruets: Warmington, *The Commerce between the Roman Empire and India*, 180-4

beautifully shaped by an artist: Varr.*L.L.* 8.31

a letter from the northern frontier: Bowman, *Life and Letters*, 130-1 (Tablet 5.2.302) the hitherto tough austerity: Hdn. 3.8.5

the house of the philosopher Favorinus: Gell. 3.19.1, cf. Front. *Front. ad Caes.* 4.12.3

special clothes: Bowman, *Life and Letters*, 120-1 (Tablet 5.2.196)

mullet in their fish ponds: Cic.*Att.* 2.1.7

lay in moderation: Motto, 'Seneca on Pleasure'

121 sense of space and well-being: Plu.*Mor.* 679e-680b. On dining habits in general, see K.M.D. Dunbabin, 'Triclinium and Stibadium', in Slater (ed.), *Dining in a Classical Context*, 121-48

community of life and mental relaxation: J.H. D'Arms, 'The Roman *Convivium* and the Idea of Equality' in Murray (ed.), *Sympotica*, 311

Carnes Vaccinae/Beef Casserole: Anthim. 3

122 pepper from India and cloves from Indonesia: Miller, *The Spice Trade of the Roman Empire*, 47-51

123 *Lepores*/Hare in a Sweet Sauce: Anthim. 13

124 *Krea Tareikhera*/Ham in a Red Wine and Fennel Sauce: Heidelberg Papyrus in Giarratano and Vollmer, *Apicius*, 88

126 *Psoai*/Pork in a Piquant Sauce: ibid., 89

a satirical poem about ancient foodies: Hor.*Sat.* 2.4.63-9 and see Berg 'The Mystery Gourmet of Horace's *Satires* 2' for a discussion of the background to this poem

vinegars made from fruit juices: Grant, *Dieting for an Emperor*, 288

127 *Ficatum Porcinum*/Fried Liver: Anthim. 21

Athletes in the ancient world: Grant, *Dieting for an Emperor*, 161-2

128 *Myma*/Baked Plaice: Ath. 14.662d-e

129 *Glaukos*/Fish in Fresh Herb Sauce: Sotad.Com. *ap.* Ath. 7.324a

impossible to identify: Thompson, *A Glossary of Greek Fishes*, 48

130 *Amia*/Fish in Vine Leaves: Ath. 7.293d

131 *Zomos*/Butter Beans in Herb Sauce: Heidelberg Papyrus in Giarratano and Vollmer, *Apicius*, 87-8

132 *Dodra*/Nine Times Sauce: Aus.*Epigr.* 19.20

133 *Spumeum*/Soufflé: Anthim. 34

134 *Oxyporium*/Tangy Salad Dressing: Col. 12.59.5

135 *Cucumeres*/Braised Cucumbers: Plin.*HN* 20.6

136 *Kolokynthe Teganistheisa*/Fried Squash: Gal.*Alim.fac.*2.3= 6.563-4K

137 *Laganophake*/Lentil Stew: Heidelberg Papyrus in Giarratano and Vollmer, *Apicius*, 88

138 *Lenticula*/Spicy Lentils: Anthim. 67
sumach as Syrian: André, *Les Noms de Plantes*, 218
Its sharp lemony taste: Stobart, *Herbs, Spices and Flavourings*, 257. This spice (from a plant known botanically as *Rhus coriaria* L.) can be bought as a powder from shops specialising in Middle Eastern foods.
the only citrus fruit: Grant, *Dieting for an Emperor*, 193-7

139 *Teutlophake*/Lentils with Beet: Gal.*Alim.fac.* 1.1.43

140 *Panis Picens*/Adriatic Bread: Plin.*HN.* 18.106

141 a banquet attended by Julius Caesar: Macr.*sat.* 3.13.12

142 *Asparagus*/Asparagus: Anthim. 54
on the French lines: Grant, *Anthimus*, 27-8
Krambe/Cabbage Salad: Mnesith.Cyz. *ap.* Orib. 4.4.1

143 *Olusatra*/Celery with Raisin Sauce: Col. 12.58

144 *Fasiola*/French Beans: Anthim. 69 and, on identifying beans, Grant, *Anthimus*, 115

145 In the refectory at Vatopedi: Kadas, *Mount Athos*, 145 and plate 77

146 *Pastinacea*/Fried Carrots: Anthim. 53
Mykai/Mushrooms in Honey: Diph.Siph. *ap.* Ath. 2.61e

147 *Tybaris*/Celery in Vinegar: Poll. 6.71

148 *Erebinthoi syn Xeroi Tyroi*/Chick-peas with Cheese: Gal.*Alim.fac.* 1.22=6.533K

149 *Erebinthoi Knakosymmigeis*/Chick-peas in Saffron: Philox. *ap.* Ath. 14.643c
    Tyros Dia Koskinou/Cheese with Honey: Ath. 14.647f

150 *Enkhytoi*/Honey Cake: Men. *ap.* Ath. 14.644c

151 *Gastris*/Nut Cake: Ath. 14.647f-648a

152 *Basyniai*/Walnut and Fig Cakes: Ath. 14.645b

154 *Oriza*/Rice Pudding: Anthim. 70
    Sesamides/Sesame Wafers: Ath. 14.646f

155 *Apioi eis Kykliskous*/Dried Pear Pudding: Gal. *Alim.fac.* 2.24.4=6.605K

BIBLIOGRAPHY

ARTICLES

Arthur, P., 'Roman Amphorae from Canterbury', *Britannia*, Vol. 17, 1986

Auberger, J., 'Dis Moi ce que Tu Manges, Je Te Dirai qui Tu Es ...', *Revue des Etudes Anciennes*, Vol. 97, 1995

Berg, D., 'The Mystery Gourmet of Horace's *Satires 2*', *Classical Journal*, Vol. 91, 1996

Bonifray, M. and Piéri, D., 'Amphores du Vième au VIIième s. à Marseille: Nouvelles Données sur la Typologie et le Contenu', *Journal of Roman Archaeology*, Vol. 8, 1995

Clark, S.R.L., 'Animal Rights', *Classical Review*, Vol. 37, 1987

Connors, C., 'Scents and Sensibility in Plautus' *Casina*', *Classical Quarterly*, Vol. 47, 1997

Crawford, D.J., 'Food: Tradition and Change in Hellenistic Egypt', *World Archaeology*, Vol. 2, 1979

Curtis, R.I., 'Product Identification and Advertising on Roman Commercial Amphorae', *Ancient Society*, Vol. 15-17, 1984-86

Darmstaedter, E., 'Ptisana: Ein Beitrag zur Kenntnis der Antiken Diaetetik', *Archeion*, Vol. 15, 1933

Davies, R.W., 'The Roman Military Diet', *Britannia*, Vol. 2, 1971

Dionisotti, A.C., 'From Ausonius' Schooldays? A Schoolbook and Its Relatives', *Journal of Roman Studies*, Vol. 72, 1982.

Fear, A.T., 'The Dancing Girls of Cadiz', *Greece and Rome*, Vol. 38, 1991

Frangoulidis, S.A., 'Food and Poetics in Plautus, *Captivi*', *L'Antiquité Classique*, Vol. 65, 1996

French, E.B., 'Archaeology in Greece 1991-2', *Archaeological Reports*, Vol. 38, 1991-92

Garland, R., 'Juvenile Delinquency in the Greek and Roman World', *History Today*, October 1991

Grant, M.D., 'A Note on Anthimus' *De Obseruatione Ciborum Epistula*', *Hermes*, Vol. 114, 1986

Halstead, P. and Jones, G., 'Agrarian Ecology in the Greek Islands: Time Stress, Scale and Risk', *Journal of Hellenic Studies*, Vol.109, 1989

Humphreys, B., 'The Way We Were', *The Vegetarian*, Vol. 6, 1997

Jackson, S., 'It Was Your Move, Claudius', *The Independent*, 14 September 1996

Jasny, N., 'Wheat Prices and Milling Costs in Classical Rome', *Wheat Studies of the Food Research Institute*, Vol. 20, 1944

Jouanna, J., 'Le Vin et la Médecine dans la Grèce Ancienne', *Revue des Etudes Grecques*, Vol. 109, 1996

Lambert, M., 'Ancient Greek and Zulu Sacrificial Ritual', *Numen*, Vol. 40, 1993

MacDonald K.C. and Edwards, D.N., 'Chickens in Africa: the Importance of Qasr Ibrim', *Antiquity*, Vol. 67, 1993

Maxwell-Stuart, P.G., 'Dating by African Figs', *Museum Helveticum*, Vol. 53, 1996

Motto, A.L., 'Seneca on Pleasure', *Helmantica: Revista de Filologia Clasica y Hebrea*, Vol. 47, 1996

Olson, S.D., 'Firewood and Charcoal in Classical Athens', *Hesperia: Journal of the American School of Classical Studies at Athens*, Vol. 60, 1991

Pelegin, C.G. *et al.*, 'Missione Archeologica Spagnola a Pompei: La Casa-*Caupona* I,8,8-9 di L. Vetutius Placidus', *Rivista di Studi Pompeiani*, Vol. 5, 1991

Perotti, P.A., '*Ius cenae* (Pétrone 35,7)', *Les Etudes Classiques*, Vol. 65, 1997

Roques, D., 'Médicine et Botanique: Le Silphion dans l'Oeuvre d'Oribase', *Revue des Etudes Grecques*, Vol. 106, 1993

Sparkes, B.A., 'Not Cooking but Baking', *Greece and Rome*, Vol. 28, 1981

van Minnen, P. and Sosin, J.D., 'Imperial Pork: Preparations for a Visit of Severus Alexander and Iulia Mamaea to Egypt', *Ancient Society*, Vol. 27, 1996

Williams, D., 'A Consideration of the Sub-Fossil Remains of *Vitis vinifera* L. as Evidence for Viticulture in Roman Britain', *Britannia*, Vol. 8, 1977

Wilson, R.J.A., 'Archaeology in Sicily 1988-95', *Archaeological Reports*, Vol. 42, 1995-96

BOOKS

Adamson, M.W. (ed.), *Food in the Middle Ages: A Book of Essays*, New York 1995

Amouretti, M.-Cl. and Comet, G. (eds), *Des Hommes et des Plantes: Plantes Méditerranéennes, Vocabulaire et Usages Anciens*, Aix-en-Provence 1993

André, J., *L'Alimentation et la Cuisine à Rome*, Paris 1981

André, J., *Les Noms de Plantes dans la Rome Antique*, Paris 1985

Beevor, K., *A Tuscan Childhood*, London 1995

Bisel, S.C., *The Secrets of Vesuvius*, Sevenoaks 1990

Blanc, N. and Nercessian, A., *La Cuisine Romaine Antique*, Grenoble 1992

Bowman, A.K., *Life and Letters on the Roman Frontier: Vindolanda and Its People*, London 1994

Buonassisi, V., *The Classic Book of Pasta*, London 1977

Carazzali, G. (ed.), *Apicio, L'Arte Culinaria: Manuale di Gastronomia Classica*, Milan 1994

Connell, C., *In the Bee-Loud Glade*, Nafplion 1980

Corley, K.E., *Private Women, Public Meals: Social Conflict in the Synoptic Tradition*, Peabody, Mass., 1993

Couffignal, H., *La Cuisine des Pays d'Oc*, Paris 1976

Curtis, R.I. (ed.), *Studia Pompeiana et Classica in Honor of Wilhelmina F. Jashemski*, New York 1988

Curtis, R.I., *Garum and Salsamenta: Production and Commerce in Materia Medica*, Leiden 1991

Dalby, A. and Grainger, S., *The Classical Cookbook*, London 1996

David, E., *Italian Food*, Harmondsworth 1963

David, E., *French Provincial Cooking*, Harmondsworth 1970

Davidson, J.N., *Courtesans and Fishcakes: The Consuming Passions of Classical Athens*, London 1997

de la Bédoyère, G., *The Buildings of Roman Britain*, London 1991

der Haroutunian, A., *Middle Eastern Cookery*, London 1982

Dombrowski, D.A., *Vegetarianism: The Philosophy Behind the Ethical Diet*, Wellingborough 1985

Edwards, J., *The Roman Cookery of Apicius*, London 1984

Etienne, R., *La Vie Quotidienne à Pompéi*, Paris 1966

Farwell, D.E. and Molleson, T.L. (eds), *Excavations at Poundbury 1966-80, Vol. 2: The Cemeteries*, Bournemouth 1993

Fermor, P.L., *Mani*, Harmondsworth 1984

Fermor, P.L., *Roumeli*, Harmondsworth 1983

Garnsey, P., *Famine and Food Supply in the Graeco-Roman World*, Cambridge 1988.

Garnsey, P. and Whittaker, C.R. (eds), *Trade and Famine in Classical Antiquity*, Cambridge 1983

Giacosa, I.G., *A Taste of Ancient Rome*, Chicago 1992

Giarratano, C. and Vollmer, F. (eds), *Apicius De Re Coquinaria*, Leipzig 1922

Girri, G, *La Taberna nel Quadro Urbanistico e Sociale di Ostia*, Rome 1956

Gowers, E., *The Loaded Table: Representations of Food in Roman Literature*, Oxford 1993

Grant, M.D., *Anthimus: On the Observance of Foods*, Totnes 1996

Grant, M.D., *Dieting for an Emperor: A Translation with Commentary of Books 1 and 4 of Oribasius' Medical Compilations*, Leiden 1997

Gray, P., *Honey from a Weed: Fasting and Feasting in Tuscany, Catalonia, the Cyclades and Apulia*, London 1986

Griffin, M., *Seneca: A Philosopher in Politics*, Oxford 1976

Grimm, V.E., *From Feasting to Fasting, the Evolution of a Sin: Attitudes to Food in Late Antiquity*, London 1996

Irelli, M.G.C., *Pompeii, Herculaneum, Stabiae: Associazione Internazionale Amici di Pompei*, Vol.1, Naples 1983

Jamil-Garbutt, N., *The Baghdad Kitchen*, Tadworth 1985

Jarratt, E. and V., *The Complete Book of Pasta*, London 1978

Jongman, W., *The Economy and Society of Pompeii*, Amsterdam 1988

Jones, R.F.J. (ed.), *Britain in the Roman Period: Recent Trends*, Sheffield 1991

Kadas, S., *Mount Athos: An Illustrated Guide to the Monasteries and their History*, Athens 1988

Kenney, E.J. (ed.), *The Ploughman's Lunch: A Poem Ascribed to Virgil*, Bristol 1984

Lamb, V., *The Home Book of Turkish Cookery*, London 1969

Laurence, R., *Roman Pompeii: Space and Society*, London 1994

Laurence, R. and Wallace-Hadrill, A. (eds), *Domestic Space in the Roman World: Pompeii and Beyond*, Portsmouth RI 1997

Lewis, N. and Reinhold, M., *Roman Civilization Sourcebook 2: The Empire*, New York 1966

Lissarrague, F., *The Aesthetics of the Greek Banquet: Images of Wine and Ritual*, Princeton 1990

Maiuri, A., *Pompeii*, Novara 1960

Marsden, P., *Roman London*, London 1980

Miller, J.I., *The Spice Trade of the Roman Empire, 29 BC to AD 641*, Oxford 1969

Moritz, L.A., *Grain-Mills and Flour in Classical Antiquity*, Oxford 1958

Motsias, K., *Ti Etrogan oi Arkhaioi*, Athens 1983

Murray, O. (ed.), *Sympotica: A Symposium on the Symposium*, Oxford 1990

Nutton, V., *Karl Gottlob Kühn and his Edition of the Works of Galen: A Bibliography*, Oxford 1976

Percival, J., *The Roman Villa: An Historical Introduction*, London 1976

Piquereddu, P. (ed), *In Nome del Pane: Forme, Tecniche, Occasioni della Panificazione Tradizionale in Sardegna*, Sassari 1991

Ricotti, E.S.P., *L'Arte del Convito nella Roma Antica*, Rome 1983

Roden, C., *A Book of Middle Eastern Food*, Harmondsworth 1970

Saberi, H., *Noshe Djan: Afghan Food and Cookery*, London 1986

Scott, D., *Middle Eastern Vegetarian Cookery*, London 1981

Slater, W.J. (ed.), *Dining in a Classical Context*, Ann Arbor 1991

Spencer, C., *The Heretic's Feast: A History of Vegetarianism*, London 1993

Stobart, T., *Herbs, Spices and Flavourings*, Harmondsworth 1977

Stewart, K. and Michael, P., *Wild Blackberry Cobbler and Other Old-Fashioned Recipes*, London 1984

Stubbs, J.M., *The Home Book of Greek Cookery*, London 1963

Thelamon, F. (ed.), *La Sociabilité à Table: Commensalité et Convivialité à Travers les Ages*, Rouen 1992

Thompson, D'.W., *A Glossary of Greek Fishes*, London 1947

Ucko, P.J. and Dimbleby, G.W. (eds), *The Domestication and Exploitation of Plants and Animals: Proceedings of a Meeting of the*

Research Seminar in Archaeology and Related Subjects Held at the Institute of Archaeology, London University, London 1969

Wallace-Hadrill, A., *Houses and Society in Pompeii and Herculaneum*, Princeton 1994

Warmington, E.H., *The Commerce between the Roman Empire and India*, London 1974

Watson, G.R., *The Roman Soldier*, London 1969

Whittaker, C.R., *Pastoral Economics in Classical Antiquity*, Cambridge 1988

Wilkins, J., Harvey D., and Dobson, M. (eds), *Food in Antiquity*, Exeter 1995

Woodiwiss, S. (ed.), *Iron Age and Roman Salt Production and the Medieval Town of Droitwich: Excavations at the Old Bowling Green and Friar Street*, London 1992

RECIPE INDEX

GENERAL INDEX

An independent publishing house, Serif publishes a
wide range of international fiction and non-fiction.

If you would like to receive a copy of our current
catalogue, please write to:

Serif
47 Strahan Road
London E3 5DA

or

1489 Lincoln Avenue
St Paul
MN 55105

or

c/o Wakefield Press
PO Box 2266
Kent Town
South Australia 5071

or you can visit our website at
http://www.serif.demon.co.uk/

Laughing
in the Face
of AIDS

The Authors

Dr. G. Edward Rozar, Jr., a former thoracic surgeon, now serves as director of a laboratory in Marshfield, Wisconsin. One of the first infected medical personnel to "go public," Dr. Rozar is active in the AIDS awareness effort, speaking across the country, through the media, and before Congress.

Co-author David B. Biebel is editor of *Physician*, a publication of Focus on the Family.

DISCARD

Laughing
in the Face
of AIDS

A Surgeon's Personal Battle

G. Edward Rozar, Jr., M.D.

with

David B. Biebel

Foreword by W. Shepherd Smith

BAKER BOOK HOUSE

Grand Rapids, Michigan 49516

Copyright 1992 by G. Edward Rozar, Jr.

Library of Congress Cataloging-in-Publication Data
Rozar, G. Edward Jr.
    Laughing in the face of AIDS : a surgeon's personal battle / G.
Edward Rozar with David B. Biebel.
            p.   cm.
    Includes bibliographical references.
    ISBN 0-8010-7767-2 (cloth).—ISBN 0-8010-7765-6 (pbk.)
    1. Rozar, G. Edward—Health. 2. AIDS (Disease)—United States—
Biography. 3. Surgeons—United States—Biography. 4. AIDS (Disease)—
Religious aspects—Christianity. I. Biebel, David B. II. Title.
    RC607.A26R68 1992
    362.1'96972'0092—dc20
    [B]   92-12924

Printed in the United States of America

Scripture references not otherwise marked are from the New American Standard
Bible. Copyright © 1960, 1962, 1963, 1968, 1971, 1972, 1973, 1975, 1977 by
the Lockman Foundation.
    Some references are from the New International Version (NIV), © 1973, 1978,
1984 by the International Bible Society.

Then they cried out to the LORD in their trouble;
He saved them out of their distresses.
He sent His word and healed them,
And delivered *them* from their destructions.
Psalm 107:19–20

This book is dedicated to
my lovely wife, Donna;
our five beautiful children:
Jonathan Edward
Victoria Kay
Jonathan Wayne
David Michael
Christina Michelle
Pastor Ed Gungor of Believers' Church
Glenn Klein
and Jesus Christ,
my Healer and Lord.

Contents

Foreword

For many years the church in America has felt itself immune from HIV, the virus that causes AIDS. Few people believed AIDS would ever enter the church, let alone infect godly people. We now know such thinking was truly wishful, part of our human nature to deny that such tragedies can touch us or our friends.

Although we may understand that the church will not remain untouched by AIDS, we still have a host of concerns and questions. What should we do when a family member becomes infected? How should a congregation respond to an infected member? What would God have us do in the age of AIDS?

Ed Rozar has acquired HIV. I know Ed personally and can attest to the fact that he is truly a godly man who loves his Lord. His genial countenance, caring nature, and spiritual character have allowed him to laugh in the face of AIDS. As you come to know Ed through these pages, you will realize that only the power given by God allows for such courage and strength. Ed's story offers inspiration and hope to those enduring hardship. But more than that, it helps answer some of our questions about how we should respond to AIDS/HIV.

Laughing in the Face of AIDS gives us insight not only into the power of God but also into the goodness of humans. With remarkable courage Ed shares both the highs and the lows. Because of Ed's intense honesty, the book speaks to our hearts in ways few books do.

So this is not as much a book about AIDS as it is a book about life. You will read about struggles common to all of us, as well as many joys and accomplishments. Although the book teaches several lessons, I'd like to highlight three powerful themes.

First, it illustrates the power of God in the face of adversity. And when I say adversity, I do not mean that lightly. Ed is the father of five lively children. Nearing the peak of his career, Ed had virtually everything taken from him. Yet he was able to realize how much more he was given.

Second, it calls us to examine our relationships with our own family members. What are our priorities? How do we respond to those who depend on us? Do we truly share our love with them?

Third, it challenges us as Christians to respond to the AIDS epidemic as Christ would have us. We are summoned to think more seriously about a disease that has entered the church and is spreading relentlessly across America, a disease that can no longer be ignored by the body of Christ.

God has equipped Ed Rozar to be an excellent spokesman for this mission. Ed is a child of God whose obedience humbles us. Ed is a father whose love of family inspires us. Ed is a doctor whose medical advice with respect to AIDS instructs us. Ed clearly points out the challenge AIDS poses and then gently with love takes away our fears and gives us courage to face this growing epidemic.

When we began Americans for a Sound AIDS/HIV Policy in 1987, it was our hope that we would never have to meet an Ed Rozar. Today I understand the critical role that Ed and others like him play in instructing us, chastening us, and guiding us to follow Christ's example in the face of this deadly foe. I thank God for bringing Ed into my life.

> W. Shepherd Smith, Jr.
> President
> Americans for a Sound AIDS/HIV Policy

Introduction

The journey you are about to embark on reveals how awesome God's grace is. As you travel along with me in this book, I hope you will be encouraged by my transition from shattered dreams to wholeness. Our family is looking forward to the future. Perhaps your view of the future will be enlightened also.

I want to thank especially Dave Biebel for putting this material together. He has invested two years of work which included hours of audio taping, and sifting through 700 pages of typewritten material. Without his dedicated efforts my story would not be in print.

Baker Book House encouraged and helped throughout the process of writing and editing the manuscript.

The people of Believers' Church in Marshfield supported us as we opened our hearts and lives to public scrutiny. Without their encouragement and prayers, the energy necessary to complete this project would not have been available. Pastors Ed Gungor, Glenn Smith, and Randy Burkhart have been instrumental in cheering me and the family along this journey. Glenn Klein and Jerry Dahlke continue to be there for me in times of need and rejoicing.

I cannot possibly mention all the people praying for us. Christians from all walks of life have taken us under wing and cared for us. The Marshfield Clinic has taken complete responsibility for my health care and continued employment.

There is no turning back, life goes on; God alone is faithful and just.

G. Edward Rozar, Jr., M.D.

1

Heart to Heart

*a*s a heart surgeon, I knew that having your heart stopped by somebody you didn't know, to make repairs you needed but didn't understand, was nobody's idea of a good time. So quite often I would sit on my patient's bed, get out a felt-tip pen and sketch on the sheets what I was going to do in the operating room.

"You'll get in trouble drawing on those sheets," the patient would protest, intently studying my artwork.

"No," I laughed, "they won't kick me off the staff!"

If the patient needed one or more bypasses, I would diagram the heart and its major vessels, and show where the particular blockages were. Then I would show how we would create conduits around those obstructions, so the heart could get the blood supply it needed.

You could almost see a light going on, especially if no other doctor had taken the time to explain the procedure. That light was partly from the patient's new understanding, but it was also because our new relationship had transformed

13

a clinical procedure into a personal experience we would both share.

I was a good heart surgeon, with good results. But I always leveled with my patients; the risk is never zero percent. Even if their surgery was more "routine," with a risk of only 1 or 2 percent, I still made it clear that to make that statistic, one or two out of a hundred patients failed to survive.

Not that I wanted to scare anybody. I wanted them to know that as far as I was concerned, every patient was unique. You can never say that even 1 percent is a low number, as if it doesn't mean anything. It means something to somebody. In fact, it means *everything* to somebody. Because 1 percent is 100 percent if it's you, it's never right to pretend that statistics like these represent anything other than real people with real and sometimes excruciating personal needs. When any of my patients didn't make it, there was a void that couldn't be filled by any other human being.

Another reason I tried to befriend my patients before we went into surgery was that I knew it was then or maybe never. As with children growing up, the time to establish that bond of trust is before the storm occurs—whether the crisis is because of illness, accident, or just the fact that adolescence has rendered them temporarily impaired.

Sometimes, even when we did the best we could surgically in our first attempt, patients would develop complications requiring us to go in again. It was always easier to sit down with these patients and their families and explain something as unwelcome as this (to us, as well as to them) if the foundation had been laid earlier. Because they knew I cared for them, not only did they believe me enough to put their lives very literally in my hands again, but they were able to approach our setback with confidence and hope.

I loved cardiac surgery. I loved the challenge. It was the peak I climbed to through thirteen years of surgical experience and training after medical school. Most of all, I loved helping patients who would have died otherwise. And I was always glad to have a heart-to-heart talk with them before it was time for me to reach for the knife.

Now that I've put the scalpel down, I want to have a heart-to-heart talk with you about infection with HIV (the virus that causes AIDS). HIV is the reason I'm not operating today. Somewhere along the line, on an unknown day—probably during surgery—I became infected. Now that I know what it feels like to be a patient as well as a physician, perhaps our chat will be even more eye to eye and heart to heart than we could have had before.

Maybe you are HIV-infected, and that is the reason you're reading this. More likely, you are not. You may not even know anybody who has this disease. But if things go the way I expect, you will in the near future, and it probably will surprise you who it is. So now is a good time to prepare yourself.

If you're like I was when I got my own diagnosis, you don't really know very much about HIV infection. I'll try to answer the questions (at least most of them) that are banging around in your mind.

You can trust me as we look at this complicated disease, though you may not always agree with my conclusions. Unlike some parties involved, I don't come to it with any political, personal, or professional agendas. All I really care about is that you hear the truth about AIDS. Much more importantly, that you come to know the Truth (that's what Jesus called himself) who is able to set us free to live and to laugh, even in the face of a diagnosis as devastating as AIDS.

There was a time when my attitude toward persons with AIDS was different from what it is today. Not that I was as judgmental as some people have been, but neither was I convinced that health-care workers (specifically, myself) should risk doing procedures that seemed unnecessary. For instance, when I was at West Virginia University as an assistant professor, we were asked to do a lung biopsy on a person obviously afflicted with *pneumocystis carinii,* a rare pneumonia that is one of the signs of AIDS. I was thinking, "Maybe it'll go away, so I don't have to put myself at risk." Little did I know that I was already HIV-infected myself.

As a Christian and a doctor, my experience with the diagnosis and treatment of my own disease has helped me see beyond statistics and symptoms to the needs of AIDS patients and their families. To convince you that I know what I'm talking about, I'll risk telling you more than you may care to hear concerning our personal, marital, and family journey with this modern-day plague.

Right from the start, I want to be clear about why I've written this book. I want to achieve one thing and avoid another. First let me say that I don't want your pity—though I must confess it feels good sometimes. As far as I'm concerned, I'm not an "innocent victim." Although I got this disease from an unidentified patient, that was part of the risk associated with my choosing to become a surgeon. Not that I would ever make light of that career. It was everything I wanted and more, maybe too much so. But I'm getting ahead of myself. When this story is over, I want you to know Ed Rozar as more than a born-again evangelical HIV-positive cardiac surgeon.

In terms of what I hope to achieve, I want to give you a deeper knowledge of what HIV is. I also want you to see what HIV can do to its carriers as well as to the people who know and love them. But this whole effort will have been wasted if I fail to convince you to stop and get in touch with the Lord. I'm confident he will show you creative ways to touch the lives of (us) modern-day lepers, just as he touched the lepers of his own day. Then, whether you're the one who's hurting or the one who wants to help, you may discover something truly remarkable that applies to any difficulty, affliction, loss, or sorrow conceivable this side of heaven—that his healing power can transform weakness into strength, darkness into light, sorrow into joy, and sickness into health.

Since our situation became public, we've had many opportunities to address the issues of AIDS. Donna and I have appeared on NBC's "Today" show, CBS's "This Morning," ABC's "20/20," CBN's "700 Club," and been featured in a multitude of other TV, radio, and newspaper interviews. I have participated in several public forums, and testified before Congress in relation to the "Kimberly Bergalis" bill. I plan to take you behind the scenes of some of those situations in the coming pages.

When I look back over all of those experiences, and anticipate those that lie ahead, three things hit me. First, many people, especially politicians and some physicians, don't show much common sense when it comes to AIDS policy. Second, if I'm accurately hearing people in the lay audiences I address, the public is clearly not going to stand for pretense and deception much longer. In my mind, what is sometimes labeled "hysteria" is the result of reasonable people demanding what's right.

Third, not everyone is happy when I mix Christianity with what they consider a purely medical issue. This doesn't bother me much, though, since it is *because of my experience with HIV infection* that my faith has become such an integral part of who I am today. I couldn't separate who I am from what I believe at this point, even if I tried. Besides, is it not more than a little hypocritical for people who have turned a clearly public-health issue into a matter of civil rights to accuse me of mixing issues?

I have had many opportunities to address different groups. When I do, there are several questions I hear repeatedly. The school kids want to know about Magic Johnson, safe sex, and condoms. Parents are desperate to keep their kids from getting AIDS through promiscuity. (Or are they more afraid that they themselves may get it?) Some people wonder if they can become HIV-infected through casual contact; for instance, from public toilets, shared utensils, mosquito bites. One person even asked me if he might get AIDS from taking prescription pills.

Increasingly, public-policy issues are brought up by both professional and lay audiences. Should there be mandatory testing of health-care workers (and/or patients)? Could the whole problem be solved if everybody was tested and those who tested positive were quarantined somewhere?

In church settings, it's not too difficult to sense unexpressed opinions, the most common of which might be: AIDS only happens to bad people. So why are you bothering us with this? We're not at risk. It's *their* problem, not ours, and it probably serves them right. Nobody in my family, or even any of my friends, has it. So let the government take care of it; I have more important things to think about.

Usually toward the very end of any meeting I address, somebody will have the courage to verbalize what everybody has been thinking the whole time: "Are you and your wife still having sex? Is she HIV-positive, too?"

Occasionally, I hear the question I love to answer: "How do you keep going—loving, living, laughing—in the face of something as terrifying as AIDS?"

In the pages that follow, I'll try to answer these and other questions. In a sense, it's as close as I can come to sitting down and having a heart-to-heart talk with you about all these things.

In a large audience, there will often be people who are really struggling. I can see it in their eyes. It may be AIDS, or it may be cancer. Perhaps infidelity or divorce or another personal loss has broken their hearts and they're groping for a little hope in their quiet desperation. These are the people I look for now, though I doubt I could have connected as personally with their pain before my own experience with this disease. They're really all around us, inside the church and especially outside—people searching for someone to believe, and a reason to carry on.

Maybe you're one of those hurting people. You've picked up this book (or somebody's given it to you), but you've been so down for so long you're afraid to believe that what you long for is really possible. It is! Peace, serenity, reconciliation, wholeness, even joy—these are all possible even in the face of AIDS. Despite this illness, life is better for me now than it ever was before.

I invite you to journey with me a little while, in the hope that as we walk together you'll see, as I have, that beyond the sometimes excruciating losses of life there is more, perhaps more than we could have known unless things of lesser importance had been stripped away.

The apostle Paul—who knew a lot about both suffering and joy—penned some words nearly two thousand years ago that are as inspiring today as they were then: "Therefore we do not lose heart, but though our outer man is decaying, yet our inner man is being renewed day by day. For momentary, light affliction is producing for us an eternal weight of glory far beyond all comparison, while we look not at the things which are seen, but at the things which are not seen; for the things which are seen are temporal, but the things which are not seen are eternal" (2 Cor. 4: 16–18).

Without doubt, before the diagnosis of my HIV infection turned life upside down for the Rozar clan, words like these made sense on one level. I believed in God and his Word and had been a born-again Christian since 1974. So I knew Paul's thoughts were certainly true and worth contemplating. But, in another way that is hard to explain precisely, I don't think this passage and others like it had penetrated much below the surface of my mind and reached my heart.

For now, maybe it's enough to say that the things that were "seen"—for a cardiac surgeon, there can be many of these, not all of them bad, either—seemed real enough and well worth investing in. The unseen, eternal things seemed to be for another time and place—specifically, later, maybe as late as when I would see the Lord face to face.

Whether my perspective and priorities got turned upside down or inside out as the result of my diagnosis, I can't quite tell for sure. I do know that it was because of this illness, not in spite of it, that God's Word, in fact, God himself, has become more real than anything I have ever known before. My hope is that you will experience this renewal, too, even if you're not grappling with something as dreadful as AIDS.

Sometimes when reading books like this, or hearing speakers describe their victories of faith, it's tempting to think that what worked for them is great, but it could never apply to you because your own faith seems so deficient by comparison. But here's a little secret: The saints of God were all sinners (a lot like you and me) who were willing to allow his Spirit to renew and empower their own.

Throughout the Bible are stories of sinners transformed into powerful spokespersons for God, but there are no saints who were magically modified as if by the stroke of some celestial magic wand. No matter who you are, no matter what you've done, no matter how old or how young you may be, and whatever your health is now, God loves you and has in his mind a destiny for you that is more magnificent than you could ever imagine in your wildest dreams.

What I'm trying to say is that God uses real people, just like you and me. To prove that, I will let my life become an open book, dog-eared and torn pages and all, in hopes that when all is said and done, you will be encouraged, strengthened, and better equipped to run the specific race and finish the uniquely designed course that is stretching out before you.

⊿2⊳

Parables and Realities

s early as I can recall, I learned about the Garden of Eden, Adam and Eve, and Noah's Ark. After all, I grew up in the church, went to Sunday school, catechism classes, confirmation—the works. Basically, though, I was just going through the motions. As far as I was concerned, stories like these were parables to teach us something, but I wasn't quite sure what for a long, long time.

Why drag the Garden of Eden and Noah's Ark into a book about AIDS? For a couple of good reasons, but I don't want to spill all the beans right now. I will say this much, however: If you want to understand how such an infernal disease could even exist, you have to go all the way back to the Garden.

If you want to see how something invisible—almost a quarter million HIV viruses will fit within the period at the end of this sentence—could threaten whole nations (as it now does in Africa) or even the whole world, just read the first few pages of Genesis. Didn't Noah's Ark save the human race from a worldwide disaster similar to what we have with

AIDS—a multifaceted global catastrophe, the impact of which no one could escape?

In my wildest nightmares, I never imagined I would become infected with HIV, the modern plague. For one thing, I was never sick, at least until 1985—and even for some time after that I felt healthy as a horse. After all, health and strength are basic requirements if you want to be a cardiac surgeon. Besides, growing up in a traditional home long before AIDS was ever heard of, I figured bad things happen mainly to bad people. Compared to the criminals I often heard about, we were pretty good people. My father was a lawyer. My mother was a schoolteacher with two Master's degrees. They were both quite strict and always right, a serious problem for a precocious youngster who figured he was right all the time, too.

As a boy I spent much energy trying to please my father, but sometimes ended up in no-win situations. Once, when chemicals killed part of our lawn, I became the prime suspect. Dad wouldn't take "I don't know how it happened" for an answer. If I didn't "tell the truth," he said, I was going to regret it. Finally, in desperation, I lied to appease him, then took the consequences just to get off the witness stand.

For some reason, I didn't end up resenting Dad as much as I might have. I don't have bitter feelings about him. As far as I can tell, I've forgiven him. The more I learn about fathering, the more I conclude that he probably didn't have a very good role model himself. But I have to agree with people who point out how much more difficult it is to develop a close, loving relationship with your heavenly Father if you have not experienced something similar with your earthly father.

Another negative result of my strict upbringing was inner conflict, especially the sense of rebellion, I had throughout adolescence. It was always my goal to become a physician, since that was what Dad wanted me to be. To express some kind of independence—as teens often do—I took up smok-

ing and got involved with some other crazy stuff it wouldn't
edify you to hear about.

I managed to concentrate enough on my studies in high
school to graduate a year early and immediately entered college in the summer of 1966. Despite my continuing rebel-
lious attitudes, I was intelligent enough to make very good
grades my first two and a half years at the University of Georgia and get accepted by the Medical College of Georgia.

After being accepted into med school, my academics went
on cruise control. All that driving and striving had finally
paid off, but I decompressed so much that I almost didn't
graduate from college. In fact, I had to go to summer school
to raise my grade in biochemistry from an F to an A. I sowed
even wilder oats during that period, increasing my smoking
to two packs a day and my alcohol consumption to a level
where it still amazes me I didn't end up killing myself or
somebody else. Once, when I was driving drunk, we ran off
the road right on campus; I bent the car's frame, but nobody
was hurt. Another time when I was in the same condition, I
ran a stop sign and just missed hitting a police officer, without even getting a ticket.

Looking back at that period, I wonder sometimes at the
way I was protected from my own stupidity. It wasn't luck,
I'm sure. I don't believe in luck, good or bad. Obviously,
God had something else planned for me. Though I didn't
know it at the time, my life and destiny were in his hands.
Not that I wanted much to do with that notion. Why drag
ideas like dependence and submission into the mind and
heart of someone so obviously headed for success?

Nonetheless, there was one guy on campus, a Campus
Crusade for Christ representative, who really got under my
skin. Their first "spiritual law," about God loving me and
having a wonderful plan for my life, just didn't compute, in
more ways than one. I certainly didn't want to hear anything about law number two, that my own sin had separated

me from God and made it impossible for me to know and experience either his love or his plan.

This fellow never gave up on me, although I mocked him relentlessly, harassed him without mercy, and continually made him the object of practical jokes. Once we even toilet-papered his dorm room. But no matter how hard I tried to ignore him, there was something about his life and something about his message that I just couldn't evade. Perhaps in my deepest self I was afraid he was right. There *was* something missing in my life, but at that point I wasn't quite ready to find out from anyone what it was. I would just figure it out myself, as I had done with everything of importance before that.

When I was a sophomore at the Medical College of Georgia, I did attend church once or twice. I'm not sure to this day why. The pastor even came out to visit, but we didn't talk much about spiritual things. Perhaps he figured I was already a believer, or else I managed to derail such discussions.

Anyhow, I sailed through medical school without much trouble, graduating in 1973. I began my internship in a small surgical program in Norfolk, Virginia, mainly because I wanted to get out of Georgia and away from home. It was time to move on, establish my own identity, live my own life.

That same summer, I met Donna Mummau, a nurse practitioner at the hospital where I was a house officer. One day I was studying in the library, and she just came over and asked my name. I had been dating a little, but Donna and I started going out together, and we've been together ever since. This, I suppose, is one of the more amazing facts of my life, since in some ways Donna and I were very different, while in other ways we were so painfully alike.

For instance, although I've always been pro-life (and we both are, now), at that point Donna was outspokenly pro-abortion. Resolving differences like that might have been easier if we hadn't both been such independent and opinionated folks who never backed down. Illogical as it may sound, after verbally fighting it out a few dozen times, we finally concluded we should either leave each other alone or get married. In 1974, we chose the latter.

It didn't take long, though, to discover that getting married hadn't erased the ego in either of us. All it took was a bad decision, one of the worst we've ever made: We bought an old house with the specific goal of redoing the whole thing. We didn't know any better, but with me a perfectionist surgeon-type and Donna a strong-willed independent woman, the sparks were flying right from the start.

Wallpapering together was a lot like mud wrestling. Stripping the walls wasn't so bad. It was messy enough, but we managed okay. Although we'd heard that couples should never wallpaper together, being the kind of people we are, we had to learn why the hard way.

As a surgical resident who spent so much time in the operating room, my mind-set was: "If it's worth doing, do it right—*exactly* right." Perfection was not to be the exception, but the rule. My compulsivity wasn't inherent or pathological; it was cultivated. When it came to matching wallpaper edges, as far as I was concerned, there was only one way to do that, too—the right way (*my* way). But Donna, not being mechanically inclined, didn't need to have it as precisely "right" as I did. The result was that we could never agree that a room, or even part of a room, was satisfactory until we had haggled over it and worked on it to the point of exhaustion.

We solved the problem not by finding a way to cooperate, but by devising ways to finish portions of the job without the other party's involvement. For instance, Donna and a girlfriend papered one of the rooms while I was working. I recall inspecting it with mixed feelings. I was glad it was done, even if it didn't look quite right.

Just so you know how intense I really was, while Donna was in Charlottesville for a weekend, I redid the whole kitchen by myself—tore out the floor, cabinets, and sink, and rebuilt it all before she came home. I stayed up all night to finish, but I was used to staying up all night, so that was no big deal.

We really had some difficulties in those early years. A surgical residency is tough enough on a marriage, without trying to restore an old house in your spare time. It's amazing that we stayed together; in fact, we alternated between fighting tooth and nail and giving each other the silent treatment.

Old-fashioned as it may sound, the reason we made it was our shared commitment that divorce was not an acceptable option. We were in this for the duration, "Come hell or high water," as my daddy used to say. In a sense, we settled into a pattern of mutual toleration and, with time, even began to accept mediocrity in our relationship as the best we could manage. In my heart, though, this perspective violated my deepest convictions, and I was never totally satisfied that status quo was the way it had to stay. Of course I didn't know that it would take a life-threatening illness before we truly resolved our differences.

One reason we were so anti-divorce was that just before we married, we had come to a position of shared faith. I don't know how Donna ever got me to that particular home Bible study, but I'll never forget the first time I went. I made the mistake of sitting on a squeaky chair. Every time I moved even a little bit, it made a very loud noise. So I sat frozen in place for over thirty minutes while the people prayed. I was trapped. I couldn't wait to get out of there. And I swore I never was going back.

But I did go back, several times, and in the process the Lord just grabbed me. I don't know how else to say it. I began to see a fellowship among the people, a closeness and concern I had never experienced before. As I listened to what they said about salvation, it made sense. I accepted Jesus Christ and invited him into my heart to be my Lord and Savior. Soon after we married, Donna and I were baptized together on a Sunday morning at Central Baptist Church in Norfolk, Virginia.

In December 1977, we rented a U-Haul truck and moved ourselves, our two dogs, and our 18-foot Larson speedboat with 115 horsepower engine to Athens, Tennessee, where I entered a general surgery practice with Dr. Bill Trotter. In some ways, it was like starting a new life. It was refreshing and I enjoyed my work very much. I was doing what I had been training to do for eight long years. And, finally, I was making enough money to pay our bills.

Right away we got involved in a good church, First Baptist Church, which is part of the Southern Baptist Convention. Each week we attended an adult Sunday school class that had a dynamic teacher. One Sunday, Bob Lambert surprised me by asking me to give my testimony, something I had never done before. I fumbled around for a few minutes, telling how I grew up in a religious home, went to church and everything, without ever really coming to know Christ in a personal way. Then I told some of my history through college, how I was searching because I knew there had to be more to life than I had discovered, and how I had finally realized that Jesus was who he said he was.

I would rate that first effort as a C-minus, but evidently it was good enough for Bob, whose motivation became more apparent when he invited me to go to India in 1978 to work with India Youth for Christ on a short-term mission trip. I would be part of the outreach teams, but not practicing medicine.

We broke into seven or eight units on that trip, going out each day to the local villages. We would go into the people's huts, and there on the walls in the semi-darkness were their "gods," grotesque caricatures of what was really the demonic. People there were hungry to know the Lord. Thousands came to Christ during that trip, and for the first time I witnessed healings and exorcisms. Although I wasn't quite sure what to think about all of it, I rejoiced to see the positive response and locked away the rest for future reference.

One thing really did hit me, though: There was obviously an intense need for surgical skills on the mission field. When I returned to the States, I asked about our denomination's short-term medical missions program. In 1979, this program took me to North Yemen, near Saudi Arabia. In 1981, I went to Ghana, West Africa, where I did more than a hundred surgeries in five weeks. Because it was so hot there, I would put a wet towel on the bed before lying down to sleep. I hardly had time to eat a meal, much less speak to any of those patients about faith in Jesus Christ.

This trip was a turning point in our life, however, not because of the work itself, but because I became acquainted with an obstetrician/gynecologist named Andy Norman who, eighteen months later, would deliver the baby who would become our first adopted son.

In 1982, Donna and I decided to go together on a mission trip, this time to Thailand, where I worked as a general practitioner and she as a nurse practitioner in a Cambodian refugee camp. In the back of my mind, I was hoping this experience would nurture our relationship, both maritally and spiritually. But while we did have a great time in Hong Kong, the mission field is hardly the ideal setting to work on a marriage.

We slept in a little hallway with a drawn curtain, but it was so hot and there were so many lizards on the wall and ceiling that it was difficult to get any sleep at all. It was no honeymoon experience, I can assure you! In addition, whether it was the accumulated stress of those three weeks or just our basic personalities jousting again, we had a real blowout on the way home over a little thing like how to fill out the U.S. Customs forms to get back in the country.

Right after we returned, my father died without our being able to talk through some of the things that still nagged me deep inside. I had to try to help Mom through this transition, so I traveled to Georgia every four to six weeks for a long weekend.

Simultaneously, I began thinking about leaving private practice to retrain as a cardiac surgeon. In January 1983 I had just returned from interviewing for a one-year thoracic surgery program in Dallas when we got a call from Andy Norman, who was now practicing in Boone, North Carolina. A young woman in labor who had had no prenatal care walked in off the street and, after delivery, said to Andy, "I don't believe that I can take care of this baby. Would you happen to know someone who would?"

Only a few hours before Jonathan Edward was born, Donna and I had decided to pick up everything and leave our nice house with its four acres, her Master's program and my $100,000 income to enter another residency at one-quarter the pay. When Andy called and asked, "Are you interested in a baby boy?" I had to stop for a minute and ask myself, "Is this really the right time to make a move?"

But because we believed God was opening doors for us, we moved to Dallas in early 1983 and started over, in more ways than one. Suddenly we two had become three—a family—with the result that Donna and I became much closer. Not only that, but my program in Dallas allowed me more time with our infant son than I would ever have had in private practice.

Without a doubt, we were becoming more convinced that the Lord really knew what he was doing. Despite our weaknesses and our strengths, he had been laying a foundation in our life together that would increasingly become more significant and more obvious in the next few years.

That leads me back to where I started this chapter, to the idea of parables and realities. The parable I'm thinking of now, however, is the one that Jesus told at the very end of his famous Sermon on the Mount.

He compared foolish and wise men, and the way they go about building their lives as they build their houses. The foolish man builds his life upon the sand, for when he hears Christ's words, he fails to act upon them. When crisis looms—when the rain comes, the floods rise, and the wind blows—neither such a house nor such a life can stand. But the wise person, having heard Christ's words, builds his life upon them, so that when the storms come, regardless of how fierce they may be, his house does not fall, because it has been founded upon a rock.

In reality, this is what preserved our marriage and kept our home and lives from disintegrating in the storms we faced in those early years—some of our own creation, and some beyond our control. Besides the problems already mentioned, we had weathered two malpractice suits while I was practicing in Tennessee. If there is anything a conscientious and caring Christian physician doesn't need, it's to be dragged into court because the results of some procedure failed to meet somebody's unrealistic expectations. However, I told the Lord that I was ready to accept his will for the outcomes.

When we were in Dallas, things seemed to level out for a while, but just on the horizon some clouds were forming again, specifically the horrendous stress of another residency, a cardiac surgery program with brutal hours and multiple responsibilities that would leave me at risk for exposure to a deadly virus that public-health officials were just beginning to understand.

3

"Fast Eddie"

*I*n June 1984 we moved to Pittsburgh, Pennsylvania where I had been accepted into a thoracic surgery residency program. My year in Dallas had been spent in a non-accredited fellowship in cardiac, thoracic, and vascular surgery, but it was well worth it and prepared me for Pittsburgh.

That first year at Allegheny was rough, much worse than I remembered my general surgery residency being. I would leave home most mornings between 5:30 and 6:00 and return at 8:00 P.M. If that wasn't crazy enough, when I was on call, I stayed right through and worked all night at the hospital, followed by another full shift before I got home again. You hardly have time or energy to wonder why you're doing this (or why you're allowing somebody else to do it to you!). You just beat yourself, like the long line of surgeons before you—trying to prove something. Just *what* is anybody's guess.

Since you've probably never been inside the doors of an operating room, let me give you a quick glimpse behind the scenes. As you look over my shoulder, you'll easily see how a surgeon might get exposed to HIV (or, more commonly, to

31

hepatitis B), especially if he or she works very fast. And *I* was fast enough to earn the nickname "Fast Eddie" when I was a general surgical resident in Norfolk. Maybe I was too fast for my own good, especially on that unknown day in the spring of 1985.

It is now 7:30 A.M., and I've already made rounds on yesterday's patients. I've taken out some chest tubes and some balloons (inserted into the large artery in the chest from the groin artery to temporarily assist while the heart itself recovers from the shock of surgery), and I've written some patient transfer orders.

Now I head for the operating room, where I take another look at the films (coronary angiograms or X-rays), scrub, put on my gloves, and prepare the already anesthetized patient for surgery. (Don't be surprised—residents open and close most of the cases in our program.) I help insert a large intravenous line, down through the patient's neck and into the heart area. Then I drape out the chest and legs, since we usually use the greater saphenous vein from the thigh for several of the bypass grafts.

Next I make an incision down the center of the sternum (breastbone), using a scalpel until I actually hit the bone. The next cut is made with a small power-driven saw, taking care to stay in the middle. Don't worry, the patient doesn't feel a thing. Actually, it's much easier than it looks, especially since this is the first time his chest has been opened. I hook the tip of the saw under the xiphoid (the back of the sternum) and *Zip! Zip!* I'm already done. Maybe you've already seen enough, but we're just getting started. Aren't you amazed how bloodless this whole thing has been so far? I'll just stop that little bit of bleeding on the edges of the sternum with some bone wax.

Now it's time to put in a chest spreader, to keep the cavity open while we work on the heart. I slowly crank open the retractor, being very careful not to break the ribs, and not to tear the innominate vein that crosses the chest at the top of the incision.

I carefully slit the pericardium and suspend it with stitches to the retractor or edge of the incision. Next I put "purse string" sutures in a circle on the aorta, the big artery that comes out of the heart, and on the appendage of the atrium where the blood returns to the heart. I leave the ends long, sliding a piece of rubber over the atrium's appendage, to be tightened down around the tubing when we go on bypass. A large tube is then placed in the right atrium after the patient's blood is thinned with heparin. Finally, I insert a small piece of plastic tubing into the aorta, secure it, and connect both cannulas to tubing from the heart/lung machine.

Everything's ready now. The patient is connected, above and below the heart, to the machine that will sustain his life while we stop his heart long enough to make repairs. I have the attending surgeon called. So far, as you see, he hasn't even been in the room.

He walks in, looks everything over very carefully, and finally says, "Okay, Dr. Rozar, it's your turn." Just what I've been waiting to hear! "Let's go," I say to the well-trained team as everybody swings into action. The heart/lung machine begins its work of pumping blood through the patient's system. The large artery arising out of the heart is clamped to isolate the heart so it can be emptied. But the heart keeps beating until it is iced down and a special drug called cardioplegia, which stops and protects it, is infused into the heart.

The heart is still now, and I look for the vessels on the heart (often hard to find because of fatty tissue) and mark them with a small incision. Next I measure to see how long a vein is needed, cut off the right length, and connect the distal end to the coronary artery below the blockage, thus "bypassing" it. After I've done this in two different areas, the third and final bypass today is done using the left internal mammary artery. The free end is connected to a vessel of the heart where increased circulation is needed. (This internal mammary artery was taken down after the chest was opened and before car-diopulmonary bypass commenced.)

Once we have finished working on the heart and every-thing checks out, we remove the large clamp on the aorta so that the heart has blood coursing through it again. The ends of the veins are then sewn to the aorta and flow is established in the "bypasses." (The origin of the mammary artery is already attached by God to the artery of the arm.) Cardiopulmonary bypass is terminated after the patient is warmed up and all sites look good. The attending surgeon leaves for another case. (Closing the chest, like opening, is also usually the job of a resident.). It is not a glorious job, but it is an important part of the procedure. Total time, skin to skin, is 3 hours, 20 minutes, longer than acceptable to me, but faster than most.

I hope I haven't grossed you out completely by that very brief and far too simplistic explanation of what I used to do—a typical episode in the workday of a surgical resident. Since I was usually involved with at least two heart surgeries a day, plus rounds before and after, the hours flew past, even if the cases were first-time procedures and everything went well.

"Redos" (what we call subsequent chest openings in people who have had heart surgery before) were another story altogether. Stuff can end up flying all over the place and whoever is doing the cutting can end up covered with blood. This isn't a problem in terms of the patient because there is plenty of blood available for transfusion as needed. But you would be appalled (and I am now as I think back) how bloody things sometimes get in there.

The second time around, the heart is usually right up against the breastbone, and we have to use a different saw (a sidebiting saw) without a guard on its blade. The surgeon must be very careful, holding the saw with one hand and guiding it with the other, as cuts are made first through the outer table (of the sternum) and then through the inner table. This is delicate business with little room for error. If you get into the right ventricle of the heart by cutting too deeply, everybody in the room, especially the patient, has a very big problem.

It is not so much the blood that may splatter on you while you work that risks the transmission of diseases like HIV or hepatitis B. More likely, one way or another you'll end up sticking yourself with "sharps": needles or maybe a scalpel. Because you use magnification (magnifying lenses attached to

the front of what look like normal eyeglasses) to be certain
the delicate sutures are placed correctly, you have a tunnel
view and a small field to look at as you work. No matter how
careful you are, you can get stuck, or stick somebody else, as
you race against the clock. If you have to look up to hand
something to an attendant or receive something yourself, you
might as well start over. The whole situation is intense: The
heart is stopped, and the length of time it is stopped is important. You know if something goes wrong, you're going to
need every extra second. So I've stuck people that way, and
I've been stuck myself, many times, either with a very small
needle or even with the big ones used to close the chest.

I hate to think how often I stuck myself while closing a
case (I participated in over 250 heart cases during my residency alone). It was just too easy to puncture my own hand
with the sternal wire needle I was trying to push through the
bone or even around it, while lifting the breastbone underneath with the other hand. For reasons that are obvious, I
would rather stick my own hand or finger than the patient's
heart.

Sometimes I had to work blind, by feel. If I got stuck, I
didn't even think about it—just changed a glove, or maybe
not, but kept going, whatever happened. I might see blood
in my glove after I finished and have no idea how or when it
got there. Even if I noticed it while still working, I would
ignore it for the sake of speed.

Anyone who sews by hand can identify with this. What happens when you're doing a stiff seam with one hand inside,
while the other pushes the needle through? Well, multiply
that by a factor of a thousand to allow for the pressure of
human flesh versus denim, and you can easily see why surgeons stick themselves so often—and why they're so concerned about doing invasive and sometimes blind procedures
on HIV-positive patients.

But that is still not the whole story of a day in the life of
Ed Rozar, resident physician. Maybe I did get infected in the

operating room, but I did a lot more than open and close cases for attending surgeons or do skin-to-skin procedures. What happened in the controlled environment of the operating room was a piece of cake compared to what I might encounter in the intensive care unit after hours. I often stood between a recovering patient's emergency and his or her sudden death.

A significant percentage of heart patients have complications, especially soon after their surgery. These problems can be minor or major, depending on the patient and the type of surgery performed. If a patient dropped his blood pressure or maybe developed a clot around the heart after surgery, I would have to cut him open right there, take the stitches out, and open the chest to expose the heart. That meant cutting wires and spreading the chest by hand—lots of opportunity for puncture wounds from metal and bone. Or if a patient went baseline (no heartbeat), I couldn't push on the chest to restart the heart because the sternum had just been wired and was now two bones instead of one. So I had to open the chest quickly and compress the heart by hand.

Once I had two patients in crisis, lying side by side with their chests open. Fortunately, I have long arms, and they were both within my reach. I can't recall compressing a heart with each hand, but when I got one patient back, the other one arrested and I just turned and went to the other bed. Those were the wildest few minutes I ever had. Fortunately, both patients survived. During times like these it would have been easy enough to puncture a glove, or get scratched or stuck in that frenzy of activity. What was I supposed to do then? Stop and change gloves? Give a lecture on "universal precautions"?

Sometimes as a resident I would be called to the emergency department. And there is no doubt in my mind that I took care of many patients who, when they were later admitted, were officially listed as someone else's. Consequently, any "look back" studies (examining the records of all patients in that institution associated with my name as a physician) might still never solve the question that seems more important to others than it is to me: Who was the patient who gave me HIV?

I'm not bitter about this, and the only reason I would want to know now is that I might be able to let that person know about his or her HIV status. Most likely, however, whoever it was is either very sick or already dead, probably the latter.

Of course, I now had acquired a deadly disease without my knowledge. I was feeling well enough that spring—chalking up any fatigue to the horrendous pace of the program, which was about to let up a little. My final year there, starting in July, would consist of a more varied schedule. I was to be on an elective rotation in July. Looking back, it would also be a time to recover from the acute, debilitating illness I had in May 1985.

Beyond that, we became the proud adoptive parents of another son in April. One day our pastor's wife called Donna and said, "A pastor-friend of ours has a woman in his church who is pregnant but wants to give up the child. Do you know anybody who'd be interested in a baby?"

"Well, yes. Us!" Donna replied, without even consulting me. Not that I would have argued against it. David was born on April 12, and we picked him up on April 15. Again, this brought us closer. Now we had two sons to love, and that, probably more than anything else, put our unresolved differences on hold.

Just two weeks after we welcomed David into our home, I traveled to New Orleans to attend a conference of the American Association of Thoracic Surgeons. On May 1, 1985, I was at a fine restaurant having dinner with my department chairman and several other attending surgeons from Allegheny when suddenly I started having a strange feeling in my neck— a cross between irritation and pain. I rubbed it, but it didn't go away. And I felt hot.

I looked around the table to see if anybody else was sick, thinking maybe it was the food. But no one else seemed to be affected. I managed to finish dinner, made it back to my room, took some aspirin, and went to bed. By the next morning, I felt bad enough to miss the meeting, though I did recover enough by dinnertime to go out with a fellow resident and his wife.

That was my last good meal for quite a while. Overnight I was sick again and feeling totally washed out. By the time I got on the plane to go home Thursday, I was miserable. That flight was the most difficult I ever hope to have, complete with fever, nausea, aches, and assorted pains. I just lay back and tried to survive it. I was one sick puppy, that's for sure.

I was supposed to work the next morning, but that was impossible. I was just too sick. Fortunately, that weekend I was not on call, so I stayed in bed the whole time. By Monday, when I showed up on schedule in the operating room, I still wasn't feeling much better. In fact, for the first time in my entire medical career, I had to be excused from the operating room to go out and vomit. When it happened again later that same week, they sent me home until I could get over whatever was wrong with me.

The next couple of weeks are still fuzzy in my mind. I remember seeing a physician at an attending surgeon's request, but I also remember that Donna had to drive me to the hospital for the lab tests because I was too weak to drive.

After $600 worth of tests, my doctor concluded I had a mononucleosis type of viral illness. The symptoms were classic of an acute HIV infection: fatigue, aches and pains, nausea, no appetite. In fact, I couldn't eat anything except Popsicles for several weeks. Even ice cream, which I had always loved, had become distasteful. That was strange, I thought, but that was about as far as I went with it. The whole thing was bizarre.

Nobody ever suggested doing an HIV screen. Apparently nobody even thought about it, maybe because as far as anyone knew, AIDS was a disease afflicting certain patient populations, and there was no chance a health-care worker could get it from a patient. (That was the information put out at the time and, in fact, continued for several more years.) Remember, it wasn't until April or May of 1985 that the blood banks started routinely screening for HIV on "banked blood," though not patients.

I got little sympathy from my colleagues, either attending surgeons or fellow residents. When you're a resident, the work is pretty cruel and grueling—almost like slave labor. I got all sorts of flack for missing work, but ignored most of it. They really expected me to just dive back into the routine. I had never hidden from work before, but now it was necessary to slow down a little so that I could recover from this "unknown" illness.

The program was doing a total of eight hearts a day, sometimes more. Since there were only two junior thoracic residents, one senior and one fellow, every warm body was needed to assist, especially since the attending surgeons counted on us to get the cases going. Then they might have one of us "do" the procedure if we were qualified and technically ready. They were really doing us a favor by letting us do so much, but with increased participation comes increased responsibility. Some attending surgeons seem to think they're doing residents a favor just by letting them be there, but at our program everything was okay as long as you put forth the effort. I suppose there was the feeling that we did owe them something, but that's true of most training programs.

One of the attending surgeons actually tried to get my week's vacation revoked because I had been out with this illness. That maneuver failed, and I took my vacation, which I spent recovering. When I finally returned to work early in June, I discovered I was now on call every other night for three weeks. I had no choice but to grit my teeth and tough it out, though I knew it would be a grueling month. Here I was just starting to feel better, even starting to eat again—I had lost twenty pounds during the acute phase of the illness.

Because I was nearly always totally exhausted by the time I had survived another thirty-six-hour stint, I would go home, crawl in a hole, and wish I could die. I was in a survival mode and felt like a zombie sometimes, but I had to be really careful because I still had to make life-and-death decisions every day. I am sure that it was supernatural strength that sustained me. "The LORD is my strength and my shield; my heart trusts in Him, and I am helped . . ." (Ps. 28:7).

One of the things that kept me going, I guess, was that I knew it would only last a month. The new "slaves" would be arriving July 1, and I wouldn't be the clinical chief anymore. I could do an elective, selecting cases to meet my board requirements, which meant I would have a lighter schedule for July.

During July, I did get a little more rest, and by August I had basically recovered. After that, I tried to ignore that episode of sickness, maybe because I was still pretty busy. I had no other symptoms to speak of, but I was never able to regain those twenty pounds, although I had returned to a regular diet, including ice cream. I wondered about that weight loss from time to time, especially when somebody would mention I looked thin. I would just reply, "Yeah, I used to weigh 170." I was down to 150, and my biggest problem seemed to be how to buy a new wardrobe on a resident's salary, with three other mouths to feed.

Obviously, I never really forgot that illness in 1985, especially the dramatic weight loss and my inability to regain weight. Every time I looked in the mirror after a shower, I was reminded. But it never crossed my mind to seek another medical opinion. I was feeling well enough again, and I had a lot more important things to worry about. What career direction would be best for me and my growing family once my residency was finished? Would I be able to pass my board-certification exams, written and then oral?

4

King of the Hill

magine holding a little premature baby, not much bigger than two hands. This tiny newborn has a hole, about the diameter of a pencil, between the two chambers of his heart (a VSD), which itself is about the size of a small orange. If somebody doesn't fix that defect, this child has little chance of seeing his first birthday. If the baby survives infancy, every normal childhood physical activity will be a supreme effort, perhaps even a threat to his life.

That's what keeps people like Dr. Robert (Gus) Gustafson operating. During a rotation from November 1985 to February 1986, I became acquainted with Gus, who was professor of pediatric thoracic surgery at West Virginia University School of Medicine in Morgantown. I enjoyed the work so much, especially working with Gus, that I seriously considered doing a fellowship (another one-year residency) in pediatric heart surgery.

A couple of things stopped me. For one thing, I didn't relish the idea of playing the resident game anymore. For another, the work was so delicate and the patients so fragile

41

that unless you have at least one expert associate, a pediatric cardiac surgeon might as well move into the hospital. Donna wasn't too keen on that idea, and I realized, too, that I didn't want my sons growing up without me.

About the biggest problem I encountered during that rotation was finding enough space for Donna and the boys to visit me on weekends. I had been provided the usual accommodations—one room. When I mentioned I had a wife and two kids and needed more space, at first they said I would have to pay for it. But on a resident's salary, we were just making ends meet. Dr. Gordon Murray, who was chief of thoracic surgery at the time, intervened and found me a small three-bedroom apartment in the faculty housing dorm. The family would come down from Pittsburgh on a Thursday and stay until Sunday. I never had time to be lonely when they weren't there, because of the immense amount of reading I had to do to get up to speed with this fascinating specialty.

Although I finally decided against another fellowship, Gus was instrumental in getting me a position as assistant professor of surgery at West Virginia University School of Medicine. So we ended up working together anyway—not too bad for a guy without the kind of credentials normally expected. I think Gus and Dr. Murray wanted me on board mainly for my clinical skills.

We moved to Morgantown in the summer of 1986. Donna wasn't exactly excited about going there, and the salary was maybe 60 percent of what I might have made elsewhere. But we reminded each other that making a lot of money was never a big deal for me anyway. One thing I will say for it, though, the position came with some good benefits, including a pension plan that put away each year an equivalent of 20 percent of my salary.

I really liked working with the residents and medical students. On a typical day we would do one or two heart surgeries, mostly bypasses, but we also did valve replacements and some lung surgery. I think I did ninety-five hearts my first year there, which was quite a few, considering that the next closest surgeon's total was seventy-five. So I made some money for the university—they knew it and so did I—and as a result I got a little bonus.

The boys were growing up so fast, and I enjoyed the time I had with them. It was fascinating to see these two together. The love they gave each other spilled over into our whole family. But my colleagues had subtle ways of letting me know that even when not on call, for instance on a weekend, I was still supposed to make rounds if I was in town.

"Aren't you coming by?" they would ask.

"I'm off," I would reply. "I wasn't planning to come back until Monday."

"Why not?"

I regret how often I gave in to the pressure to make Sunday-morning rounds on patients and as a result miss church, but I still had enough time off to satisfy us. We managed that winter to do something we had wanted to do for a long time; we learned to snow ski, at Canaan Valley, West Virginia—a great place for kids.

We also enjoyed the water, and by our second summer in West Virginia had fallen in love with sailing. One weekend in August, we all spent three nights on a sailboat with another young couple. We rented a thirty-five-foot sailboat near Annapolis and sailed the Chesapeake Bay, though we almost returned with one less Rozar. Jonathan and David were playing tug-of-war with a rope, Jonathan in the galley and David on deck. Suddenly, Jonathan let go and David went flying. Fortunately for us, I was sitting there beside him, watching them play. I reached out by instinct and snagged him just before he would have flipped overboard.

We returned home with the same number of kids after that trip, but it wasn't long before our "quiver" filled up all at once. For some time we had been trying to adopt again, through a local agency. We learned in the process that if we wanted to get a young child, the only way would be to take either one with special needs or a sibling group. We had requested siblings, if possible.

At one point three girls had been available for adoption, but we didn't get them. We learned later that we were considered "too intelligent" and our kids "too motivated" for these three girls to fit into our family. The social workers felt that they probably wouldn't be able to "adjust." Another set of parents got the girls, and then wound up giving them back. I don't know what happened to them, but such is the world of adoption procedures, as anybody knows who's been through it.

We really didn't know what the Lord had in mind during this time of disappointment. It was disheartening to Donna, and I must confess I was hurt by the agency's rationale. But then, out of the blue, we got another call. Would we drive down to Beckley, West Virginia, about three hours south? A social worker there had three children she wanted us to meet.

I'll never forget that day. Before I tell you what the kids were like when we took them in, I assure you that today they are all doing fine, and we're very proud of the progress they have made. Our family has grown together by God's grace and all the kids love each other. It is amazing how they get along, considering their various backgrounds and genetic makeup. Jonathan Edward continues to be the leader and having four siblings has helped him mature. David is our video and computer kid who loves all the interaction with so many kids. Victoria has developed into a beautiful girl and has taken on the "mother hen" role when she relates to the three younger children. Jonathan Wayne continues to be very active. He is our "jock" but a very precious boy. Christina has also developed into a beautiful young girl. I suppose she will always be our "baby."

On arriving in Beckley, we checked into a motel. Soon the social workers came with the three kids. It was quite an experience. Christina, sixteen months old, sat quietly on the bed. She had no expression on her face and did not respond to affection. Jonathan Wayne (he was already named before he became a Rozar), who was almost three, was simply hyper—running back and forth from room to room. Four-year-old Victoria just wanted to sit and watch TV. She didn't yet know her colors or the names of animals.

Christina, who had been in a foster home different from the one Jonathan Wayne and Victoria were in, brought a letter with her describing a very regimented schedule—at 9 o'clock you have to do this; at 10 this, and so on, almost as if life in that home had been organized entirely around her needs. She was still on the bottle, but the worst thing was that somehow her little stuffed puppy dog had been left behind. She screamed bloody murder for several hours that night—the kids stayed with us overnight at the motel—and we didn't know why.

That wasn't the biggest surprise, by a long shot. The next day—Sunday—the social worker showed up in the morning with all their toys and clothes. Overnight, our family of four had mushroomed to seven, without our even having a chance to go home and think it over! The local head of the private adoption agency was livid. Evidently, procedures had been bent. "You're not supposed to bring those children home—they never do that," she said. "You're not supposed to have those children now."

I've concluded that it would have been light-years easier to have had triplets, and I'm not sure how anybody survives that! The adjustment required of everybody during the next few months defies description. For some reason, Jonathan Wayne became violent, destroying things like antique furniture. It seemed he couldn't stop until whatever it was he was attacking was broken.

I couldn't even get near Christina for six months. She would just scream, or alternate between screaming and sitting on the bed with no expression. It was really bizarre, and it took eight months—maybe a year—before we could become close.

Victoria still just wanted to sit and watch TV.

On top of all that, Jonathan Edward and David had to adjust, too. David rebelled, regressed, and lost a lot of ground when the other three kids arrived. Jonathan Edward was still too young to have his own bedroom, so for a while we had three boys in the same room, using a set of bunks and a youth bed.

Perhaps the biggest conflict for the first two boys in our family was about ownership. I don't know how often we heard, "That was mine before you came," whether in relation to toys, games, or even the bedroom itself.

Of all the shocks to our family stability, however, the most disturbing came about eight months after the last three kids moved in with us, a time when our lives had finally hit some kind of normalcy. Our lives were suddenly thrown into turmoil when someone filed a complaint of child abuse. One day in the spring of 1988, we got called down to the child protection agency (CPA), where one bitter woman presented us with a list of complaints. The most serious one was the charge by an unidentified witness (the accused in such cases have no right to know their accuser) that David had been seen with bruises on his bottom. You would have thought we were in Hitler's office, being branded as high criminals. This dictator had a long list of demands, including that we put the children in school—a nonreligious school (we were home-schooling). The younger ones must attend day care, and we were not to use any form of corporal punishment on the children.

The woman at CPA had us over a barrel, and she knew it. The last three kids hadn't yet been legally adopted. And now there was this formal complaint, and we were being investigated. Without doubt, it was her goal to take those kids away from us.

Nonetheless, I must admit I was less than cordial in my response. "You can't do that," I replied, waving the paper in her face. "You're infringing on my rights. This is America. I won't agree to this. It's garbage! You can try, but we'll fight you all the way."

Donna kept telling me to cool it, but I wasn't listening. "No way," I said. "This is wrong. We have to stand up for our rights."

I let it be known that if somebody tried to take away the kids, I would sue. "We'll be glad to go through this investigation," I said. "I'm going to get a lawyer, too."

It was a very hostile confrontation—one of the most difficult spots I've ever been in. This woman was trying to destroy us, especially what we stood for. To me, it was as simple as that.

To be fair, it's possible David did have a few mild bruises on his bottom. He had been having a tough time for months, rebelling when the others came. But, in our own defense, he was born with what are known as "Mongolian spots," bluish splotches on his buttocks, which might easily be taken for bruises by someone who had never seen them before (we found out later who it was).

I told that CPA woman about David's spots and that they were well documented by his pediatrician. "So this is all libel and slander," I shouted. "There's not a word of truth to it. We don't abuse our children; we love them." When I finished, that woman's face was about the same color as the spots in question.

At a cost of several thousand dollars, we retained a Christian lawyer, who thought we might have to take it to the Rutherford Institute and focus on the religious-freedom aspects of the case. We had many people praying, too, because this kind of thing is not just a personal attack, it is spiritual warfare.

Talk about being paranoid, we knew the CPA had the power to come get the children, no matter what I said. So we were concerned about not spanking the children, because someone might hear them carrying on and report us again. But we sometimes did have to spank Jonathan Wayne because, even after all that time, he was still a wild colt in need of a corral. Of course, I love him to death, and we've had some great times together, snowmobiling at the farm and things like that. It took us a while to get there, however.

Sometime later—and I'm glad I wasn't home—the CPA worker showed up at the house. Donna said she was like a totally different person. She just sat on the floor and played games with the kids and then left. Although that was the last we saw of her, it was a very tough period, especially after everything we had gone through to take these children into our home. To feel like criminals, afraid to live the way we knew was right, was a test—another very strong test of our foundations.

But again, we emerged intact. The storm just made us stronger. A week before Thanksgiving of 1988, the judge, who had perhaps heard we were about to move to Wisconsin, where I had accepted a position at the Marshfield Clinic, scheduled us to appear before him.

What a scene that was! Here we were in a typical small-town West Virginia courthouse, standing before a judge who had five kids of his own, for a hearing that would decide the fate of three children we had come to love deeply. The kids were crawling under the table, and the judge was laughing. David sat on the judge's knee while he asked us a few questions. Interestingly enough, he never asked us about the allegations of child abuse. One of our favorite photos has all of us crowded around that judge in that little courtroom, with everybody smiling and very happy, including him. Before we left, we finalized everything, and Jonathan Wayne, Victoria, and Christina were officially Rozars—ours forever. The charges of child abuse were dropped and the case was closed. Thank you, Lord.

That one word, *ours*, is the key to that whole transition. When we moved to Marshfield, a friendly dairy town of 18,000 set among central Wisconsin's gently rolling glacial hills, everything became *ours*. We moved into *our* new house together, a beautiful two-story, four-bedroom brick house with blue-gray siding, big enough for everybody to have his or her own space. The full basement was great for *our* home-schooling. The wooded lot with its big backyard meant there was room for a gym and a sandbox and a clubhouse and a swing set for *our* kids to share with *our* neighbors. This family-oriented kind of community—where people are less impressed that you are a cardiac surgeon than whether you've been to your kid's Little League game—was *our* kind of town—home. Without a doubt, we were on top of the world.

In terms of my work, I was now making more money than I ever thought I would, but that just meant we would have more to give away. I was busy, too. Despite its rural location, the Marshfield Clinic is one of the largest and finest heart-surgery centers in the country. As I recall, I did four hearts the first week, plus an emergency consult my very first day. In the first five months I probably did forty to fifty heart cases, but I was also doing pulmonary consults and some lung surgery.

In spite of that, I still had time to work on a paper about a special incision I had developed to save the chest wall muscle in thoracic procedures. I had done maybe fifteen cases that way, but it wasn't quite enough to publish.

I was on call every night during the week, but lived only several minutes from the hospital. On weekends, if I wasn't on call, I didn't have to worry about the patients at all. Because there were three other cardiac surgeons who shared call, you were free from Friday afternoon until Monday morning on the weekends that you were off. This freedom was a greater benefit than a large salary.

Besides having three out of four weekends off, there were
other benefits. Life, disability, medical, and dental insurance—the works—was part of the employment contract.
This factor was to be far more providential than I ever could
have guessed when I took the position.

During the winter, we went skiing, trying to teach the
two youngest boys to ski. We went to Powderhorn, in Michigan's Upper Peninsula, and had a lot of fun. The kids learned
to ice skate, too. And we went sledding. Since I was on call
only about one weekend a month, I had a lot more time
with the family.

Physically, I was fatigued and had more back trouble than
ever. So, in January 1989, I had a complete employment
physical by a physician who later felt bad that he didn't see
the HIV. But all my lab work was normal, except for a
slightly elevated lymphocyte count. Everything else was okay.
I attributed my weariness to the move and the recent legal
hassles, but mostly to the fact that surgery is always so tiring
that you don't think anything about it, unless you're so
totally wiped out you can't move. Since I was now doing
every procedure myself, skin to skin, a little fatigue was nothing to worry about.

If anything *was* clear, it was that God had abundantly provided for us and had chosen to bless us more than we could
have imagined. Everything was as if I had written out, "This
is what I want to do, Lord. Can you fix it for me?" He did
it—almost like the happy ending to *The Ed Rozar Family
Fairy Tale*.

But one day in April 1989, when I was between an open-
heart case and a lung case, our fairy tale got fractured by
fourteen words said to me over the phone. A few weeks earlier I had decided to change a whole-life insurance policy that
was costing about three hundred dollars a month into a term
policy through the American College of Surgeons (ACS).
Besides all the forms to fill out, a perfunctory blood test was
required. I had sent it in without giving it a second thought.

Then came the phone call. The ACS representative asked, first, if I had applied for insurance. "Yes," I replied, wondering only vaguely what the problem might be. "I don't know how to tell you this," he hesitated, "but your HIV test was positive."

Stunned, I hung up the phone, my normal decisiveness suddenly overwhelmed by a multitude of questions, like a black cloud in the middle of a sunny day. *How can this be true? I'm healthy as a horse. This can't be happening. There must be some mistake! I am in a no-risk group.*

Stifling the emotional eruption for a moment, my scientific mind needed facts and some solid, informed advice. Believe it or not, what came to my mind first wasn't myself, my wife, or my kids. It was: *Should I operate on my next patient?*

Quickly I called Dr. Doug Lee, an infectious-disease specialist. After we talked it all over, the best route seemed to be to submit two more tests, anonymously, one to the local lab and one to a lab in Minnesota. Doug was confident it was just a false positive. After all, how could it be true? I didn't fit the HIV profile. At this point, there was no reason to cancel any surgeries, certainly not until the lab results were back.

Next I called Donna, who was downstairs with the kids when the phone rang. "A pathologist from Dallas called today to tell me my HIV screen was positive," I told her.

"Oh," she replied. "Oh—you're kidding me!" It took a moment to register.

"No," I responded, as calmly as I could manage, looking out at the gray early spring sky and wishing I knew more answers myself. "I've talked the whole thing over with Dr. Doug Lee. We're sending out another sample. Maybe it's just a false positive."

I hung up, and sat at my desk, trying to collect my thoughts: *Everything is down the drain, all washed up. My career is over, maybe my life is over.* I didn't know much about AIDS yet, but I knew it spelled death. *What about the kids? What about the house? What will we do if I can't operate?* My mind was wheeling a million miles an hour. In a matter of minutes, I had tumbled from the top of the hill—in charge, in control—to the bottom. Despite Doug's reassurance, I had an intuition that in the near future I would become more a patient than a physician.

In those quiet moments, I reached for the one thing I knew I could trust, my Bible: the Word of God. I kept it in the office to read while waiting for patients to stabilize. My mind was confused enough that I can't recall what I read. But when I put it down, I had a sense that God was there, and because of that, I didn't need to be afraid.

There had to be some trembling. My epinephrine level and heart rate were probably sky-high. As a surgeon, I lived with crisis all the time, but this was my crisis, which certainly put it in a different light. But that day, at least, there were no tears. I had to get back to work. A patient was waiting, the staff was standing by. If I was going to become a patient myself, so be it. For the next couple of hours, however, this surgeon would have to put his skills on automatic pilot. I would have to depend on an inner peace "that passes all understanding" to keep my hands steady and my mind focused on the task I had trained so long and hard to do.

5

Life on Hold

lmost immediately, the local lab report, using the ELISA test (the initial test for HIV antibodies), confirmed the ACS report. From then on, I had no doubt I would have to give up surgery. But somehow we held on to what hope we had through the intervening weekend, awaiting the definitive Western Blot test results that should be back by Monday. I was on call both weekend nights and making rounds on thirty to forty patients twice a day, so the time flew by. But I'll always remember it as the longest weekend of my life.

Donna and I were going through the motions of living, working, and doing things with the kids. Our life was on hold, as if we were in a dream or a trance. You wake up in the morning, walk into the bathroom, look at yourself in the mirror, and wonder if it can possibly be real. And you ask yourself, a thousand times a day, *How can it be real?* You might even whisper, "God, I'm glad it's not real."

Reality hit, full force, that Monday, when Doug brought the results to my office. I could see it in his face before he said the words. And no doubt he could see what I was feeling before either of us spoke. "The Western Blot is positive, too," he said quietly. "I'm sorry."

Now what? I wondered. I could hear Doug continue talking, though my mind and emotions were now threatening to disconnect.

"We'll have to get some others involved," he said. When I nodded, he added, "I'll talk it over confidentially with Reed Hall (the clinic's general counsel). He'll need to call around to see what's happened elsewhere, but he won't find anything. There's not yet been even one report of reverse transmission from a health-care worker to a patient. I don't see why you can't keep operating until we get a ruling."

At that point I wasn't in any mood for an argument, but my thought was: *Even if it's one chance in a million, or one in ten million, that's one too many.* For that one person it's a hundred percent, as it was for me.

Only a few days later, I laid down my surgeon's knife for the final time. It was as much a legal and ethical question as anything else. I knew it was both the prudent and the right thing to do, whether or not a nationwide search had turned up a precedent. I closed that last case with a sigh of regret that I hadn't achieved my potential. *What a shame,* I thought. *What a waste.* It wasn't as if I was ending my career at the normal retirement age. *Here I am, forty years old. They just spent all that money to recruit and move me here. I won't even be able to pay them back for that.* Funny what mixed thoughts go through your mind at such a time.

It was a lung case, as I recall, not that difficult by comparison to some others I had done, but each case had been important to me in a special way. Some had been emergency situations where the patient would have died if I had not made the right split-second decisions. Yet even the most "minor" procedure challenged my know-how. Each case was not just a name on a chart, but a person, and I had always enjoyed talking to my patients and their families. Saving lives and helping more people get better is why I had gone through that grueling retraining experience.

Now I was sad and frustrated, wondering whether it had been worth it. "You're useless now," I told myself. "Finished!"

More than anything, I had a feeling of emptiness, futility. Instead of contemplating a new chapter in my life, I found that somebody had ripped out the rest of the pages. In an emotional sense, I had been violated and felt helpless. I had gone from being a capable and respected heart surgeon to nothingness. Even my M.D. had no meaning anymore.

In the midst of my discouragement, two men were like shining lights. Reed Hall, the clinic's counsel, kept saying, "Don't worry, Ed. We'll find something for you. And don't worry about insurance. All of the health, life, and disability insurance will be kept in place. You need it now more than ever. If the disability is not approved for a year, we'll pay your salary. You have more important things to think about."

My other pillar of support was Dr. Doug Lee, who right from the start was as positive as possible, despite mounting lab evidence that my immune system had been compromised for some time. My blood count showed T4-cells (white blood cells processed through the thymus gland) at 230 (normal is 1,000), with a T4-T8 ratio of 0.15 (normal is 1.0). I'll have more to say in the next chapter about how HIV works, but the loud and clear message for me was: Get help, as soon as possible! I knew my risk of opportunistic infection was great. The main help available at that point was a relatively new drug called AZT, which we decided to start as soon as possible: April 28, 1989, at 11:00 A.M.

As Doug and I traced my history, it became increasingly clear that my initial HIV infection had occurred during my residency at Allegheny General Hospital. Working forward from that period, he computed something else, that my life expectancy was now only about three years—1992! It was time for him to make a house call.

I was in and out of the den during Doug's visit to our home, since I still had patients in different stages of recovery and every few minutes I would be paged to call the hospital.

Once, Donna was in tears when I came back. Later she told me that Doug had been very candid. "Enjoy the summer," he said, "because I can't promise you'll have another one." She could hardly believe her ears. On the other hand, when somebody levels with you like that, it's highly unlikely you have misunderstood what's been said. I guess it was Doug's way of saying, "This is serious. You better get your house in order, just in case."

On the other hand, he tried to paint as bright a picture as possible of the way things might go with AZT, which had shown some promise of delaying the onset of AIDS in asymptomatic patients. "You can improve," he told me. "You're going to feel better than you have in a long time. I hope your immune system will stabilize. You're probably not going to have any side effects."

Besides *my* health, Doug was also very concerned about Donna's HIV status. Considering the fact that we had been enjoying intimate sex the whole time I had been infected, he wanted to ensure at least three things: Donna should get tested as soon as possible; she should have her own internist monitor her situation; and we should be very "careful" from now on in terms of sexual intimacy.

I think if there was anything that lit Donna's fuse, it was this. But I should let her say it in her own words:

> That bothered me the most, that this thing had even invaded our bedroom. That made me really angry. I could cope with all the other things, but to think that this unseen invader had now stolen something that was so good. How can it do that? Here was such a positive part of our marriage and there had never been any fear, there had never been any problem, and suddenly HIV comes and just ruins it all. I just felt it wasn't fair.

With all the stuff being written in the popular press, it was hard to figure why she was still HIV-negative when I had been infected since 1985. Maybe it was the providence of God. If it was, did we dare test providence further by continuing as before—or even by continuing with the use of a condom, with its reported annual failure rate of at least 15 percent?

This problem is far more complicated than it might seem on the surface. I tell you about it not because I want to—we're really quite private people—but because some can't understand why, with all the latex barriers available today, anybody could be dumb enough to risk infection with a deadly disease for a few moments of pleasure.

Donna and I are spontaneous people, so beyond the fact that sex with condoms is less enjoyable, it is also far less impromptu. Within a marriage where two people are firmly committed to each other, it is very difficult to remove this aspect without diminishing the broader mutual meaning that the sexual act seems intended to have. It's near impossible, believe me, to relax and enjoy sex—even if you're using all the protections modern science has to offer—when in the back of your mind is the word: *transmission, transmission, transmission.*

Perhaps this has not been such an issue for us as it might be for others, since for a while I was so sick I didn't have the energy or interest required for sexual performance. But I certainly had a need that sex seems designed by God to help fulfill—a need for intimacy. I was lonely, often quite discouraged. In a very real sense, I was dealing with the death of my dreams. And, as Rebekah comforted Isaac after his mother's death, I needed a similar kind of comfort from my wife.

On the other hand, I think we men often overlook the importance this part of marriage also has to our wives. They need that closeness, too, perhaps even more than we do, so it's no wonder Donna was so offended when this illness suddenly threatened me, and therefore her, in many ways.

Early on, we gently argued about "safe sex." This may not seem as humorous to you as it is to us, looking back, but one night she protested: "It's not going to kill me," and I replied, "Oh, yes, it will," feeling like a leper or worse. Total abstinence would have been the simplest solution, of course, and perhaps the most prudent for the sake of the children. But I think the best long-range solution is to find creative new routes to intimacy and closeness, as some physically disabled people have done.

For a long time after I got the Western Blot report, I felt a bit paranoid, and not just in terms of Donna. When I needed some dental work, I wasn't sure what to do. But Doug Lee was able to find an oral surgeon to do a root canal, and then a local dentist was more than willing to treat me after that. I also wondered if I should get my medical treatment out of town, to be sure my HIV status didn't reflect poorly on the kids. I didn't want them ostracized in any way because of what was happening to me.

Because I worried about transmitting the disease to the kids, Doug assured me—and everything I read confirmed it—that there had only been one confirmed case of casual transmission within a family. That case probably occurred because of the way a mother handled the diapers of her infected baby. If we would just observe common rules of cleanliness within the home, we should be fine, Doug said.

But how could I make five kids who loved to play Wrestlemania on Daddy understand that some of that was going to have to be toned down? Or how could I explain that they could only kiss me on the cheek now, and vice versa?

Not only that, how would I explain to them that I wouldn't be doing surgery anymore? Or, especially, how the same God we had so often credited with making them Rozars instead of orphans might one day allow them to become fatherless again? Who would take care of them? Would they have enough to live on? Would Donna have to sell the house? The list of unanswered questions seemed endless at first—mostly about the unknown and unknowable future.

When I took it one day at a time, I was better able to keep my life in perspective. Two days after starting AZT, for instance, we had a nice day in church, in spite of the malaise and nausea that was starting to develop from the medication. We took a pleasant family walk that evening, too. Later that night, as I put Jonathan Edward to bed, we recited the books of the Bible together and then I sang him the Lord's Prayer.

Jonathan Edward, who was then six, was really the only child old enough to begin to comprehend what was happening. One morning I took him out for breakfast, and we had a long, long talk. I tried to explain that I was sick and wouldn't be able to do heart surgery anymore because I wouldn't want to risk making my patients sick when I was trying to help them.

But the little guy knew how much I loved surgery. "Won't they let you do even one more, Dad? Just one?" he asked.

I fought back the tears and tried to get past the lump in my throat. "No, son. Not even one. This sickness I have is pretty serious. In fact, it may someday take my life." I watched his face to try to read his reaction and didn't have to wait long. "Well, then, Dad," he said, "you should be happy, not sad, because if you die you'll be with Jesus!"

Kids can be so matter-of-fact! His insight cut right through the mental and emotional fog I was struggling with. Of course, he was right, even if he didn't understand all the implications of what he had just said. I smiled and gave him a big bear hug, thankful that God had brought him into my life.

But there were other times when I fought the tears and lost, especially in those first few weeks while we waited for the disability question and other financial matters to be resolved. Although I kept going to work, making rounds on any of my patients still in the hospital after surgery, after a couple of weeks I really didn't have much meaningful work to do. That, on top of the problems I was having with AZT, was probably the main cause of my first real weeping in a long, long time.

I was sitting in the office in the dark, feeling sick and self-pitying as I thought about the kids, about leaving them in the world without a father. Who would mold them, tell them about all the hazards out there? *What are you going to do, God? I do believe you're sovereign, but I need to know how this is going to work out.*

There was some Christian music playing on my little radio, as tears ran down my face. *Oh, God, I can't leave these kids. I don't want to leave them. You brought these children into my life—and now you're going to take me out of theirs? Although our home's not perfect, and I'm not a perfect dad, I want to see them grow up and get excited about life. Am I going to miss all that?*

Almost as quickly, I added, *God, I'm probably being selfish. But is it really selfish to want to be with them and see them get through high school and graduate? That would be such a great thing!*

I went around and around with that. I knew I needed to put my whole trust in the Lord, but I wondered what he was going to do. *I had* put my whole trust in the Lord, and he let this happen. Even when he saved me, he knew it was going to happen. Even before I was born! *Lord, when I was born, you knew all this was going to happen, yet you guided my path through all that foolishness as a youth, and you brought me this far. So, Lord, I have to believe you know what you're doing.*

As a rule, surgeon types don't cry too often, either because of our training and everything we've experienced in terms of life and death and blood and gore, or maybe because that's just the way we are. This episode in the office was new to me, I assure you. Maybe it had something to do with the fact that without the clear-cut role I had had all these years, I didn't really know who I was anymore.

It's strange, but I wasn't worried that somebody would walk in on me. This was a private matter between God and me. Although I sometimes was tempted to think I had been abandoned, I always felt that he was there with me. Actually, I think—as a part of me—he was helping me release some of my emotions.

In that sense, my situation was a good thing. I was becoming acquainted with, and more honest about, other parts of myself, as if different layers of this former cardiac surgeon were being peeled away. I sometimes wondered whether there would still be anyone home when all the layers were peeled away.

One of the first layers to go was my personal privacy. Because I was a health-care worker, once my status became known, it was impossible to avoid public scrutiny, not only by my medical colleagues, but also by the Wisconsin Public Health Department, which by law had to investigate. The woman who interviewed me took what amounted to a "strip down" history. She wanted to probe into my life as far back as 1980. She was very persistent, grilling me for two hours about such matters as sexual promiscuity, homosexuality, and IV drugs.

When we started, I kept my guard up. But after she had asked all her questions without coming to any clear-cut conclusion—except that this case didn't fit the usual HIV profile—I had a chance to tell her how I was dealing with the illness. We even talked about the importance of faith in the face of this disease. When the interview was over, I think we had become pretty good friends.

Early on, I wasn't really talking to too many people about my diagnosis. But when the opportunity arose, I tried to express what I really believed. After my colleagues had been notified—without my knowledge and consent—one of them passed me in the hallway and kind of hung his head, without saying anything. I thought that was rather strange, since he had been so friendly up to that point. A half-hour later he returned, apologizing for not saying hello in the hall.

The issue of confidentiality is complex, especially in the health-care setting. My perspective, and that of my colleagues, may be different. However, the need for the clinic physicians and staff to know versus maintaining the privacy of our lives was an issue that never became that important. As we were always open about the situation, God's grace prevailed.

As we talked, I had an open door to tell this doctor how my faith was helping me through this crisis, that Jesus Christ had become my Sustainer. It was a really good conversation, the first specifically spiritual talk he and I had ever had. In the end, he said, "We're really going to miss you. I'm sorry this happened, and I certainly don't understand why. But let me know if I can do anything for you."

Moments like those pulled me up from the depths as I struggled to make sense of what was happening, and to discern what new directions God might have in mind for me. I was beginning to see how he could resurrect a significant ministry from the ashes of sorrow I was sitting in at that point in time. I began to hope that it wouldn't all be doom and gloom, and then the tomb. Could my God, who had overcome the tomb, help me overcome HIV, transforming my helplessness into helpfulness for someone else?

6

Dr. Rozar's Wild Ride

lmost immediately, some of our biggest questions were answered. My medical disability was approved in a matter of weeks, and the clinic would provide my full salary for six months. My medical care would be covered under the HMO, and if it ever was needed, the hospital's hospice would be available. The sizeable life insurance originally provided as part of my employee benefit package would be kept in effect.

Through it all, in spite of our fears, the Lord seemed to be saying, "How can you doubt my ability to take care of you in every detail?"

Although I didn't really have to work, I kept going to the office. It was partly through force of habit, but also my sense of obligation to do something doctor-like with my time as a way to repay the clinic's generosity. I had worked only about five months before I went on full disability on May 1, 1989.

Because I was used to working long hours, it seemed strange to be free—though I really was not. I couldn't put my career as a physician down. I had quit operating but everything in me resisted giving up being a doctor. For a while I still had some patients and patient families to care for, but I couldn't reveal anything about my own illness for fear of unnecessarily alarming them. Some of the cardiac-surgery patients would even stop by the office with a wound problem. I took care of them, though I didn't want to make that a habit.

Especially during May, I spent much of my "down time" in the office trying to sort things out, wrestling with occasional depression and sadness. Sometimes I would just sit at my desk, meditating, reading the Word, searching for some hope and help—and talking to the Lord, mostly about the kids. For a long time, I perceived this disease as more of a problem for them than it was for me.

Reading as many journal articles about HIV infection as I could put my hands on, it was easy enough to become resigned to an early, excruciating, slow death. On the other hand, I longed to stay around to help our children through adolescence, so much so that sometimes wishful thinking made me even question the diagnosis. Here I was, reading the awful facts about a disease I couldn't see, which had only become apparent through lab tests I never witnessed, done at a time when I had apparently been healthy. Once I even asked Doug, "Where is this thing?" When you're a surgeon, it's all the more difficult to become a prisoner of something you can neither see nor fix.

Why? HIV is a silent killer and you can get HIV without knowing it (as I did, or as Magic Johnson, Kimberly Bergalis, Arthur Ashe, or others have). Then, while you still feel healthy and appear healthy, you can transmit a disease worse than death to others—perhaps *many* others if you have sex with multiple partners or share contaminated needles while using IV drugs. There are other ways to get it, but these are the most common. "Innocent" victims (health-care workers, patients, and newborns) are also at risk from people with HIV, whether or not the diagnosis is known.

Yet, in spite of all the well-publicized warnings, some people are still risking acquiring HIV in exchange for a few minutes of pleasure. Are they betting that, as with so many other diseases, medicine will soon find a cure or even a vaccine for HIV? A vaccine may be developed someday, and I hope it is, so that those who are uninfected who insist on living an immoral lifestyle can be protected from their stupidity—at least from HIV infection. There is no vaccine, of course, to protect them from such other consequences as guilt, remorse, poor self-image, and the downward spiral where such activities inevitably lead.

A vaccine still won't help the millions of people already infected with HIV. And, from everything I've read and every informed person I've talked with, the possibility of a cure being found is still nearly zero. This is because of several things, including: (1) the way the virus attacks the immune system, incorporating itself into the DNA and then reproducing itself; and (2) the fact that it may mutate, once it has effectively taken over the immune system, making it harder to track down.

Nonetheless, the media seems ready to grasp any straw of hope the researchers toss out. I think this is mainly because if there is anything the children of the sex-and-pleasure revolution resist, it's returning to the only thing that could virtually eliminate AIDS within one generation—abstinence before marriage, and sexual faithfulness to one uninfected partner after marriage. Additionally, of course, IV drug abusers would have to either stop doing IV drugs or at least stop sharing needles.

For some time there was a lot of hype about the drug AZT being able to turn HIV disease into a manageable illness, like diabetes has become. I've taken AZT for a year, and it didn't have that effect for me.

These reports didn't mention that nothing available now (or even on the horizon) will tear down the wall of isolation that HIV infection builds, separating you sexually and in other ways from the people you love, and also from society, for the rest of your life. The fear of transmitting or acquiring HIV will exist until every HIV virus has been eradicated from an infected person's system. Even if that could be accomplished, could it be proven?

The material I studied graphically described how, generally speaking, AIDS patients die a horrible death, as infections and cancers that their body normally would fight off slowly sap their strength and vitality and finally take their lives. These diseases are called "opportunistic" because they take advantage of the opportunity provided by the person's compromised immunity to enter the body and make the person sick.

AIDS is called a "wasting" disease because it often kills people very slowly; in other words, they waste away. If you have observed this process in a person with AIDS, you know what I mean. Sometimes it has been made so public, nobody could miss it. This was true in the excruciating case of Kimberly Bergalis, who died in late 1991 after being infected through dental procedures. My own loss of twenty pounds in 1985 was another example. I've never been able to regain that weight, no matter how much food or how many calories I consume. I don't know why HIV disease has this effect, but perhaps it changes the body's metabolism in some fundamental way. There are whole villages of people in Africa— where AZT, acyclovir, and other high tech treatments may never be available—who are dying from "slim disease," as AIDS is known there.

Of all the horrifying possibilities I studied, the worst is called "dementia." Unlike many diseases, HIV can penetrate the central nervous system (CNS), so that a patient can slowly "lose his mind" while slowly losing his life. The idea of ending my life demented caused me the most concern. My own mother has been in a state of dementia for some time from Alzheimer's disease, and I have seen my kids' inability to relate to her in a meaningful way. They don't even want to touch her. I, like most HIV sufferers, would much prefer to die quickly, with my wits about me, than to have that one last impenetrable barrier erected between me and others, especially the little people I love so much.

As Donna and I both became AIDS-informed during those first few weeks after diagnosis—by reading and by watching videos—we discussed the question of "artificial" life-sustaining measures, should I become totally incapacitated. We agreed that despite how bad it might get, life would still be God's to give or take away, so I would always get food and water, even if it had to be administered artificially.

Believe me, although these are matters all spouses should discuss (and write out their wishes in that regard), just thinking about them in the context of my illness was subtly depressing. We did go so far as having a new will drawn up. We then decided that reading so much about AIDS and knowing so much medically about the "possibilities" wasn't really doing us that much good. It would be much better, emotionally, interpersonally, spiritually and even physically, to focus on more positive things.

Physically speaking, the treatment I received—AZT— proved far more troublesome than the disease itself. I kept trying to go to the office, but I was miserable; afflicted with dry skin and severe itching, anorexia, and general malaise. I was also constantly nauseated, with a terrible taste in my mouth. Maybe you've had that feeling: the combination of wanting to vomit but not being able to. I battled that constantly until I finally found an antidote: Coca Cola and lemon juice.

Those days were some of the hardest of my life. One evening, when I had stayed home all day because I was too weak and sick to do anything else, I was lying on the couch in our den, just off the kitchen, while everybody else was having supper. Suddenly, I was crying, feeling sorry for myself, and hoping that nobody would come in and see me like that. The radio was on, tuned to one of our local Christian stations. As I wept, the words of a song ministered to me: "He will not leave you this way." Embracing that thought, I gained new strength, dried my tears, went around the corner, and ate supper.

After I had been on AZT for about five weeks, we took a trip to Pennsylvania to visit relatives and do some sightseeing. It was during that trip that I hit the bottom. There I was, in somebody else's bed, sick, with no local physician to call on (maybe the local doctors would rather not get involved with HIV—you never know). The family was in and out every day, doing their own thing, having family reunions and a basic grand old time. But I couldn't join in because I had barely enough energy to get out of bed.

I had a fever, alternating between being hot and having chills with uncontrollable shaking—to the point where my teeth were chattering and I had cramps in my legs and soreness everywhere. I couldn't get out of bed and lie down on the sofa, just for a little change, because the house was full of people and I didn't want to bother them. I had stashed my private supply of liquids in the refrigerator, but I didn't want to take up too much room in there either. And if I had to use the bathroom, I didn't want to take too long because many other people needed access to it.

On top of all that malaise, I wondered what the relatives thought about my illness. Would they burn the mattress after we left? Were they afraid they might get HIV from the toilet seat, or from the dishes or utensils we shared—even though they had been washed? Were they mad I had dragged my family, and all of *them,* into what seemed like a stigmatized black hole?

It didn't help much, either, to read in the local papers while we were there about a fellow in his seventies who had just died of AIDS acquired through a blood transfusion during heart surgery. He had had a prolonged course of dying, and right after he died, his wife was diagnosed HIV-positive.

My personal agony (mostly physical, but emotional, too) got so bad that one day I said to the Lord, "If it's going to be like this, if I'm going to be this sick just from the medicine, not my primary illness, please either get it over with, or heal me. I don't think I can handle this anymore." I figured if I could get this sick just from the treatment, the disease itself was going to be far worse.

I would lie there thinking, *Things are backward here. This expensive medicine ($7,000.00 a year) is making me sicker.* Yet I was resigned to following my physician's advice. I had gone from being the doctor to being the patient, from being in control to being helpless, from being self-reliant to having to depend on somebody else's decisions and to follow his directions.

Maybe you're used to that, but I certainly was not, and I had no idea how dehumanizing being a patient can be. My role-reversal began the day I had to let somebody stick me for the test to confirm my HIV status. Since then, it's never changed, though my experience as a patient has had such ups and downs that if graphed, it would look like the stock-market curve. For a comparable experience, board the world's largest roller coaster or go to Disney World and take Mr. Toad's Wild Ride.

For about two months on AZT I really struggled, sliding lower all the time. Then all of a sudden in July, I woke up one morning and felt fine, super—no side effects, and lots of energy! I thought, *This is great! Now I can get on with my life.* I cut the grass, trimmed the trees, did all kinds of odd jobs that had gone undone for weeks.

Fairly soon, however, it became obvious that my bone marrow had stopped working. For about two weeks I had experienced a kind of "remission," but now if I was going to survive, I would have to have blood transfusions, regularly. It's one thing to have somebody stick you for a blood test, but entirely different to spend six to eight hours on your back while the IV drips somebody else's blood into your vein. Being a doctor made those days doubly difficult. The nurses, of course, knew me, and when they had to insert the IV, I think they were a little afraid of not getting it right in the first time. Maybe they were afraid of getting stuck themselves. I don't know. But even when what they were doing really hurt, I never let on.

On top of that, since it's a day-long procedure, I had to use the rest room from time to time. The image that really sticks in my mind to symbolize my role-reversal is Ed Rozar, M.D., pushing his IV pole into the bathroom, just like any other patient.

Once, when I was lying on the cot and getting a transfusion, one of the other doctors walked by the door. Although he glanced in, and I was sure he recognized me, he just kept right on going, without even stopping to say hello. Now that I was Patient Rozar, I guess he didn't know how to relate to me anymore. Because of HIV, there was now some invisible partition between us.

Donna happened to be with me that day, and it really teed her off, but I tried to help her understand that I wasn't offended, even if I was disappointed. Doctors are busy people, after all, and this man was one of the busiest. Later that day, while I was still being transfused (four units takes a long time) Donna met that fellow in the hallway. Since this time he couldn't escape, he mumbled something semi-apologetically about being awfully busy and hoping I would understand.

I don't think it was a lack of concern. And I couldn't really expect an outpouring of empathy, since I had been there only five months. Maybe my colleagues simply didn't know what to say. In fact, what can you say to a budding cardiac surgeon who all of a sudden can't operate anymore?

Besides Doug Lee, my physician, there was one other doctor who did reach out to me that summer—Scott Erickson, a six-foot-three internist who is at least as much at home in the boundary waters of Minnesota as he is in the Marshfield

Clinic. Scott knew just what this doctor-patient needed to get back on his feet—trout fishing!

When I say that, you probably envision an *Outdoor Life* calendar-type picture of a perfectly decked out angler, hip-deep in a crystal-clear mountain stream, calmly watching his perfectly placed dry fly settle over a waiting rainbow trout.

Unless, that is, you're familiar with Central Wisconsin fishing, where King Musky, Queen Walleye, and Prince Northern Pike rule over a piscatorial court comprised of panfish like the delicious crappie. Hardly anybody there takes brook-trouting seriously, for at least two reasons. First of all, the fish are generally fairly small—a twelve-inch native brookie is a monster! Besides, the beaver ponds and back-woods streams they inhabit are inaccessible to all but the most determined fishermen, who are undaunted by the swarms of hummingbird-sized mosquitoes that also inhabit the same locale.

Scott is that kind of fisherman, I discovered. The first time he led me through the cedar swamp to the Mecan River, I wondered what I had agreed to. We were at least a mile from nowhere, and I had spent a lot of money on waders. Believe it or not, the decision to spend that seventy-five dollars had been very hard to make, considering my prognosis. It better be worth it!

We weren't purists about it, either, choosing lightweight spinning gear and small spinners for bait. But even expert fisherman Lee Wulff couldn't have made a clean back cast with a fly rod in that swamp, where cedar, spruce, and poplar trees reached out from both sides of the ten-foot-wide creek to effectively canopy the creek throughout the year. Not infrequently, we would have to climb out and walk on the bank just to make progress upstream.

There was something about being out there, knee- to waist-deep in the gently flowing, slightly murky water, that was cleansing to the soul and the spirit. After a few minutes in that chilly stream, it was almost as if the cares of my world were swept away, erased by elements that had been flowing here since long before my troubles ever came to be. And they would still flow long after my troubles had been forgotten.

But there's a nibble! I sense it with my index finger, barely touching the four-pound-test monofilament line. *Let him take it. Don't set it yet!* My heart beats faster. *There!* I whip the rod tip upward with a wrist motion, and the five-foot light action rod bends as the trout rushes downstream, then upstream, then sideways, shaking its head to dislodge my hook until I gently slip my left hand under its belly.

I gaze at my prize for a moment, absorbed by the artistry of a ten-inch brook trout, its green and black mottled back just breaching the surface. Orange and yellow and purple dots decorate its heaving sides as I lift it higher, toward my creel. Now the bright orange belly comes in view. *This one is a native, no doubt,* I think, with a certain sense of accomplishment for having captured it. And then I see its delicate fins, nearly as colorful as a monarch butterfly—orange, with a black stripe in the middle and a white stripe along the leading edge.

Amazed at the unassuming yet intricate beauty of this creature, I reassure myself: *Another proof there is a God. How fortunate I am to know him, and even more to be known by him. Like this fish, my life is in his hand—or else this doctor is in deep, deep trouble.*

7

Life in Overdrive

*t*ruthfully now, what would you do if you thought you had only three years to live, maybe only one of them in reasonable health? That's not a bad question to ask yourself, even if you don't have a terminal illness. But it's totally different when you see it in black and white on a legal document. When you think you're dying, every day—maybe every issue—takes on a different sense of urgency.

When I started feeling well enough, we put our life into overdrive. I had agreed to retrain in a similar but noninvasive field of medicine, peripheral vascular studies. Compared to cardiac surgery, it wasn't much of a challenge, but it would give me some use for my M.D. degree, and I could continue serving the clinic in some way, at least for a while.

One of the secondary benefits of this decision was that in the fall of 1989 I was able to take the whole family with me to retrain. We drove first to Detroit in September, for a one-week course in vascular technology. A month later we drove to Seattle for more retraining, a three-week trip during which we visited some national parks, including Mount Rushmore, putting more than four thousand miles on the van. All this was on the heels of June's three thousand miles of traveling to Pennsylvania to visit family and a trip to northern Minnesota for a church family camp over Labor Day weekend.

Throughout this period, I was getting transfusions every three or four weeks. In all, I've received more than thirty units of blood—like some kind of medical vampire! In fact, we had to stagger the trips to allow for the transfusions.

We were driven people, trying to beat my doctor's estimate that I might only live until 1992. So we squeezed three or four years of family activities into one—just in case. Not that we sat around the table saying, "Wouldn't it be wise to run ourselves ragged this year because Dad might not be able to travel next year?" But, interestingly enough, when we stopped to take photos, Donna often volunteered to work the camera so I could be in the picture.

One other factor in all these travels was that they took me away from Marshfield to places where people didn't know me and where I wasn't reminded daily of what I was missing. This tension was mainly internal, since nobody in Marshfield pressured me about the illness. But had I been at home, I would have felt obligated to go to work, where I would have seen all the heart and thoracic surgeons coming and going, busier than ever—without me.

If you want to identify with me, just think of something you really love to do—jog, cycle, play tennis, bingo or shuffleboard, fish or hunt with your buddies, or participate in a quilting bee—whatever. Now imagine you've had a stroke. How would you feel, sitting there in a wheelchair, watching, listening to all the friendly chatter and banter you used to relish so much. Give that feeling a name, and you're getting close to where I was, because operating was my life.

"Disappointment" is close, but mix in some "emptiness" and "frustration," too. It felt like part of my life was gone, as if somebody sneaked into the kitchen overnight and cut out a piece of the pie. Only now that I couldn't bake another pie, the missing part was irreplaceable.

Looking back on those rather frenetic few months, maybe the process of having my layers peeled away had reached the father/husband level. I wanted so much to give the kids as many happy memories as we could fit into whatever time we had left together, even if they were a little young to really appreciate some of the things we did.

One thing's for sure, though: Thinking I was dying helped me appreciate my family more than ever before. Now, almost more than anything else, I wanted to see us become a close-knit, loving, caring unit, committed to common principles and goals.

Being a surgeon is like being in many other professions or jobs—in the sense that you go in early, work hard all day, and get home twelve to fourteen hours later, exhausted. When you're in that mode, the family just sort of goes along on its own track while you concentrate on being their provider. Before my illness, I hadn't been an integral part of the family during the week. I simply wasn't home most of the time! And even when I *was* there, I had a beeper on, and the telephone could ring at any moment, so it was nearly impossible to be totally at home and not partly somewhere else.

Once I began to stay home more, I began to see more clearly what family life was supposed to be like—a 24-hour-a-day involvement, not just from 6:00 P.M. to 10:00 P.M. I developed a new perspective on the children, especially how they could minister to me, and me to them. Our relationships became more important, and my role as a father, rather than primarily as a breadwinner, became more pressing. I began to fully appreciate Donna's role as a mother and "nurturer" of the family. I became far more focused on building into our kids the kind of character and discipline they would need to carry on without me. That was one of the biggest pressures I felt, as if I could somehow condense parenthood, protecting them from temptations that they wouldn't really face for years.

I probably I was too hard on them, too intense, an over-reaction complicated by the fact that I was around them more, so I knew what was going on. On top of that, especially when I was taking AZT, I wasn't feeling good. I might be nauseated, for instance, just when they wanted to turn my bed into a trampoline—with me on it! They didn't understand the situation, and I was sometimes too demanding and impatient.

But that was more than irritability from being sick. I felt that if I didn't control them now, how would they learn? If they didn't learn discipline and respect from their father now, it might never happen. So, if they were being disrespectful, acting up, or not eating well at the table, I not only focused on their present actions, but also on what they might become if they didn't shape up. I tried to explain, "I want you to grow up to be godly boys and girls, to respect your elders, to obey and control yourselves. I may not be here later to teach you, so I want you to learn now."

In reality, my approach was unfair to them. I pushed too hard. I tried to make them grow up too fast. Before I became sick, I figured—like most parents—that I would have time later to help them develop and mature.

Donna and I had our share of conflict about this. Having me around the house all day long made her life much more difficult in many ways. Now there was one more person to think about, especially when I was sick. It was more an expression of her love than I realized at the time that she generally put up with my expectations and demands. But once in a while, when I was being unreasonable or at least unrealistic in terms of the kids, she would remind me, "Just let them be children, Ed. They can't be adults yet. If we push too hard, we might win the battle but lose the war later."

My dilemma was that I had to relinquish what I as a doctor prized most—control. In terms of my family's future, and even my own, the outcome was in the hands of God, not mine. I had become God's patient, and he my heart surgeon, sitting on my hospital bed, drawing on the sheets, trying to help me understand what he was going to do. More importantly, he wanted me to trust him.

I don't know if I was a good patient or a difficult one. But I do know that, once we got past the initial large hurdles about finances, I spent a lot of energy trying to understand what this illness meant. What could be done about it? What had God said about it in his Word? Where was I, from his point of view? What was his perspective?

I began to seriously search the Scriptures, looking for every possible promise to claim, every case similar to mine, every message my Divine Healer might be trying to communicate to his twentieth-century patient. I read voraciously because I was hungry to learn not only what he said in his Word, but more importantly, how to know him better, to get as close to God as one human being could possibly get.

I had read the Bible through at least three times before, but this time through it seemed to come alive. It was more real, more relevant, more practical. I was learning that the Word of God really is "living and active and sharper than any two-edged sword, and piercing as far as the division of soul and spirit . . . able to judge the thoughts and intentions of the heart" (Heb. 4:12).

In the Book of Job, I found a kindred spirit, adopting his policy of not charging God with wrongdoing, although, like Job, I had many questions and only a few answers. I concurred with him, a man perhaps even more afflicted than I, that, "He knows the way I take; When He has tried me, I shall come forth as gold" (Job 23:10). And I affirmed his trust: "Though He slay me, I will hope in Him . . ." (Job 13:15).

Hundreds of other passages nurtured my soul during those days, slowly pumping strength into my weakness, as if I were receiving a spiritual transfusion. I could almost hear God whispering, as he did to the apostle Paul, "My grace is sufficient for you, for power is perfected in weakness" (2 Cor. 12:9). And I echoed Paul's declaration: "Therefore I am well content with weaknesses, with insults, with distresses . . . with difficulties, for Christ's sake; for when I am weak, then I am strong" (v. 10).

The prophet Isaiah spoke directly to my situation, "Behold, God is my salvation, I will trust and not be afraid. For the LORD GOD is my strength and song" (Isa. 12:2). Also in the Book of Isaiah was a story so like my own that it seemed to be a message straight from God. "In those days Hezekiah became mortally ill. And Isaiah . . . came to him and said to him, Thus says the LORD, 'Set your house in order, for you shall die and not live'" (Isa. 38:1).

But when Hezekiah cried out to God for mercy, he received an additional fifteen years of life. Would he do the same for me? Did I dare to ask? Why not? Our God is the same yesterday, today, and forever. So I prayed, very specifically, for twelve more years, long enough to see my oldest son through high school. I thought, *If I can just stay around and help him mature until he gets through high school, then he can become the leader in the family and help take care of things.* Of course, I wanted to see all my children grow up. I suppose, by my human nature I would have asked for more after the twelve years were over.

The more I immersed myself in the Word, the more I discovered that the coin of affliction has two sides. Every testing is also a hidden opportunity to show that our faith is real; more than that, to prove—to others as well as ourselves—that *God* is real.

My first major presentation on the topic of AIDS was at a special conference in June 1990 in Wheaton, Illinois, sponsored by the Christian Medical and Dental Society. But before I tell you what I said, I need you to understand that getting up in front of any crowd, much less an assembly of my peers, to discuss something as intensely personal as my HIV status and all its implications is not something that the old Ed Rozar would have wanted to do. But once I started working on my presentation, I had more trouble figuring out what to leave out than what to say. I had so much I wanted to discuss, not so much about AIDS as a disease, but about how God could turn such an apparent tragedy into an opportunity for ministry.

I wanted to exhort my colleagues to stop and take stock of their lives *before they were forced to do so.* If they were at all like me before diagnosis, their whole lives were planned all the way through retirement. Had they considered that God might have something totally different in store? It's so easy for physicians to think we are the masters of our own destinies—potters instead of clay—and this may be even more common among surgeons, who so often function like mini-potters: rebuilding, reworking, rearranging. Surgery is an awesome vocation, but it's just too easy to let success ruin your sense of humility.

Putting that talk together was a real turning point for me. I had to solidify my thinking about such basic things as: Who is God, really? What is he like? What are his promises? I spent days on that program, wrestling, redoing, adding new stuff almost right up to the time I spoke. But, during that sorting process, my hunger for truth—and for God, who *is* that truth—intensified. When I finally got it organized to my satisfaction, the talk, which included slides, was infused with Scripture, almost forty references in just a few pages.

I wanted to be crystal-clear that my hope and courage did not come from myself, but from God and his Word. Left to myself, I could never have found the right perspective. But I did find it in Psalm 39:

Lord, make me to know my end,
  And what is the extent of my days,
  Let me know how transient I am.
Behold, Thou hast made my days *as* handbreadths,
  And my lifetime as nothing in Thy sight,
  Surely every man at his best is a mere breath.
  (vv. 4–5)

I wanted to open some eyes and hearts to the implications of this plague and to call for compassion from my colleagues. I hoped the message would hit home: that my disease is real, and what happened to me could happen to anyone. I wanted them to realize it was time to get involved, to reach out and touch people with AIDS the way Jesus touched the lepers of his day. I had needed my illness to change my attitude toward HIV-positive folks, to see them as creations of God. Maybe I could save someone else the agony of learning the same lesson the same way.

AIDS patients are on the threshold of eternity. They are lonely people who often don't have the support of family or friends. It's a tremendous opportunity to minister, but one has to stop and take the time. I told my audience they had to be there and listen, though it's difficult to reach out when there's nothing more to be done medically and there are so many other patients to care for.

Since they were physicians, I told them about my symptoms and treatments and the challenge of becoming a patient. During my first year after diagnosis, my T4-cell count had fallen from 230 (normal is 1,000) to 30. I described the effects of AZT, and the failure of erythropoietin injections to stimulate my bone marrow. After three weeks of extremely painful injections, I was glad it had failed. With the dropping T4-cell count, we started a monthly treatment of pentamadine. "I don't know if you've ever taken inhalation therapy," I said, "but the plastic by itself tastes awful, and pentamadine is extremely bitter." I reminded them that many doctors aren't really aware of the side effects, dehumanization, and outright discomfort their patients experience when they follow their physician's orders.

I described other medical details, too. In April of that year, yeast began growing in my mouth—a very frightening experience! I ignored it the first time, but then it came back. A week later I had developed such a severe cough that it would wake me up at night, and I wondered if I was going to end up with a hernia. I dragged my feet about getting an X-ray, until Donna called Doug and I had to admit what was going on. We looked at the films together, and there was pneumonia all right, but probably not pneumocystis.

Because I was on AZT for HIV, Nizoral for the yeast, and Doxycycline for the pneumonia, sometimes I felt like a walking pharmacy! Donna seemed more concerned about my pneumonia than I was. She even asked me if I was disappointed. "About what?" I replied.

"It looks like it's started," she said. "When's your first bronchoscopy?" Both of us, at that point, were prepared for the worst, a gradual decline, probably marked by numerous pulmonary problems. I told the audience I had thought about what was coming, too. I was going to get the oldest pulmonary specialist in the clinic to do the procedures, rather than a young guy. That way, if he got infected, it wouldn't seem quite so bad. That may have been a crazy way of thinking, but I was really concerned about spreading this disease.

My first presentation was well received, but if I gave it today, I would try to communicate a simple but profound lesson I'm still learning. It goes something like this:

Friends, there is more. There is more to life than being a physician who happens to be a believer. Sometimes we modify the word *Christian* with adjectives like "sincere," "born-again," "devout," or even "Spirit-filled." But that's just window dressing. A Christian is a Christian. A Christian physician is a Christian who happens to be a physician.

There is more to faith than Sunday school and church and rushing home to see the ball game on TV. We need to get serious about who God is, and what he desires for us and requires of us. He's not the "man upstairs," or the "big guy." He is the Creator—*our* Creator. He is our Father—Abba, Father—in reality, he's our loving Daddy. He wants us to be whole in him, no matter what the circumstances. He requires our faithful obedience even when the actions involved might seem illogical, impractical, or worse.

In the same way, there is more to marriage and family life than being a good provider and taking everybody on nice vacations while accepting relational mediocrity as "good enough." A Christian has the opportunity and responsibility to "press on" for everything God desires for him or her.

My priorities were rearranged for me through this crisis. Will it take that to rearrange your own to the point where you earnestly seek his will *before* going ahead, instead of asking him to bless your decisions *after* they're made?

I would conclude a talk with this challenge: "Examine your foundations, now! Once the storm begins, you'll be so occupied with it that you won't be able to get underneath and shore up the weak spots." (This revelation truth came from one of Pastor Glenn Smith's messages as associate pastor of Believers' Church. I have used this example many times in impressing on people that only with the Lord is one's future secure. And I would echo an unknown author's words, printed in *Our Daily Bread:* "I thank you Lord for bitter things; they've been a friend of grace; they've driven me from paths of ease, to seek the Father's face."

When I finished that June 1990 conference, I was exhausted and exhilarated at the same time. At the close of my talk, perhaps a hundred of my colleagues gathered at the front of the auditorium to pray for me. It was the first time I felt so affirmed, accepted, and supported. More significantly, though, an important change was taking place within me.

Until my diagnosis, I had thought my mission was to be a cardiac surgeon. Then, from the day I put down the instruments until that conference, I had lacked a real sense of direction. But being there was like turning the page to the beginning of a new chapter. Or, to use another analogy, it felt as if the dark clouds were being blown away and the sunshine was coming through. All of a sudden I saw a new horizon I hadn't imagined—a vista dotted with people needing to hear a voice of faith and hope in the midst of this epidemic, whether they were patients, their families, or health-care workers.

When I thought about it, I realized that instead of being near the end of something, I was at the beginning of a new adventure. Who better to carry this message to physicians, legislators, and lay people—and all Christians? I could look at AIDS from both sides, patient and health-care worker, without a hidden agenda or a self-serving motivation.

I wanted to tell the whole truth about AIDS because I knew that facts would ultimately overrule both hysteria and self-interest. It was obvious to me that good science, good medicine, good public policy and good AIDS education must either be built on truth or be bankrupt (and in this case, lethal).

Yet, as my willingness to speak out became more broadly known, I discovered that not everyone was happy to hear me say that with this disease, as with any disease, it is always better to know where we stand than to be uninformed and risk the consequences. Knowledge, not ignorance, had become a focal point in my way of looking at HIV—and I hoped it would be that way for others.

God was showing me that the last and greatest adventure in life was not dying, but living. The fire within me was started by a tiny spark. Over the next year and a half, it would become a roaring blaze, fed by the Word of God and the prayers of his people.

8

Hype, Hysteria, and Hope

In terms of my illness, the rest of 1990 was pretty quiet, but I kept giving my presentation in both medical and lay settings as the opportunities came along. In July 1991, however, the whole thing exploded. Several articles appeared in major medical publications, and we received local and national newspaper coverage. After that, it wasn't long before Donna and I were sitting in the "green room" of NBC's "Today" show.

Here's how it happened. I had participated in an AIDS panel in May at the Marshfield Clinic, where I simply stated the facts as well as my beliefs. In the midst of the discussion, I said, "We've been talking a lot about the disease, but not one thing has been said yet about sex. Let's clear the air. When AIDS began, 80 to 90 percent of the people involved were homosexuals. Most of the rest were IV drug abusers and bisexual men."

Now, if you want to get some mail or phone calls, that's all you have to say. I was accused of gay-bashing, being homophobic (whatever that is) and proselytizing—because I had also shared how my faith was sustaining me.

However, there was such good response to the honest
and open discussion that the clinic offered the panel again,
and this time the media came. Not much new was said but
we did touch on some pressing problems. Interestingly
enough, all the media interviews that day focused on a
homosexual on the panel who had lost his job and whose
lover had already died of AIDS. It irked me a bit, but I recall
praying, "Lord, that's fine. If they don't want to interview
me, so be it."

But the next thing I knew, TV Channels 7 and 9 from
Wausau came down on separate days to interview and tape
me for their news programs. That same week a crew from
Channel 11 in Minneapolis traveled here to do a segment on
my situation. These were pleasant experiences, and I was more
than glad to be involved. At that same time, there was a big
flap in Minneapolis about two local HIV-positive physicians.

A week later, when I was at a summer fishing camp with
Jonathan Edward, NBC-TV was calling, as well as CBS.
Channel 11 (an NBC affiliate) had sent a clip of my interview to New York, and the network had aired it Friday morning, July 12. The initial Centers for Disease Control (CDC)
proposal on HIV testing for health-care workers was due to
be released, and they wanted both Donna and me to appear
in person and as soon as possible. CBS would interview me
the same day and show it as a live interview the next morning.

I have to be candid with you: Flying into New York and
being treated like celebrities was like a fairy tale. We were
met at the airport by a big, black limo that took us to a very
nice hotel. A team from a Pittsburgh TV station was waiting
for us—trying to scoop the others, I suppose—but we didn't
give them an interview because we wanted to honor our first
commitment to NBC. The next morning, when we headed
for the studio at 6:15, the Pittsburgh cameraman was waiting
in the lobby. So we got filmed going to another limo. *Big
deal*, I would have thought, had I seen that on the nightly
news. But being there was a totally different matter.

Now I'm going to tell you a trade secret—at NBC the "green room" (where you wait to be next on camera) is actually green! At CBS, it's a different color even though they still call it the "green room." I have been told that this phrase comes from Shakespearean times when the actors would wait in the green shrubbery before going on stage.

Faith Daniels did the interview for the "Today" show, and she was super. Nobody mentioned that the CDC director, Dr. William Roper, would appear just before us from the Washington, D.C., studio. That was a little ironic, since if the CDC and others charged with disease control had taken HIV seriously enough at first, I might never have been infected.

NBC's studio is beautiful, with wood paneling and inlaid marble and lights and cameras everywhere. There are actually three sets side by side: one for the opening, one for news, and the third, where we waited on the sofa, more informally decorated, like a living room.

After a short introduction of my HIV history, Faith began the interview by asking, "Was there ever any question in your mind what you would choose to do [after diagnosis]?" I responded with the fact that I stopped operating as a cardiac surgeon because I felt it was the moral and ethical thing to do. She went on to ask what I thought about the new CDC guidelines requiring more patient and health-care worker testing, and what I thought the answer to the HIV problem was as far as physicians go. I said I felt that the guidelines did not go far enough, but that I was encouraged by their appearance, and as far as our profession was concerned, I was hopeful that we would be able to police ourselves.

For some reason, I wasn't nervous, maybe because I had been doing similar interviews for a few months. Donna seemed a little more tense with it all, but she did very well, nonetheless. Ms. Daniels spoke directly to Donna's heart: "Donna, it must have had a tremendous effect on you and the children." Donna responded that many positive things had happened and that there had been abundant opportunities to share where our hope comes from.

In fact, our interview was going so well, it was continued after the break. Faith made a very profound statement how ironic it was that physicians, whose mission was to save lives, could put their patients at risk. At the end, Faith said, "Your courage is inspiring," but I don't know exactly what she meant. Maybe she was thinking of my positive attitude toward my illness, or about wanting to express my views instead of hiding in a closet and waiting to die. However, if she was thinking about my point that health-care workers doing invasive procedures owe it to themselves and their patients to know their HIV status, and to retrain if it is positive, I don't see that as courageous. I was just stating what is obviously the right thing to do.

Before we knew it, the interview was over, and we were off in the limo to CBS, where Paula Zahn taped an interview of us for a program to air the next day. The studios there are comparable to NBC's, with the exception that in the "holding room," people can watch monitors that are tuned to their competitors.

Although the basic stuff Paula wanted to cover was similar to what we had talked about at NBC, she built on it a little. After our introduction and a brief summary of our situation, she wanted to go deeper. "We've got two stories here," she said, but there wouldn't be enough time to fully discuss our personal story as well as the ramifications for my profession.

We covered questions ranging from patients' rights and my opinion of the CDC guidelines, to whom Donna "blamed" for my infection. Paula did make a very interesting comment early in the interview following my comment that the CDC guidelines were overdue: "If doctors had any inkling at all that they carried the virus, they should quit doing surgery."

The fast-paced world of sound-bites and quick-fixes can't adequately explore the multifaceted plight of an HIV-positive, born-again former cardiac surgeon, his wife, and their family. I don't want to seem ungrateful; it's just the reality of TV news coverage. Everybody, from the limo drivers to the makeup people to the interviewers, treated us like royalty. One of the funny things was that the CBS segment of Health Watch was sponsored by a denture adhesive: "Orafix really sticks." I hope that our message "stuck" as firmly with the TV viewers.

By evening, we were home in Wisconsin again, and the interviews almost seemed like a dream, except for the message on my answering machine to call Dr. Bill Roper. And the next day, there we were on the tube on the CBS "This Morning" program. For average Americans, this was heavy stuff.

After that, the dike broke, and we were overwhelmed with so many requests for interviews, panel appearances, and the like, that the whole summer of 1991 was a blur.

We flew to Pittsburgh, where my story was front-page news for some time. Here we were, chauffeured around again, this time in a white stretch limo. I'll never forget Donna saying, "I could get used to this!" I just smiled back and said, "Don't." But I was glad she was enjoying herself.

In Pittsburgh we did an hour-long, live TV talk show, "Pittsburgh Talking," on WTAE, during which I had total freedom to talk about anything. Adam Lynch did the show, and it was a rewarding experience. I knew there were people there from the Pittsburgh Academy of Medicine, and the director of surgery at one of the hospitals was appearing with us.

But I was more nervous about a particular guy in the audience. He wasn't dressed very well, and he had a long earring hanging off one ear. *He's a plant,* I figured. *He'll try to drag us off into the homosexuality smokescreen, for sure.* When the time came for questions from the audience, however, I learned a big lesson about prejudging people when he asked, "Dr. Rozar, can you tell me how your faith has sustained you through all this?"

Adam Lynch started the show with the statement that "for the last several weeks, only Barry Bonds and President Bush have had more publicity on Pittsburgh television." The reason was that Pittsburgh is most likely where I got infected, and the hospital where it happened was very unhappy with all the notoriety and interest in the situation.

More public appearances followed, and in August we appeared on "The 700 Club." Both Donna and I came away with the impression it hadn't gone nearly as well as in the secular setting. Maybe it was because Pat Robertson's first comment was, "You don't look so bad!" Normally, I would take that as a compliment, but it goes right to the heart of the whole problem with HIV transmission. Often, people who are infected *don't look so bad.* In fact, they can look pretty good. Too good. Ask Magic Johnson and Arthur Ashe.

Overall, it just seemed like Pat and I were not on the same wavelength. He wanted to talk about testing, the public-health officials "deceiving" us, and "this homosexual lobby," who were to blame for bringing this plague on themselves and us. I tried to buffer that, to show him it wasn't just a homosexual disease. But isn't it ironic that on a major Christian TV program I felt obliged to say this? Why? Because anti-homosexuality convictions (which is consistent with Scripture) have kept many conservative Christians from thinking clearly about HIV.

I did have to do some educating during the segment with Pat Robertson, but the Lord blessed the time, and the Holy Spirit gave me wisdom. Looking at the tape later, it seemed to have come off very well.

I used to be confused about the homosexuality issue myself, until I realized that the list of "bad people" in the world begins with me. It is just as unrighteous (or self-righteous) for the uninfected to make light of this disease (and people who have it) as it is for those who acquire AIDS by violating God's moral laws! To me, the logic is clear enough, even without bringing in the drug abusers, hemophiliacs, children, and others, including health-care workers like me, who have acquired AIDS in some other way.

That is not to say that we shouldn't do all we can to protect others. For instance, on August 23, I had a chance to address the CDC in Atlanta, the primary agency responsible for developing guidelines to contain HIV within the health-care community. Although the CDC has no regulatory power, its guidelines are usually enacted into law by the various states and federal statutes. Their proposals had just come out, so it was an ideal time to say I thought the statement was too weak, and why. There were maybe twenty to twenty-five people present, and they were cordial enough, even if I was disputing their guidelines. Maybe they let me say my piece because for once they were not being blasted by an activist. Here was a "real person" who happened to get pulled into the AIDS debate through no choice of his own, except to retrain in surgery at precisely the wrong time.

It was exciting to meet some key players in our national strategy to combat this plague—people I had been reading about for years. They wanted to know how I was dealing with the illness, how I got it, what I thought about health-care workers with this disease, mandatory testing, and the new CDC guidelines. These guidelines suggested that health-care workers involved with invasive procedures should know their HIV status. If positive, they should withdraw from doing invasive procedures, unless a peer-group panel decided they could continue. Continuing, however, would require the informed consent of their patients.

I said they should be more stringent, more clear-cut regarding do's and don'ts, instead of "what if's." I didn't think the panel idea was enough. In my opinion, an HIV-positive surgeon should do something else, period. There is no good reason to compromise on that. It's the right thing to do.

"The American public doesn't trust you," I said. "They perceive the CDC as not taking the ball with this thing in the 1980s, and this is the time, with these guidelines, to reinstill public trust [and physician trust] in the CDC. The problem is, right now, everybody who's HIV-positive is hiding, fearful they might lose their jobs once their HIV status becomes known. So there has to be a safety net to catch these folks. Otherwise we're going to drive them further underground."

HIV infection is an extremely complex health issue, probably like no other in history, yet the variety of groups interested in this disease is truly amazing. I finally realized that many of the agendas and so-called solutions are based on wrong motivation and/or misinformation. When I became acquainted with Americans For A Sound AIDS/HIV Policy (A.S.A.P.), I began to see what role I could play in helping inform the public. Later, I accepted an invitation to be on their advisory board. Shepherd Smith, the president of A.S.A.P., had asked me if I would testify before a congressional committee on a bill regarding more diagnosis of HIV. The initial date was cancelled for political reasons. We were told that a room was not available for the hearing. Were those politicians who were against HIV testing hoping that Kimberly Bergalis would die before the hearing?

However, on September 26, 1991, I addressed the congressional hearing on what has been referred to as the Kimberly Bergalis bill. Kimberly Bergalis was one of the patients infected by her dentist in Florida. The bill would require testing of health-care workers and patients. I'll never forget walking into that austere hearing room, with the congressmen on the committee sitting up there above us, and all the media people filling the room behind us. The main thing that struck me was the sense of an evil presence there. There was something not quite right about the whole atmosphere.

When Kimberly Bergalis was wheeled into the room, there was an explosion of flashbulbs, and a near-hysterical frenzy among the press. Kimberly looked somewhat refreshed, but was obviously very compromised physically. She made her statement, which lasted only about twenty seconds, but will probably stick in the mind of anyone who saw her. Then her father, George Bergalis, spoke. This confrontation had the appearance of Custer's Last Stand.

Originally, this hearing was supposed to be just for people who favored the bill, but its opponents (mainly Democrats) had managed to postpone the proceedings.

After the Bergalis's testimony about six people gave the opposing side. It was the same old nonsense: "We can't afford testing." "It won't make any difference." "What do we need to test for?" "What are we going to do with HIV-positive health-care workers?" "Aren't alcoholic and drug-abusing doctors more dangerous?"

One thing that seemed significant to me was that after George and Kimberly Bergalis left, all the Republican committee members left, too, except for California Republican William Dannemeyer, sponsor of the bill. He stayed the whole time. Many of the Democratic committee members stayed and gave unsupported, negative comments about the bill. Evidently many congressmen had already made up their minds before the hearing even began, but they needed the kind of media exposure that would portray them as concerned about the rights of the uninfected. It burned me up to see those guys leave. Not only did I believe what I had to say was important, but I had traveled at my own expense, interrupting a family vacation to be there.

But I gave about a five-minute statement anyway, which went something like this:

> This is a medical disease that I know a lot about personally, since I'm HIV-positive from doing surgery. This is not primarily a question of civil rights, as if AIDS deserves such status.
>
> In medical school, the very first principle we're taught is *primum non nocere,* Latin for "first of all do no harm." That's why I quit doing invasive procedures and got retrained in

another medical field. Once I knew my own HIV status, the only right thing to do was to avoid putting any patients at risk; even one is too many. We hear all kinds of statistics about what chance there is of reverse transmission. But even one in a million is too high, especially when that one person is you.

We are wallowing in a sea of ignorance, by our own choice. It's almost as if we don't want to know. That's dumb, but it's been a consistent perspective from the beginning. When you link that with selfish motives among both high-risk groups and physicians, you have a full-blown disaster. That's how we got where we are. When are we going to do something about it?

Putting blinders on—or keeping them on—won't solve anything, for the doctor or the patient or the general public. There is no other disease where we act as though we prefer that patients not know their status. In the history of plagues, there has never been, until now, a communicable disease the carriers of which were protected by the law. It would have been irrational then, and is irrational now. To spend billions of money on AIDS research without including the starting point of diagnosis through testing is absurd.

My testimony was over before I knew it. The opposing view was stated by Dr. Hacib Aoun, who had been infected from a broken lab vial and then kicked out of his training program. In spite of his own history, he said, "We don't need testing. HIV-infected workers can continue working as usual."

Although I didn't want to destroy Dr. Aoun, I made the point that he was not a surgeon, nor had he ever practiced surgery, so he had no idea of the degree of risk for either a health-care worker or a patient. His theory might sound nice but it is unrealistic. Surely he and others must know that "universal precautions" cannot be followed 100 percent of the time.

I felt the trip was worth taking, even though the bill failed, mainly because it was opposed by certain special-interest groups, including the American College of Surgeons and other groups of people who don't like anybody telling them what to do. For one thing, I wanted to support the Bergalis family. Together we visited the White House, where the Bush administration chose to totally ignore us. The reason for that is unclear, but I suspect it was politically motivated. While I was in Washington I also visited the Family Research Council and spoke at the Concerned Women of America national meeting.

The Bush administration was not the only group to distance itself from those who support HIV testing. CNN's "Crossfire" program cancelled an interview they had tentatively scheduled. That was okay with me, but George Bergalis, who was to appear with me, refused to be a guest when he learned I had been unfairly excluded. Maybe the whole thing was an answer to prayer, because by that time I was pretty beat and just needing to get back to my family.

Although other opportunities to present my views became available, they were generally oriented toward conflict and confrontation. The Oprah Winfrey show, for instance, wanted me to appear, but I knew that if certain activists were on stage or in the crowd, they might transform discussion of a serious public health issue into a civil rights circus. The issues involved are far too important to let them get obscured by media hype or special-interest group chicanery.

One invitation we did accept, however, was from ABC's "20/20," because the format of the show would be less combative and on our own turf. In November they sent a crew of five production people, the producer, Diane Forbes, and Lynn Sherr to Marshfield. Filming was done first at the clinic and then at our home, where the actual interview was held. It was easier to express ourselves, even to *be* ourselves, in this kind of format.

I will never forget Lynn's reaction when we got to the house, which they had totally rearranged to shoot those forty-five seconds that you may have seen on January 31, 1992. Here was this beautiful but somewhat stern woman who had interviewed many people, saying, "Where are the kids? I hope they'll be around." In fact, when the kids showed up, the whole thing lightened up. At the end they had our whole family walk down the street holding hands. We haven't done that in a million years! We usually look like a herd of cows when we go for a walk—three or four out front and a couple more bringing up the rear, with the dog in between.

I think what impressed Lynn most was hearing me say: "You know, life is so great! We don't have to crawl in a hole and give in to this disease. We can still choose to live every day, one at a time, as fully as possible, with God's help."

She asked me many questions and the answers came easily. In fact, she said, "This was great! Just great!" Yet—because the team spent several hours at the clinic and three to four at the house—we were surprised to see how little they used. The issue of HIV infection in health-care workers was never really addressed. I would not have taken the time or energy had I known that it would be such a one-sided presentation. Although I disagree with the viewpoint that opposes testing and retiring HIV-infected health-care workers, I am willing to hear them out. The public needs more open discussion and arbitration, not reporting that reflects bias and limited information.

One of our favorite programs was done for "Physicians Journal Update," which airs on the Lifetime cable network. Filming was done at the clinic and at our home. The real issues were addressed, and they also included our personal side. I suspect the audience that viewed it was already convinced of the need for more "routine" testing and practice modification for HIV-infected health-care personnel.

Ed and Donna, 1991

Christina, Jonathan Wayne, Jonathan Edward, Victoria, David, 1989

1980

Surgery in Ghana,
West Africa

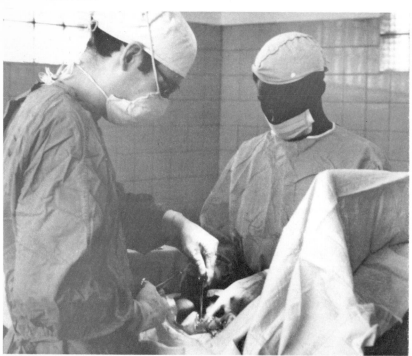

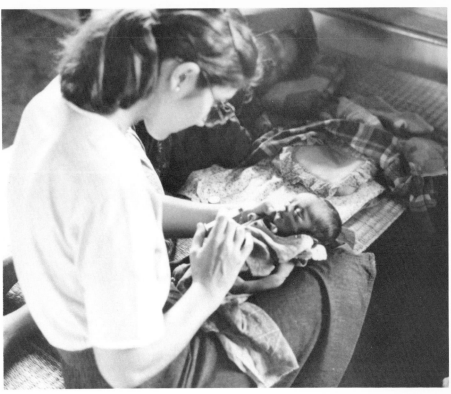

Serving in Thailand refugee camp 1982

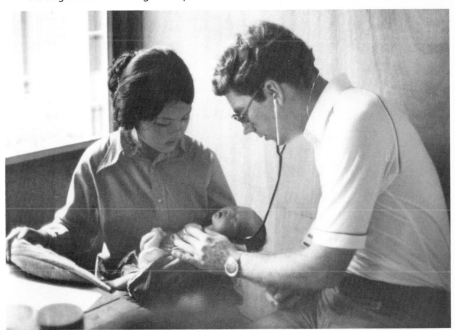

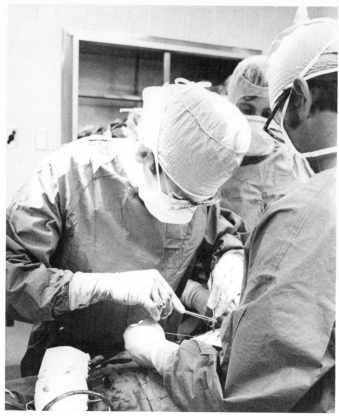

Fast Eddie, Norfolk,
Virginia, 1977

Jonathan Edward,
#1 Son, 1983

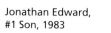

I can see your
tonsils, Dad!

David Michael
joins the family,
1985

Storytime

Judge Larry
Starcher finalizes
adoption papers
for Victoria,
Jonathan Wayne,
and Christina,
November 1988

Suppertime, 1987

1983

Time to move
the firewood,
late fall, 1988

Valley Forge, Pennsylvania, November 1990

November 1988 Weekend trip to Pittsburgh.

Ed discusses writing a book with David Biebel

David Biebel

Winter 1992 vacation at Ski Brule, Michigan

Lake Michigan beach on way to Detroit, 1989

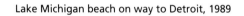

9

Everything You Wanted to Know— And Were Not Afraid to Ask

verywhere we go, people from reporters to laymen to young people, ask lots of questions about AIDS. Since we can't devote a chapter to each concern, perhaps the best approach is to choose some of the most common ones and give you a brief response.

1. What's the difference between HIV-infection and AIDS—and which do you have?

AIDS (**A**cquired **I**mmuno**D**eficiency **S**yndrome) is the end stage of infection with HIV (**H**uman **I**mmunodeficiency **V**irus). In other words, HIV is the AIDS virus. It gradually disables a person's immune system until infectious agents such as bacteria, fungi, other viruses, parasites, and some cancers are able to cause illness or even death. In a healthy person, these intruders would be recognized and destroyed by the body's natural defenses.

Because HIV works slowly, the symptoms of AIDS often develop over a long period of time. For years there was an intermediate classification: ARC (**A**IDS **R**elated **C**omplex) to describe HIV-positive patients with certain symptoms but not full-blown AIDS. In early 1992, the CDC proposed that anyone whose T4-cell count fell below 200 (from a normal 1,000) should be classified as a person with AIDS.

According to this new classification, when my HIV status became known in 1989, I already had AIDS, even though I had no obvious AIDS symptoms. Over the next two years, my T4-cell count fell to nearly zero without my developing the more severe manifestations of the syndrome (group of symptoms) known as AIDS.

2. How close are we to finding a vaccine or cure?

I have met Dr. Bob Redfield of Walter Reed, who published an article in the New England Journal of Medicine (June 1991) about how work is proceeding on a vaccine that seems to have some promise. But there are many problems to overcome, so I think it will be years rather than months before a vaccine is perfected, if it ever happens.

This is a tricky virus, not like the one that causes polio. HIV changes; it becomes resistant. And once it's in the body, it gets incorporated into the patient's molecular structure and then reproduces itself. It is nearly impossible to isolate and destroy without killing the patient in the process. The only "cure" I can imagine at this point would be through divine healing.

3. Have you met people whom the Lord has physically healed of AIDS?

Not personally, although we're beginning to hear accounts. For instance, a 1991 issue of *Charisma* magazine included the testimony of a young man who was healed. Certainly God's will is to do this, since he is more powerful than any disease process. In fact, I have received my healing. This happened not because I'm some special person who deserves it more than others, but because of who God is. (See chapter 12.) The Word of God is very clear on the issue of healing. If Jesus could raise Lazarus from the dead, in effect reversing all the processes of decay that three days in the grave would bring about, routing out HIV from my system would be mild by comparison. It matters not to me how he does it, whether by miracle or by medicine, for all healing is in his hands. More than just physical, healing involves the soul and the spirit. The amazing fact is that the Lord provides strength during these times.

4. As a Christian physician, what are some of your thoughts about Magic Johnson's disclosure in late 1991?

You don't have to be a Christian to be disappointed with his initial press conference. I think he started speaking before he himself was educated about "safe sex." Furthermore, Magic downplayed any reference to abstinence, so for President Bush to call him a hero tended to cloud the issue. I'm glad he came forward with his diagnosis, but he lost an important opportunity to educate millions of fans, especially young people, about the dangers (and immorality) of sexual promiscuity.

Right after that, I accepted an invitation from a local school nurse who said, "Ed, can you come down? Kids are coming in saying safe sex is okay." I put it to them straight, you can count on that. You should have seen their faces when I rolled up my sleeve and showed them the HIV-related shingles I had at the time. "You don't want to get this," I assured them, "or any of the other much worse problems that go with HIV infection. And you don't have to, either. If you'll just save sex until marriage, and remain faith-

ful to an uninfected spouse, there is almost no chance that
you'll get it."

5. What is the risk of patients' acquiring HIV from health-care workers?

So far, there are very few documented cases of patients
who became infected from exposure to infected health professionals. The chance may be only one in a million—but
nobody really knows for sure. This is because an exchange of
body fluids must occur to transfer the virus, and the only
way this happens is in some type of accident during an invasive procedure.

In reality, health-care workers are more at risk of becoming infected from their patients than the other way around.
So I favor testing patients prior to invasive procedures,
when possible, and certainly when they admit to engaging
in high-risk behavior. (Of course, patients are not always
truthful about that.) It's always better to know these facts
before beginning treatment—and to prevent transmission
to others.

6. Should there be premarital testing for HIV?

That depends on what kind of behavior patterns the
prospective bride and groom have had and whether they are
willing to be truthful. (Rent or buy the video "No Second
Chance" from Jeremiah films to see the intergenerational
agony one family endured because of this.) People who are
getting married should have a physical, at which time they
can discuss HIV testing with their doctor. The safest course
is for anybody who has ever been sexually active with *anyone*
but the intended spouse to be tested. At stake is the health of
both the marital partner and any children who result from
the union.

7. Why haven't the American Medical Association (AMA) and other medical groups done more to protect their members and the public?

I am not a member of the AMA. (I dropped my membership because of their pro-abortion stance.) Normally they endorse CDC guidelines, but when the testing proposals came out, there was a lot of resistance. Regardless of how loudly some medical professionals protest that the risk to patients is less than this or that, I believe that what really drives them is the desire for autonomy and self-preservation (otherwise known as greed). However, I am encouraged that the AMA has moved in a more responsible direction toward HIV testing.

The American people are driving this issue now! Some call it public "hysteria" but at least the once-silent majority is finally being heard. HIV is not a disease like syphilis or gonorrhea, which is usually cured by an injection in the hip. It is subtle and diabolical in the way it spreads, because the majority of people who are HIV-infected don't know they have it. There are probably at least a million cases in this country alone, and some say that is a very conservative estimate! Only ASAP has been outspoken about efforts to protect the public from this epidemic.

8. Aren't you angry that you got an HIV infection from a patient?

You might get a different answer from Donna, but I've never held it against whoever it was. That patient probably didn't even know he or she had it. (In 1985 we were just starting to test for HIV.) I've even talked with Jonathan Edward about this, because I thought when he got older he might develop a deep resentment toward all homosexuals and drug addicts, groups within which AIDS has been most prevalent. However, if anyone is to blame, it is members of the medical establishment who dragged their feet in terms of keeping health professionals informed.

9. Do you favor mandatory testing for health-care workers and patients?

I favor mandatory testing on a periodic basis depending on geographical assessment of risk factors. For example, when a recent patient sample was done of emergency-room patients in a northeastern city, 7 percent were found to be HIV-positive. If that number were coming in with cancer, strokes, or the like, we would be moving heaven and earth to find out what was causing it and how the cause could be controlled. But if patients come in with HIV, we just send them back out, thinking "Isn't that awful?" Therefore if a health-care worker is in a high-incidence area, he or she should be tested frequently.

Not long after my visit to the CDC, the American College of Surgeons came out against the guidelines. I believe that physicians should regard their profession as a sacred trust on behalf of their patients. We owe it to our patients to have regular medical care ourselves, especially if we are HIV-positive, so that someone else can be sure our judgment is not clouded. We need checks and balances in regard to HIV, just as we have with physicians who have problems with drugs and alcohol.

In some health-care settings, such as general medicine and nursing, there are many noninvasive procedures performed for which retraining may not be necessary. However, health-care workers with HIV will fall through the net, unable to find something else to do. That's where details like disability insurance and workmen's compensation have to be worked out. It's going to cost money, but that is no reason to keep us from doing what is right.

I say to my fellow surgeons that it is illogical not to want to know your HIV status, for your own good as well as the good of your patients. "First of all, do no harm." Most of us dislike having nonprofessionals tell us what to do. I know that, and so do you. But shouldn't we do this on our own?

Testing has to do with knowledge versus ignorance. To provide the best treatment, we need to know everything we can about a particular patient—family history, what medications are being taken, past diseases and surgeries. All that information is important, as is knowing a patient's HIV status—and our own.

10. Aren't people afraid of what might happen if the test shows them to be HIV-positive?

That is a very poor argument against testing! Wouldn't you want to find out if you are infected, so you can get early treatment and take precautions against getting certain types of opportunistic diseases? You can also be careful not to transmit it to other people. Surely you would want to have this information and use it in the best interest of others and yourself.

It's pretty simple, really, but the other side comes on very strong with some inane reasoning: "We can't afford it." Or "It violates my privacy." And so on. I say that the fear of diagnosis must never override the need to know. Good, sound medicine is based on facts, not emotions.

11. What do you think the general public really wants here?

People want to be confident they're not going to be exposed to this disease through a health-care worker. I think they deserve that consideration. Although the risk can never be reduced to zero, they want to see that something has been done to make it as low as possible. So far, they don't see it being done.

The public is waking up to how the agenda for AIDS has been politicized and manipulated by various special-interest groups. As a result, the real threat of the disease has been kept hidden. For example, some homosexual activists have resisted the idea of testing because it "violates civil rights" or is "an invasion of privacy." Others cite discrimination against homosexuals as the reason there has been inadequate funding of AIDS research and treatment programs. On the other hand, at first some public health officials were saying there was little chance for a patient to transmit the virus to a health-care worker (and vice versa). They knew it could happen at the time, though they said something different. They also lied by implying that AIDS was a problem only for homosexuals and IV drug abusers.

So the public says, "Whoa, you lied to us. Now we don't believe anything you say." It is going to take a while to regain public confidence. I think the CDC is on the right track, but, unfortunately, they don't have the cooperation of some of the medical groups.

12. But isn't AIDS still really a homosexual disease?

AIDS can no longer be viewed as a threat to only such "high risk" groups as homosexuals and IV drug users. It is *everyone's* problem now, as my own case has proven! Not only are health-care workers its potential victims, but HIV is being found in increasing numbers among heterosexuals, as well as in babies born to infected mothers. Nevertheless, some people (especially conservative evangelicals) seem to think, "We can stop this plague right now by dealing with the sinners who caused it!" As if it's not *our* problem, and the way to stop it is to do something about "them." Well—and I want to emphasize this clearly—nothing is going to completely halt HIV's gradually increasing death-grip on humanity until the Lord returns. But there's a lot we can do to control its spread.

I'm thinking globally here, not provincially, like many North American Christians often do when they consider

HIV disease, as well as other things. Even if someday a vaccine or cure becomes available here, it will almost certainly not be readily available in the Third World, where AIDS will continue to march on.

It is also very presumptuous—and *untrue*—to say that HIV only happens to "bad people." Morality alone does not guarantee immunity to this or any other disease so long as we live in an imperfect world.

Worldwide, believers and nonbelievers alike are suffering (and will suffer) because of AIDS. Regardless of how these patients acquired the disease, it is simply not right to turn our backs on them and their families as if they brought the plague on themselves. If I read the Bible correctly, we are *all* sinners and under God's judgment. And people are going to keep sinning until the final coming of God's kingdom. However, for the Christian the penalty has been paid by Jesus.

If God can include an adulterer and murderer like King David in the very lineage of Jesus the Redeemer, we ought to pause and look in the mirror of our own consciences before we write off those "bad people."

13. If abstinence and/or marital fidelity—not "safe sex"—is the answer, why don't more doctors preach it?

I hate to be this blunt, but I think it's mainly because they are reluctant to deal with their own immorality. Having grown up in an era of sexual freedom, they don't want to restrict their own activities—and it's pretty difficult to convince others of something if you really don't believe it yourself. As far as I'm concerned, you can apply this same thought to politicians, preachers, and other public figures who resist proclaiming the surest way to keep AIDS from spreading: abstinence before marriage and faithfulness within marriage.

14. Should Christian medical personnel treat AIDS patients, even if it means risking their lives?

That's a difficult question with a simple answer—yes. Jumping into a raging stream to save somebody is about as risky as treating somebody with HIV disease. Yet, especially if you are a Christian, you wouldn't think twice about jumping into that stream, even though you know there's a potential to lose your own life in the process.

Christian health-care workers ought to be leaders in this role. I met a dentist who actually recruits AIDS patients, though in a quiet way so he doesn't scare off his other patients. He sees that as a ministry, and that's the attitude we all should take. Not everyone will want to work only with AIDS patients, but I think we Christians ought to be leading the way by showing our compassion, and not by words alone. I don't mean Christians should be reckless in any way. God gave us a brain to process facts and use them wisely. In this case, that means taking proper precautions.

15. I'm a Christian health-care worker who believes that God has called me to minister to AIDS patients, even at risk to myself. But aren't there family issues involved?

I think we've rarely had issues of this magnitude brought before us, although Christians have always been willing to minister to victims of hepatitis, leprosy, tuberculosis, and the plague. Of course, some physicians ran and refused to get involved with these and certain other communicable diseases. I can't answer for them.

This is a highly personal issue that depends a great deal on spiritual maturity. Because the transmission risk is never zero where HIV is concerned, it should also be a decision agreeable to your spouse. Doing invasive procedures on HIV patients, whether in surgery or nursing, will involve some risk. If your spouse agrees that the risk is worth taking to have a ministry to those patients, I believe you should accept God's call and use your medical skills on their behalf.

16. Where do precautions end and risks begin, and how does faith in God blur that line?

Take the setting of a missionary health provider who doesn't have access to double-gloving (maybe there are no gloves at all or none without holes), or who has to reuse needles that cannot be properly sterilized. In that case, you completely rely on the Lord. I've been in situations where needles must be used hundreds of times. Or scalpels are so dull, you have to put your whole weight on them to make them cut through the skin. Yet they can't be resharpened. Because gloves must sometimes be reused and repowdered, you never really know what their status is.

But those things don't seem to be that important if it is clear that God called you there. So you rely on his power and protection. I don't mean that you jump into the raging stream without knowing how to swim, for we should never "test" God. We just have to be in the Word, confessing and believing it, and then go about the work he puts before us. When I was on the mission field, it never dawned on me to be concerned about catching a disease—and I never did.

17. Do people look at you differently than they did before?

I suppose some people look at me and think, What a shame. How do you do it? You used to be a cardiac surgeon and now you have to deal with this. My answer would be that being a cardiac surgeon is great stuff, but it's not the whole world. It's not even the top of anything. The top depends on what God wants you to do. As far as I'm concerned, the guy who cleans the church is just as important as I.

One problem with cardiac surgery is that you sort of get pushed there up a long, tough road. You really pay your dues, so you enjoy the fact that people look up to you. It's hard not to believe you've earned their respect and deserve it.

My way of validating that respect was to try to always do the best I could for my patients. I never considered myself any better than anybody else, though I enjoyed very much what I did, as well as the benefits. You have to guard yourself against pride whether you're a surgeon or a preacher, or maybe even a very good janitor.

Although I would much rather still be operating, God has given me an opportunity to do something else, medically and in other ways. I want to be an example to HIV-infected health-care workers and anyone else who is impacted by this disease, showing them that even in the face of AIDS, life goes on. In fact, impossible though it may seem, in spite of HIV infection, or perhaps because of it, life can be better than it ever was before. If this revelation encourages one person to come into the kingdom of God, then the process will have validity for me.

◿ 10 ◺

Becoming a Soul Doctor

*i*n the world's history of plagues, AIDS could end up being the worst ever, and not just in a physical sense. It has the stigma of *leprosy*, the transmission characteristics of *syphilis*, the natural history of *tuberculosis* and the prognosis (at least so far) of *the bubonic plague*. Additionally, its long-term global socioeconomic impact may be greater than all the wars ever fought.

In times of plague, responses to its victims have ranged from desertion to persecution to compassion. In the Middle Ages, many physicians and clergy fled the cities during a plague. For example, in London's plague of 1665, when nearly 70,000 died, only 13 doctors stayed to care for the 200,000 citizens who were left in the city. Modern people with HIV infection have experienced similar abandonment.

Persecution and scapegoating is society's second most common response to plagues. In Milan, Italy, in 1630, two men—a barber-surgeon and the commissioner of health— were accused of spreading disease by means of deadly ointments. The city senate ordered that their flesh should be torn with red-hot pincers, their right hands cut off, their

bones broken, and that they should then be put on a tor-
ture wheel for six hours before being burned at the stake.

In the late twentieth century, HIV-infected people are
persecuted more subtly but no less unfairly. They may have
their employment and health benefits cut off instead of their
hands. To my knowledge, none have been burned at the
stake, but in Florida one family's house was destroyed by
arson. Nobody needs to put HIV-infected people on the
wheel. They're already being tortured enough.

Persecution and abandonment have always been ways to
disenfranchise the poor and the plague-prone. The net result
is a fragmented and demoralized society in which any epidemic will continue to spread. Sound familiar? How else can
we understand—more than a decade into this plague's history—our nation's continuing failure to develop a rational
approach to AIDS, a multifaceted (political, public
health/medical, educational, and ecclesiastical) policy and
agenda? Compassion is the only helpful response to those
afflicted by a plague, and the only one we should allow.
Physician William Boghurst remained in London to care for
patients during one severe plague. His conviction was that
professionals must accept the responsibilities as well as the
benefits. Ministers must preach, captains must fight, physicians must attend to the sick.

When HIV-infected people are treated with compassion,
not only do *they* benefit, but those who help them are
rewarded in less tangible ways (active love always receives
more than it gives). As this happens, societal disruption is
inhibited and even reversed, because hysteria cannot be maintained in the midst of composed, courageous people who
are calmly caring for the afflicted.

Besides these practical arguments for compassion, we who
claim to be followers of Jesus of Nazareth have in him the
example of someone who touched the lepers and ministered
to all the disenfranchised of his society. To him, their needs
were not a burden; they were an opportunity to bring God's

comfort, grace, and presence into the life context of people who knew nothing but despair.

I know it is difficult to think of AIDS as anything other than a threat, a crisis you may be living with already, or one that is lurking on the horizon. But did you know that in some Eastern languages the word *crisis* combines the root words for "danger" and "opportunity"? AIDS is obviously a danger, but might it also be an opportunity in disguise? It has been for me, and I'm convinced it can be for you, too, whether or not you are HIV-positive.

In the final few chapters of this book, I want to examine four facets of this one theme—"AIDS as an opportunity"—without discounting the fact that for me, for you, for our society, and for the world it is also a dangerous crisis of monstrous proportions.

Because I want to reserve my most personal thoughts until last, we will look first at AIDS as an opportunity for both health professionals and others, especially those within the church. Then I'll share some rather painfully gained insights about HIV-infected persons and their families. After that, I'll take you behind closed doors into my own family and marriage, concluding with an even closer look at the one component of this whole danger/opportunity that has kept me from going over the edge in a personal sense.

In terms of health-care workers, including physicians, compassion is increasing, but it has been a slow process and there is still a long way to go. By compassion, I mean more than sensitivity in terms of individual patient needs—and AIDS patients usually take more time and energy than those with other diseases. Even more basic is the humane choice to treat HIV-infected people rather than referring them elsewhere.

At the risk of being labeled "homophobic" (a meaningless term), I think the militant behavior of the homosexual community has worked against its own best interests and the rest of us in the area of AIDS-related concerns. I cannot fathom

how they can believe that the way to engender compassion
for HIV-infected people is by disrupting public gatherings,
abusing elected officials, holding noisy parades, and carrying belligerent placards.

This combative activity confuses rather than clarifies the
issues of AIDS patients, many of whom are not homosexuals.

Compassion and the Health-Care Professional

I would choose medicine again as a profession if I had it
all to do over, especially if I could know at the start what I
never learned about illness before becoming HIV-positive. Of
course, I wish I had known more about AIDS when I was
retrained, so I could have been more careful. Because nothing was said about it to us residents, I just went on my merry
way.

Perhaps AIDS is one reason there is a nursing shortage
and fewer qualified people applying to medical school these
days. But, as far as I'm concerned, becoming a health professional is still one of the most fulfilling callings. The key
word there is "calling." In the age of AIDS, you may not
make it if you enter health-care work in search of wealth or
power, or even because in a purely human sense you care
about people and want to help them. You will eventually
become cynical, burned out, or both—unless you truly feel
called to be a caregiver.

When I talk to Christian medical groups, I often ask a
simple question: "Do you have an upward calling from
God? If so, what is it?" One of the rewards of following
Jesus Christ is becoming convinced that your profession is a
divine calling. This is the key to understanding what kept
the apostle Paul going in spite of the discouragements and
hardships of trying to carry Christianity to a pagan world.
How else can we explain his joy and contentment, even
when imprisoned?

If you are a Christian who has chosen a health-related career, are you just working like the rest of the world, as if the opportunity to minister through medicine is merely a job, a way to earn a living? That's the way it was for me once, although I did try to take a personal interest in my patients. Before HIV rearranged my life in so many ways, I seldom stopped to ask myself, "What am I really doing here?" I was cruising along, enjoying the ride and even deeply grateful for God's providence and grace. But I had blinders on. I was so focused on repairing people's hearts that I often missed the equally if not more significant opportunity to minister to their deeper needs, to help repair their souls and spirits. I cringe to think of the eternal consequences of this omission, especially for those who died during surgery. I was trained as a technician, a specialist in body repair, and that was my main concern.

To minister effectively to HIV-infected individuals as a medical professional, you must ask yourself this question: *"What am I trying to accomplish through my relationship with this patient?"* The disease model you learned in your training will eventually prove inadequate in the face of the frustrating, long-term, irreversible decline you will see in many of these patients. If you think that your only role is to cure disease, AIDS will have you for lunch. You will quickly begin looking for somebody you can really cure, rationalizing that "I should be a more productive steward of my hi-tech training and skills."

Interestingly enough, that same frustration's other side is where the real opportunity for ministry through medicine begins. But, to pursue it, you have to view a patient wholistically: body/soul/spirit, existing in a web of horizontal and vertical relationships constantly in need of maintenance and repair. Sometimes there is *nothing* you can do physically, beyond trying to make your patient more comfortable—and the medical treatment you offer may have just the opposite effect. But you can *always* be a "soul doctor," if only through a simple prayer, reading an encouraging Bible passage, or just sitting with him or her silently for a while, a partner on the pilgrimage of pain.

One opportunity AIDS gave me was to learn firsthand that pain has many faces. It might be the pain of hearing the ear-nose-throat specialist's trocar needle crunching through the cartilage of my nose because he needed to culture the bugs causing a year-long sinus infection that the antibiotics hadn't touched. Or it might have been the pain of not being able to do things I used to do and the feeling that now my life was useless.

Having to strip down and put on a gown for an upper-gastrointestinal and gallbladder ultrasound brings its own kind of pain. Or being ignored, even ostracized by your friends. Or wondering if you should go swimming in the public pool with your kids, or hug and kiss them like you used to. Or wondering how much your illness is going to drain your family's physical, emotional, and financial reserves before it's all over. There is also self-pity, confusion, loneliness, emptiness, doubt, fear, and the sense of isolation that is a side effect of feeling abandoned by others as well as God.

Pain is pain, and even when there's no pill, surgery, or cure available, health professionals can always help in some way if they fight the temptation to withdraw when there's nothing more that can be done medically. I know you have too much to do, and many other patients—some of whom God may even cure through your efforts. However, beyond the thoughts of failure and inconvenience lies a seldom-charted territory of discovery—for you and your patient, especially if he or she is a believer. There is no doubt in my mind that as people get nearer to death (or even think they are), if they can get past all the negative stuff that can go with dying, they begin to see realities much more clearly. The jewels of wisdom they have to offer could never be found by search or study—only by being there and listening.

Some dying patients have a vision of heaven or angels, or even of the Lord himself, and will share it with you. I urge you to accept these experiences as special gifts. How else could you know such things, except by lying there yourself? Through your patient's situation, you may be blessed and touched by a deep sense of the reality and presence of the Divine. Treasure such gifts forever, for they are priceless.

Sometimes there may be only abject suffering, overwhelming and apparently meaningless. Even then, by choosing to enter into that pain, you will diminish your patient's hurt and sorrow. And you will be blessed as you struggle to understand, for any believer who embraces this search with an open mind will inevitably end up gazing at the cross, where the guiltless Redeemer cried out, "My God, my God, why have you forsaken me?"

The Church and Its AIDS Ministry

In the midst of all the mental groping and grappling that comes to any health-care worker, those who are Christians should also see this disease as an opportunity to lead, convict, convince, inspire, and educate the church about the need for other believers to take on this ministry. Of all institutions, the church is the only one designed by God to be a caring community, representing him in a tangible way in a world that has always been hurting. Why else would the church be called the body of Christ? Surely it is God's intention that we who claim allegiance to him carry his unchanging love to the very people sought out by his Son during his earthly sojourn.

As far as I can tell, the conservative branches of the North American church have failed so far to minister adequately to HIV-infected persons, *for several unacceptable reasons.* In the early days of AIDS, probably because the disease was perceived as a homosexual problem, the evangelical perspective was generally more judgmental than it is today. One of the reasons this self-righteous attitude is changing is illustrated by the story of a conservative pastor's daughter who became infected through her boyfriend at a time when the policy of her father's church was to have nothing to do with "the sinners" who contracted AIDS. Only the most sanctimonious would dare bar his own flesh and blood from the very help she would desperately need in the next few years.

Unfortunately, the more typical story thus far has been like that of one young pastor and his family. His wife was infected with HIV through a 1985 blood transfusion during the birth of their first child. Subsequently, she gave birth to another child, who was born with AIDS, although some babies born to infected mothers remain uninfected. This pastor first became a bereaved father, as the child slowly succumbed to the disease. Next, the church he was serving asked him to leave. Soon after that, he became a widower.

The point here is that AIDS is coming to your town, to your schools, to your church and maybe even to your family. This is no longer debatable. Because it's *our* problem already, the question is not: "If it comes to us, what shall our *policy* be?" The proper question for the church to be asking is framed in terms of human need, not theological principles: "How can we touch the lives of people with AIDS and their families in the name of Jesus Christ?"

To do this effectively, there are at least three more bridges to cross after a church acknowledges its responsibility for an AIDS ministry. These are credibility, sensitivity, and capability. Setting up programs and hiring people to represent the congregation is not enough, even if it is a start. One reason some churches are so ineffective today is that many laypeople think that "ministry" is what they pay their pastors to do, instead of what their pastors should be equipping *them* to do.

The only way to bridge the credibility gap is for as many members as possible to get personally involved in a ministry to AIDS patients. I'm not talking about the "politics" of AIDS here. Some Christians think they've gotten "involved" by writing letters or making phone calls, or maybe even providing financial support. But you cannot really understand this illness by staying at a safe distance and shooting arrows, thinking you're doing the "right" thing. Jesus said ". . . whatever you did for one of the least of these brothers of mine, you did for me" (Matt. 25:40 NIV). The *right* thing is to get down and get dirty. Until you've done that, despite how sympathetically you speak about HIV-infected people, your words are meaningless, and people listening will say, "What do you really know about it?"

Sensitivity, like credibility, is not something you can manufacture, either. It means knowing someone's specific needs and caring about that person. So you have to do more listening than talking, a difficult challenge for any Christian who is used to handing out advice laced with pious platitudes and Bible verses. AIDS patients may need and want *some* of that, but sensitivity means sharing your faith gifts on their turf, according to their timing, and at their request.

If listening is difficult for some lay Christians, it is doubly difficult for the clergy, who are so used to holding forth in situations they control, such as in church or at a funeral or even in visitation. Few of them are very prepared for a cardiac surgeon to walk unannounced into their office one dark day in May and say, "I really need to talk to somebody, pastor. A few weeks ago I learned I'm infected with the AIDS virus, and my life feels like it's been turned upside down."

When I said that, my former pastor just sat there with his mouth open, totally shocked for a few moments. Then he said, "I don't know what to say." That's not a bad place to start, because there may be nothing you *can* say that will fix things. But, if you start like that, you might add ". . . but I love you, and we'll do everything we can to help." Then you might say, "I've read some and thought a lot about this disease, but would you help me better understand what it means personally? Please, tell me everything you've been experiencing, and how I can help."

Anyone who wants to minister in the name of Jesus to people infected with HIV needs first to go before God and examine his or her attitudes toward AIDS, toward the patient, even toward death itself. I'm not talking about numbered prayer arrows you aim at God to tell him this or that or ask him for such and such. What you will need is wrestling, agonizing prayer, because getting involved with AIDS will chew you up and spit you out if you are not ministering in the power of the Holy Spirit. If you ask, "Lord, show me how to deal with the problem of AIDS," you will never help anybody. But if you ask, "Lord, show me ways to really help people with AIDS," you are headed in the right direction. Ask God to act through you. Take into your heart and put into action the realization that Christians "abide in Him and He in us, because He has given us of His Spirit" (1 John 4:13).

Sometimes the first response to an HIV-infected person is to reach for the pastoral-care Rolodex, with its list of problems and solutions. But AIDS is too complicated for an A-B-C approach. It is neither appropriate nor helpful to reel off such simplistic answers as "All you have to do is pray. Then follow these five steps [or go through these three stages] and everything will be hunky-dory."

An effective AIDS ministry involves *everybody:* the patients, their families, the church at large, and its clergy. "Why?" questions abound, but nobody can really answer them. So the only helpful answers are relational and personal: "I care about you and hurt with you, brother [sister]. You're not going to face this alone, because I'm here, and I'll be here until you don't need me anymore."

Now, that's light-years more helpful than stopping by just long enough to say, "Call me if you need me!"—with the last word hanging in the air as you turn to go. You can bet the farm the patient is not going to call, even if he has one foot in the grave, because he knows what you would say: "Sorry, I can't come right now, but be sure to call again."

But what are some practical ways to help? Why not begin by looking for a need you can meet and then just do it? For example, the gutters on our house needed cleaning and in my condition there was no way I could get up there. So one day our sixty-year-old interim pastor showed up and said, "I'm going to clean your gutters." And he climbed up on a ladder in the rain and cold and did the ones he could reach. One of the deacons came over after that and cleaned the second-story gutters, also without our asking.

That's the kind of help AIDS patients need. Take them a meal you've prepared, something that can be frozen in case they don't need it right then. While you're there, discreetly observe other things that aren't getting done, either because that person hasn't the strength or is so depressed he can't get motivated. For instance, offer to do the laundry or the cleaning, or to repair something that may not be working quite right. Ask if a ride somewhere is needed, or if you can do some shopping or pick up some medication. Invite him or her to go on a picnic with your family, or maybe to a ball game or concert. Things like this speak volumes, while pious platitudes with no real feelings to support them are just so much sound and fury, signifying nothing—except to you.

Ask yourself, "What would I be willing to do for this person if he were my brother or sister? Genuine kindness has as its root the idea of being of the same kind: "kindred." If you can reach the point of treating an infected person as a relative, you've come a long way. In fact, like the good Samaritan in Jesus' parable, you demonstrate the meaning of "love your neighbor as yourself" whenever you show kindness to a wounded traveler on the road of life.

One other thing: If you really want to show that you care, how about a hug? This disease has such power to isolate infected people from their families and friends. They will

feel reconnected with the living, instead of the dying, if
somebody reaches out to them in that way.

That's the way it felt to me when I started going to a different church. Believers' Church and World Outreach Center in Marshfield provided me with a living gospel that nourished me both spiritually and physically. The pastor and
congregation welcomed me with hugs, acceptance, and
expectation. I described this feeling in one of the few poems
I have ever written:

The Hug
God drew me here,
this World Outreach Center.
At first, a Handshake, a Hello.
Then laying on of hands.
Next,
A Hug: Brother, let's sit down and talk.
How are you dealing with this?
Late night discussion by way of modem?
Does the Holy Spirit traverse electronic wires?
The appointment: another Hug
But I have AIDS!
Hang on, Revelation's coming!
God wants me healed!
Listening, Praise, Encouragement, Prayer and a Hug.
Family!
This is His plan:
"Thy Kingdom come, on earth as it is in Heaven."

△ 11 △

Letting Your Love Grow

S tudies have shown that people with terminal diseases are most afraid of two things: that they will die in great pain or that they may die alone.

Medication is no guarantee that an HIV-infected person will not die in pain—short of narcotizing the patient into oblivion. There are so many variations of end-stage AIDS that nobody can be sure how it will be until that time arrives. However, the family and friends of a patient can alleviate the second fear by making this commitment and keeping it: "We are with you in this and will be until it's over." Faithfulness like this provides the context for love to grow, even if it has not been there very much in the past.

On the other hand, love's growth is stifled if an infected person just withdraws or sits back and waits for help to come. He must reach out to people, let them inside his thoughts and feelings. Sometimes, patients will have to minister to others, giving out even when their own tank is empty. We who are infected may have to help *others* think positively, giving *them* hope, even when we ourselves may be

121

sliding toward the edge of despair. Real love grows in two directions.

"Dear Patient . . ."

First things first: HIV-infected people have to be realistic. Once you know you're HIV-positive, you can't just go about your business as if nothing has happened. It's a new chapter in your life. Ignoring it or denying it will not help. You first need to find a physician you can trust, somebody you can call when the office is closed. This should be someone who will level with you about the twists and turns that lie ahead of you, and will covenant with you (an old concept, but the basis of good medicine) to go there as your fellow traveler.

Another aspect of that "realistic" approach is acknowledging that your lifestyle will change, in terms of nutrition, for instance. There may be activities you'll no longer be able to do, and medications with unpleasant side effects. For me, accepting new limitations has been very difficult, maybe because there never seemed to be anything I couldn't do if I put my mind to it. Times have changed! For instance, once I was taking a shower when my blood count was so far down that my blood pressure plunged and I had to stagger to bed and lie down quickly before I fainted. There have been many times I was sick from AZT to the point of not being able to eat, although I desperately wanted to regain those pounds (I lost twenty pounds originally and ten more with chemo) I had lost since 1985. Even relatively "minor" things like the chronic sinus infection I had for more than a year (despite four rounds of antibiotics) really wore me down. Besides putting up with all the yucky stuff that kept coming out of my nose, the inability of my system to dispatch such a simple bug was another frustration and a less-than-subtle reminder that I was infected. That got old pretty fast for a guy who was used to being healthy as a horse.

The list goes on. There was a pesky eye infection that would sometimes be bad enough that I couldn't see very well. The idea of going blind is frightening to anyone, but the eye infection also kept me from reading what had kept my head above water, the Bible. I remember praying, "You know, Lord, if something happens to my eyes, I've got tapes of the Bible to listen to. I'm ready."

But the worst things I faced giving up were activities I wanted to do with the kids, such as hunting and fishing. I wondered if I should risk getting so far out in the woods that I might not be able to make it back. Once when I took the kids fishing on the farm in southern Georgia, just walking down to the lake nearly killed me, and I wondered, "Should I be doing this?"

AIDS changes the way you look at everything! Yet hidden in all this upheaval and change was the opportunity to see life and its meaning with more clarity. For instance, I used to be as compulsive at home as I was in surgery. The precision needed in my work carried over into the home as an insistence that there is a right way to do things, to schedule activities, to keep the house, and so on. Sometimes I treated the kids and Donna as if I were a king, and they were my subjects. (I am not happy or proud about telling you this.)

I always had a list of projects, especially things needing repairs. It was a never-ending list, because as soon as we fixed one thing, another would get broken. Five kids and a dog will take care of that! Even after I got sick, I maintained my list, so there was always a vague anxiety that if I wasn't fixing something, I hadn't looked hard enough. You can imagine the kind of conflict I brought into our home, now that I had hours available every day, instead of saving up my projects for the weekends. To get beyond that, I had to real-

ize that some of those things I was so focused on wouldn't
matter a lick in five years, maybe even in one year.

Realism, however, doesn't mean being fatalistic about
everything. Whether sick or well, all of us must learn to be
realistic about things that are actually important. Sort these
out, using the new discernment that becoming an HIV-
infected patient can provide. Then you'll begin to appreciate
the basic things you took for granted before: health, freedom, love, life itself.

To do this, you'll have to deal with the intense loneliness
and fear that AIDS brings. Its propensity to isolate—even
to the point of isolating you from the real "you"—will have
to be faced. Otherwise, you'll give in to feeling like a leper
and allow an invisible wall to be built between others and
yourself.

The underlying problem is that someone who hasn't been
there can never really understand our situation. We who are
infected with HIV need to tell others how we feel, and that
takes more energy than we think we have. But the invest-
ment will be worth making in the long run, because it may
help heal the hurt that those who really care about us carry
as they participate with us in whatever bad things AIDS is
doing to us at the moment.

I have been on both sides, as observer and patient, and I
believe it's almost as hard to suffer with somebody you love
as it is for the patient himself or herself. One thing's for sure,
though. You'll do a lot better with this if you prepare yourself for it. The fact is, people react differently, even to the
same pain or loss.

Both sides have the option of withdrawing, and with
AIDS the temptation to do so is very strong. As family
members look into the future and see only pain and sepa-
ration, the natural thing to do is to protect themselves by
withdrawing, at least emotionally if not physically. I've seen
this happen, even in the health-care setting. Here's a patient
with HIV in the bed; a doctor walks in and stands way over

there, and a nurse comes in and stands in the far corner. If they do get any closer, you get the feeling they are hiding behind an invisible shield. Observing this withdrawal is nothing like having it done to you, I promise you. This common reaction does not mean that health-care workers are afraid of contracting HIV from a patient. Rather, it is a result of dealing with their fears about what is to come.

We who are infected with HIV need to gently invite our caregivers to find a way to bypass that emotional wall. They may be struggling not only with a sense of impending failure to help us, and the guilt that goes with that, but also with the practicalities of dealing with our infections, cancers, GI problems, central IV lines, or feeding tubes. The reality is that the whole scenario with respect to the physical problems can become almost intolerable for a caregiver.

Because of our illness, the people caring for us must daily enter the distressing world of our loneliness, confusion, debility, pain, and a multitude of weird things that a compassionate mind would hope could never happen to the human body. Is it any wonder they sometimes feel ambivalence, an approach-avoidance conflict of enormous proportions? They care, but they hurt, too.

Perhaps it seems easier to just get mad at them, to feel so sorry for ourselves that we withdraw inside ourselves to hide and wait to die. But why do that when there's so much living yet to do? Even if you choose to *live,* as I have, don't be surprised if some of the people who care about you don't jump on your bandwagon and vigorously cheer you on. After all, they've been gearing up for you to die, which means trying to handle their present sorrow and still reserve enough energy to get on with their own lives after you're gone.

What I'm trying to say is that dismantling the fences begins with us. Can we identify with the bystanders? Where are they coming from? Can we try to understand their emotions? No matter how it feels, it's not us patients they hate, or something we've done they're so angry about. It's AIDS.

So maybe it's time to say, "I love you," to family members or friends who are at our side, instead of waiting for them to say those words to us first. Try this: "Thanks for being with me today. Thanks for just caring." And if people come to mind who haven't been around in a while, write them a note that invites them in: "I'm sick of just thinking about dying. I need you to help me live."

There are risks in this open and honest approach, however. For one thing, the more love we invest in a relationship, the more heartbreaking it is to say "Good-bye." This perception has some validity, so it requires both patient and caregiver to reach out in faith. There is also the risk that a vulnerable request for love may be rejected. When one is already stripped naked emotionally, it hurts all the more to have somebody turn and walk away.

But these risks are worth taking. What else is more meaningful and lasting than love? Investments in people are eternal; investments in objects will just die with us. Love cannot be conquered by such a flimsy thing as AIDS. Embracing caring relationships is the only way to laugh, instead of cry, in its face.

If you're infected with HIV, broader risks are worth taking, too. For instance, reach out to try to help all those in need, whether through education or by trying to give them hope. In the world we live in, AIDS is only one of many problems. Once I got beyond self-pity, fear, and despair, and made myself available in a public sense, I discovered that many people, not just HIV-infected ones, are searching for a way to make sense of their lives. I guess they figure if I can keep going, I might know something that could help them.

It was a little surprising, but once I decided to share the values system and lessons I had learned through my illness, I didn't have to go looking for opportunities. People found me, both laypeople and medical professionals. I remember one medical student who came up after a talk I gave and said, "I thought things were tough for me, but hearing you and seeing your attitude puts my problems in a different light."

A little warning, though: Helping people is exhausting. You may have only two minutes to try to comfort a total stranger who has just told you, "I'm dying of neuroblastoma, with three months to live. Please tell me how to rise above it." He would like to have your advice condensed into five easy steps, but that's not what it's about. Handing out prescriptions like some fast-fix spiritual dispensary is useless. Instead, say—like one pilgrim telling another—"I've found some passes through the mountains of pain." Then let the other person know the route you've taken.

More importantly, I try to answer a sometimes unexpressed question: "Where does the power to traverse such awful terrain come from?" A panel was held recently in LaCrosse, and an infected young man was talking about how the power within you is the key to getting over the depression and despair. Sounds like the film *Chariots of Fire*, whose main character was a Christian with strong enough convictions to turn his back on an Olympic medal if it meant violating the Sabbath. In his sermon, he asked the question "Where does the power to run the race come from?" His answer, "From within."

But this is only a half-truth, for if the power comes from within and is of our own making, it simply does not, cannot, and will not hold up in the face of AIDS. On the other hand, there is an internal *supernatural* power available to run any race or cross any mountain, if a supernatural being lives within us (more on this in chapter 13).

While it's true that we all have a certain amount of "power," the difference between what we can produce *on our own* and what we can draw on *from an unlimited source* to face something like AIDS is the difference between trying to power a modern submarine with the most sophisticated internal combustion engine ever made instead of a nuclear reactor. You might make it out of the harbor just fine, but with time your power source would expire—and you and everybody else in the ship would perish.

Speaking of all the others in the ship, let me end this chapter with some thoughts about the people who care for HIV patients, and may be caring for you. Mark 4:35–41 NIV records an incident wherein Jesus and his disciples were crossing the lake and a "furious squall" arose. Jesus, exhausted from a long day of ministry, was sleeping in the stern. Now there's a perfect portrait of peace: power under control. But the disciples—seasoned sailors—began to fear for their lives to the point where they woke him. First Jesus rebuked the wind and spoke to the waves, "Quiet! Be still!" After all was "completely calm," he rebuked his disciples for their lack of faith.

This story shows that the power from within (the disciples' expertise) will be *inadequate* unless it is linked to the power that comes from the Lord. But my main reason for bringing it up comes from one little phrase that might be overlooked: "There were also other boats with him" (v. 36).

When we're fighting for our lives (as the disciples were), we tend to forget that the same storm is rocking the boat of many others, including family, friends, and even the larger anonymous community of mankind. As John Donne wrote, "No man is an island, entire of itself; every man is a piece of the continent, a part of the main. . . ."

The people in the other boats were just as involved, worried, and overpowered by the storm, which Jesus used to teach them where the real power comes from. This power is what we need to bear troubles so great that it feels like we're about to go under—a conviction anyone caring for an HIV-infected loved one is likely to have felt at some point, too. It may be a mother rocking her adult son, now reduced to infancy through dementia, or a father holding his dying baby girl who became HIV-infected before she was born. Perhaps it's a wife wiping her husband's brow as he shivers and shakes uncontrollably from an AIDS-related fever. Or it's the husband who holds his wife's hand as she gasps for breath in the terminal stages of *pneumocystis carinii* because she contracted AIDS in a blood transfusion.

"Dear Caregiver . . ."

If you're a caregiver for an HIV patient, you are needed far more than the patient may let on. Thank you for caring that much, when you could have simply turned away—like some have done—to get on with your own life.

Beyond reminding you of the ultimate source of your power to run, walk, or crawl through this difficult journey, I will suggest two other things that will help. First, give yourself permission to hate this disease, not the person you're caring for, or even the one who infected him or her. Perhaps you've been taught to accept all things as from the hand of God, to never question and certainly never to dispute what appears to be his will. But I think it's much healthier—emotionally, physically, and spiritually—to be positive about one's faith and negative about AIDS.

To me, AIDS seems particularly demonic. Just look at the way it works—deceiving our God-given immune system until it can no longer defend us from microscopic intruders our macrophages (cells that protect against infection) would normally gobble up. If it isn't okay to hate something this diabolical, I don't know what "righteous indignation" can possibly mean.

Second, let yourself risk loving, even if it seems like committing emotional suicide. If you really love a person with HIV infection, you will affirm that person's life instead of preparing for his or her death. The latter may seem more practical and realistic, but it certainly is callous to say, as one person said when he called to inform me of a mutual friend's death from a heart attack, "I guess you'll be joining him soon!"

"No way!" I replied. "By his stripes I *was* healed."

I plan to be around for a while, and I'm claiming life instead of resigning to death. Nobody has to tell an AIDS patient that death is a possibility. But how many are willing to say that healing is just as possible? God wants to bless his children, but we must believe and claim what he has said. If God cannot conquer AIDS, then I say, with other Christians, "Get yourself another God!"

It took a while for me to see things this way, and it was mainly through two men who risked loving me after my diagnosis became known: Ed Gungor, pastor of the church I began attending in 1990, and Glenn Klein, a friend who's been discipling me. As Glenn started reaching out to me, I told him, "You're taking a risk." He knew what I meant, that I wasn't talking about his risk of infection but something even worse—a broken heart.

"Whoa," he replied. "I know what you're saying. You and I get close, and then you die, and I'm heartbroken. But that's not going to happen. I believe you're healed."

In chapter 13, I'll tell you more about these men and what they have taught me about faith. To wrap up this chapter, I will focus on some practical ways to show your love to a person with HIV infection:

Be readily available, either in person or by phone. Sometimes your HIV-infected friend or family member will have a bad day and just needs to know that somebody cares and is there, *really* there, for him or her. If you're a Christian, what you are doing is concretely representing the Lord. Although God is the real pillar of strength, his presence and power reach out through every person who says, "I'm here for you because I love you."

Realize that saying "I love you" must imply your willingness to pay whatever price that love requires. Jesus said, "Greater love hath no man than this, that he lay down his life for his friends" (John 15:13 NIV).

I'm quite careful to whom I say these three little words, and equally selective about whom I believe when they are said to me. You can't give me a greater gift than love, but words and reality are not identical. We're either in this together or we're not. If we are, I may need you more than you can imagine. If we're not, don't lie to me, to yourself, or to God.

Be prepared to share the silence, deafening and threatening though it may be. When you are quiet, you can enter my pain without tramping all over my soul. Trust me—you don't have to talk. You don't have to reason this through with me, though both of us may need to reason it through with God. Do you really think you can make some sense of it without separating yourself from me?

Oratory isn't needed here; fluency doesn't matter. I may be so sick and tired that I not only can't talk, but I can't listen either. I may not be able to converse intelligently, nor do I care to. So just be here with me. That's enough.

Whatever you do, don't say you know how I feel, because you can't know how I feel, even if you have AIDS yourself. Everybody is so different that no two people can possibly feel the same way, even about an experience they have shared.

Identify with me, but don't tell me all about your problems even if you hope I'll then forget my own. I have no interest in competing with you in terms of *your* pain quotient versus *mine.* Tell me some good news, please.

Keep it simple. Bring me a damp washcloth for my forehead if I'm burning up with fever, or straighten the bedding if you like, but don't fuss over me too much or I'll wonder if you're more concerned with acting concerned than whether I'm receiving what I really need.

How about reading to me, from a book or magazine or, especially, from the Bible? Almost anything will do, as long as it's not about AIDS. Or maybe you could write some letters for me. I've just been too tired lately, although every day that passes adds to my guilt at not answering my mail.

There are also many bills over on that table, but I haven't had the energy to balance my checkbook in weeks. Will you help me catch up with that?

And one other thing: Would you pull your chair right up next to my bed, and hold my hand for a while? Or perhaps just sit close and pray. Thanks. I need that more than almost anything else right now.

12

Starting Over
While There's Still Time

Like any other life crisis, AIDS can be either a wedge that separates people or a powerful glue. Left alone, people can as easily be driven apart as drawn together by this illness. Without the grace of God, the marriage of Ed and Donna Rozar might be just another statistic by now, and I might still be as distant from my own kids as I was before. Instead, these relationships are stronger now than they ever were.

The simple fact is that stress of this magnitude tends to exacerbate problems that already exist, whether openly or under the surface. At first it may unify two people and their family, galvanizing and bonding them against a situation that threatens all of them. But most of us, when faced with the grinding pressure of AIDS (or cancer, Parkinson's disease, or similar debilitating illnesses), are tempted to run away, either physically or emotionally. This reaction is normal (being tempted isn't wrong in itself), and it's hard not to give in and say, "Too bad, but I'm not going to get bogged down with your problems. I've got things to do, places to go. I'm sorry you're dying, but I don't want to be part of it. So long."

To make it through this, however, we have to be realistic about how much we are willing to give, or—to turn it around—how little we are willing to give up. AIDS requires more time, energy, and personal presence of caregivers than I could possibly put into words. That's been true for us, although I haven't had some of the horrid problems others in my situation have faced.

If you're involved with AIDS, either as a patient or as a family member, your relationships are in danger, whether you realize it or not. The good news is—I'll say it again—every crisis is also an opportunity in disguise, even this one.

I have already told you how early on (when all we could think about was the process of my dying), Donna and I put our family life into overdrive, trying to cram three years of living into one year of rushing around—for the children's sake as much as for our own.

What I haven't told you yet is how things changed once I began to focus on living rather than dying, on being a father rather than being my children's memory. It didn't happen overnight, and much of it had to do with my evolving faith. But it also involved some key practical issues, like the fact that all of a sudden I had a lot more time on my hands.

When I was doing surgery, my marriage and family got the leftovers in terms of my time and energy. The long hours and constant pressure required my best efforts and my most focused attention. Lives depended on me all the time, it seemed. Even when I wasn't on call, if I was in town, how could I ignore the needs of my patients?

Since May 1989, I've gone from a secondary role as a father to understanding what being a father really is. This transition didn't happen overnight, and it wasn't always smooth; changing habits never is! My typical day is much different now, although I still go to the peripheral vascular lab four days a week to evaluate the technicians' studies and dictate my findings and recommendations.

I still get up early—5:45 A.M.—but instead of rushing off to make rounds before surgery, I wash down my medications with a drink made from aloe vera concentrate, and Sun Rider products. I haven't become a natural-foods fanatic, but I am eating smarter because I want to give my system every advantage I can.

I've cut out white sugar and flour and usually skip caffeine drinks, including coffee, tea, and colas. My sugar intake is way down, as is my consumption of red meat. But when a nutritionist said I should stay off milk products, too, I said, "Hey, I live in Cheese Land!" Nevertheless, I have learned to drink soybean milk.

When I am able I go over to the church at 6:30 A.M. for one or two hours of praise and worship, immersing myself in God's Word and especially focusing on healing Scriptures. By the time I get home, the boys are usually up, so we eat breakfast together. The girls straggle in later, unless they're going out with me for breakfast, which we do once every week or so—their choice.

Usually I get to work by 9 or 10 A.M., and stay until around noon, depending on how much dictation there is to do or if there are meetings to attend. I'm home for lunch almost every day—something that never happened before—and I return to the clinic in the early afternoon if there's still work to do.

Our favorite family time comes after supper. We play board games, Foosball, or Ping-Pong, and we read. The kids are always going to the library, so there's a book lying next to just about every chair or couch in the house. We have many family-type videos for us to watch, since network TV watching is almost nonexistent at our house.

Like me, the kids are really into computers, so we're always playing some game like "Scorched Earth," with its tanks, other weapons, and mountain peaks to shoot over. It can get pretty competitive, because whoever wins a round gets to buy more weapons. Sometimes I cheat in reverse because otherwise they get too upset and say things like, "Dad, why did you have to blow me away? You don't ever let me get a shot!"

We play checkers, and I want to learn to play chess, because Jonathan Edward and David want to play. Other times after supper, we wrestle, if I'm feeling good enough. When they all pile on me at the same time—the usual arrangement—I'll shout, "Help! You're killing me!" Sometimes I wrestle them down and yell, "Doggie pile on Jonathan Wayne (or Victoria or Christina)!" Of course, I'm protecting the victim underneath me the whole time. They like that game, but usually it's three boys against me. And the bigger they get, the harder it is to stay on top.

When it's finally time for bed, I try to leave them each night with a simple prayer. "Thank you, Lord, for another day. We trust you'll give us a good night's sleep. Thanks for watching out for our family. Thanks for being who you are."

Sometimes they'll want to be more specific, like when Jonathan Wayne prayed: "Oh, God, please make it snow tonight so we can go skiing tomorrow." In the morning there was snow on the ground, so he said, "I prayed for it! God answered my prayer." Who was I to argue with that?

Quite often I go into their rooms when the kids are asleep. I touch their heads and pray for them, "Lord, thank you for these lives, that they're part of our family. Give them wisdom and help them become godly boys and girls, men and women."

I have gone from, "Lord, I know you're going to take care of them after I'm gone," to, "Lord, I'm looking forward to seeing my grandchildren. But, Lord, give me love like yours so when I see those grandchildren, I won't be seeing my own unresolved negative stuff coming out in them."

One thing I particularly enjoy with the older kids is going out to the farm in midwinter to look at the stars. We use a computer program, "Skyglobe," to plot the heavens as they appear from our locality. It's neat to watch the kids matching the stars to the chart and getting so excited about naming the constellations—something I never shared with my own father. I have a little trouble sharing it with them, too, but only because they can pick out the formations easier than I can.

Jonathan Edward will say, "Look, Dad, there's Leo the Lion. See his front leg and his tail?" He can see it, but I need one of those cans with holes in it to see it right. That might seem impossible if you live in a city, but in midwinter in mid-Wisconsin the stars seem so clear and bright in that jet black sky that you want to try to touch them and almost believe you can.

In those "teachable moments" I remind them of the almighty God who created all this. "Look at that!" I say. "Look what he made for us. He did it for his pleasure, but also for ours, so it doesn't cost a thing to stand here and enjoy it." I don't get too preachy, but just try to flow with it. You don't have to say much to kids in times like those. God has his own way of reaching them at their level, even about these deeper things. But if I were still doing cardiac surgery, I might have missed so many opportunities to tell them what I so earnestly want them to embrace in terms of faith.

Many other teachable moments can occur because I have more time with them now, time that the older ones especially value, perhaps because they see other kids whose physician-fathers are rarely home. Jonathan Edward said once, "Dad, if you were still operating, you wouldn't be able to do all these things with us."

By contrast, sometimes our brief exchanges focus on my illness and their fears. For instance, in the late fall of 1991 Jonathan Edward said, "Dad, I sure wish you didn't have this." As I recall, that day I was physically down, and he was identifying with me. Without making light of it, I tried to explain, "Honey, it's not a perfect world. Life isn't fair."

Kids understand that, I think. In their own world, little things don't always go just the way they hoped, and a minor setback becomes a tragic disappointment. Those "little things" seemed silly to me before, because, after all, I was a cardiac surgeon with more important concerns. But now that I've had some setbacks of my own, I can identify with theirs. "Let's take what we have," I say. "Deal with it and see what God is going to do. Life isn't always fair, but *he* is!"

Sometimes our interactions are humorous, like the time David came down early in the morning, saying he was too sick to make his bed or eat breakfast. In the past, because my life was so rushed, I might have ordered him to toe the line, but now I had time to play along with him a little. As an expert diagnostician, I knew his problem: CDS— computer deprivation syndrome. So I felt his head and said, as I shook mine solemnly, "Maybe you *are* a little sick. Do you think playing on the computer for a while would help you get better?"

"Sure, Dad," he replied, seriously enough that I had to fight to keep from laughing. "I think that we could eat breakfast after that."

Occasionally we overhear them talking about my illness, like when we were traveling cross-country and Jonathan Edward made some comment about "Daddy dying," and Jonathan Wayne asked, "Who's going to die? *My* daddy?" Jonathan Edward replied, "Yeah, didn't you know this sickness he has is going to cause his death?" His brother sat there, stunned, repeating, "*My* daddy?"

Donna told me that a couple of the kids have specific concerns, such as: "When Daddy dies, we want you to get married again—because we need a daddy." Obviously, our own struggle with the disease has immersed them in some pretty serious questions for children under ten.

Donna has been open and matter-of-fact with them right from the start. After all, the six of them spend so much time together, there's no way she could hide the truth even if she wanted to. Early on, she sometimes wondered how God could leave our children fatherless twice, but she still tried to field their questions truthfully and faithfully, without overwhelming them with data.

Once in home-school devotions, the verse for the day was "Ask and it shall be given; seek and ye shall find . . ." and the question to discuss was, "Have you ever asked God for anything?" Jonathan Edward became very angry. "I ask God every day to heal my daddy, and he doesn't do it." She tried to explain about God's timing, and the kinds of answers he gives, and how the fact that I was so well was an answer to our prayers.

As often as possible, Donna has used their lessons to build their courage and resolve. When they were studying history, she pointed out how the fathers of many famous people died when they were still quite young. "Remember how George Washington's father died when he was only eleven?" she said, showing them that orphaned kids don't have to be devastated for the rest of their lives.

But children can also be quite practical-minded about death and dying. Jonathan Edward once asked, "Dad, who's going to get the computers? You have to make a list now—we don't want to be arguing about that. And, Dad, have you decided about those guns? Who's going to get the .44 Magnum? I'd like that, but don't forget to write it down."

There is no doubt that although our oldest child is still only nine as I finish this, our children's view of life and their hopes and dreams have already been affected in a major way by my illness. Even though I plan to be around for thirty more years, Jonathan Edward will probably not pursue his earlier dream to be a heart surgeon like his daddy because he doesn't want to get AIDS. Now he wants to be an internist.

David, who often goes along with me to the office, loves to play doctor with my Dictaphone, imitating my reports even though he doesn't really know what they're about. He still wants to be a doctor, too, but he wants to be like me: a dictator! No longer does he want to be a belly surgeon. The reason for the change: AIDS.

I'm glad they still have some interest in medicine, but what my family needs not in the least is another *dictator*. Of all the layers of myself that AIDS has peeled away, my domineering spirit was the last to go, perhaps because it was the hardest to perceive and deal with. Thankfully, I had help, or I might have just continued being limited by this blind spot and hurting the people I love the most, especially my wife.

From my perspective, Donna and I seemed to be on different wavelengths for quite some time. I needed her more than ever before, but there just seemed to be something missing in our relationship. Sometimes this was so frustrating that I felt like splitting. If I was going to overcome this disease, I certainly didn't need strife and contention. I needed peace to be able to get on about my business and get my healing manifested. When our friction took the form of an argument, it usually centered on the idea of supernatural healing. I was contending for my life, and I tried to help her understand. Why couldn't she believe the best with me—my best, our best, our children's best? Little did I know then that our lack of a relationship was the basic problem.

Finally, Donna met with Pastor Gungor (at his urging). I prepped him for a theological dispute about supernatural healing. Instead, as they talked, Donna took the risk of telling this man, who had become one of my best friends, the truth about us. She didn't have any problem with healing; she believed that God is God, and he can do anything he wants to do. Something else was bothering her.

The real problem was that, as far as she was concerned, we didn't have a marriage—in fact, we had *never* had a marriage. From day one, my obsessive-compulsive, driven, and overbearing personality had squashed her. I had effectively quenched the possibility of our becoming "one flesh," which has to be based on mutual respect. She had stayed with me all these years not for affection, romance, security or anything else we shared or enjoyed, but simply because she felt the Lord had told her to do so.

So, it wasn't that Donna couldn't believe in my healing. Deep inside, *she didn't want me to be healed,* because AIDS had become her ticket out of a bad situation. She wasn't going to abandon me, but she wasn't about to pretend our marriage was wonderful, either.

Pastor Ed was shocked, but it wasn't until the following Wednesday that he dropped the bombshell on me. "Donna and I had a long talk last week," he began, "and as far as I can see her problem isn't with supernatural healing," he began. Then, as he looked in my eyes, friend to friend, he continued, "She *believes in it,* all right—but, she doesn't *want it* to happen to you."

My mouth dropped open. I was floored and overwhelmed with emotion at the same time. Tears came to my eyes as I wondered what he could mean. I felt like I had been kicked in the chest by a horse. My death was seen as vindication for the failure of our marriage.

"I love you, Ed," he said, "but I've only known you since the Lord's been softening your personality and building your character, partly because of your struggle with AIDS. But Donna is carrying a lot of hurt. She has a wounded spirit—and if she's told me the truth, I can't say I blame her."

"I don't think I understand," I said. "What did she say?"

"Mostly stuff about the way you've treated her and the kids—ordering everybody around, making impossible demands based on unrealistic expectations. I don't want to get in the middle of the specifics. But I couldn't believe I was hearing about the same guy sitting here in front of me. I couldn't believe you did all these things and still thought of yourself as a Christian."

"What can I do? Is it too late?" I asked.

"It's never too late," he said. "But one thing's for sure. You two need to get away, and you need to start over. You should tell her you're sorry if you hurt her, and you're willing to do anything to renew your marriage toward where it's supposed to be."

As I stood up to go, I said, "You know, it would be a lot easier just to die."

"I know it, brother," Pastor Ed replied. "It would be, but that's not what God wants for you."

I drove home, still in shock, but also relieved to finally see why we had had such conflict once I started thinking I would be healed. It was still only ten in the morning when I got home, but I asked Donna if we could talk for a few minutes. We went into the study and closed the door. Little faces did appear through the glass panes, but amazingly enough, that did not distract us.

"I'm sorry for all the hurt I've caused you," I confessed. "Pastor Ed told me some of the things you talked about, and he recommended that we get away by ourselves, spend some time alone together somewhere, and see if we can get our relationship back together. He'll find somebody to watch the kids."

Donna agreed to the plan without a lot of comment, and the following Tuesday we drove to Wausau. The Rib Mountain Inn is a nice condo-type motel. Our place came with a fireplace and kitchen. A nice, secluded setting—just what the doctor needed. We went out to eat that night, enjoying the longest and best dinner we've ever had, even when we were dating. (We've had several outings like this since then, and it has been great.)

"I want to start over if you are willing," I began. "I want us to have a marriage that reflects the plan God has for us as a couple." I don't know how I would have handled it if she had said, "Forget it!" She got pretty teary-eyed at that point, and so did I. Even though she never came right out and said yes, it was obvious that she was willing to try. We talked about the fact that it might not be easy at times, but God would sustain us through the rough spots.

After three hours at the restaurant, talking, eating, and enjoying each other's company, we returned to our room. I built a fire, and we talked for another three hours. "I need to hear your heart," I said. "Help me see what I've done wrong. Show me what it will take to have a relationship that will work."

Donna proceeded to give me a history of our marriage, from things she had struggled with to things I had done (or left undone), much that I had either forgotten or repressed. Obviously, the scars were still there for her, along with a lot of pain. "Whatever it takes to heal our marriage," I said, "I'm willing to do it. I'm contending for my life, and I need your help to win this battle."

I'm not really sure why she believed me, except perhaps she had already seen some changes taking place within me. Not that I was any kind of perfect husband yet, but she knew something was different. She decided to risk believing me— a little hesitantly at first, but far better than rejecting me. "I'm going to wait and see if this is real," she said. Fair enough, as far as I was concerned. Nobody should expect everything to change overnight because of a few words. During our encounter, one thing that Pastor Ed had told me kept popping up in my mind: "If she thinks she is right about something concerning your marriage (even though you think she may not be), she is." This advice came in handy; it was far easier to see where she was coming from by accepting as true what she said rather than trying to defend myself. Her "charges" were acknowledged as true, and I spent a lot of the time turning the other cheek. However, this is what God's love is all about. It really was not that difficult as I wanted our marriage to be healed. The Holy Spirit's prompting and restraining was the key to the success of our beginning over.

I have to thank my pastor for helping me understand about *agape* love—what it really means to love people unconditionally, to see them as God does. He values them all, even people like me who have done atrocious things. I thought when I convinced Donna to see Pastor Ed that he would fix her up and tune her in to my needs. What happened was almost exactly the opposite, one of the biggest turnabouts in *my* life. "Be forgiving and humble yourself," he had urged me. "Be more of a servant to your wife and kids." I absorbed his book, *Supernatural Relationships* and as I daily read the Bible, I began to comprehend my role as husband and father.

So now, after the rebirth of our marriage, when I'm helping by washing the clothes or the dishes or cleaning house, I'm not muttering to myself about those messy kids who are just going to clutter it up again when I turn around. Instead, I try to think about Jesus and how he got down and washed his disciples' feet—a pretty dirty job for the Son of God—without saying, "Now, guys, how about keeping these feet a little cleaner next time so my job will be easier." Sometimes I even find myself singing as I work.

I'm still far from perfect, but it's been fascinating to see how God is healing those wounds and bringing us closer together as a couple and as a family—though I must confess that being HIV-positive really gets in the way of marital intimacy!

Donna and I are much more open and spontaneous now. We sit and talk, which we never did before. I'm still pretty much a loner, so I struggle with that constantly. But I'm thankful I wasn't an active cardiac surgeon when this relationship bombshell burst, because I doubt I would have had the time or energy to really work it out.

As far as I'm concerned, experiencing this renewal has made it all worthwhile. I would rather be where I am today, with HIV infection, than where I was before, especially in terms of my marriage and family relationships. AIDS is still a curse, but God can turn even a curse around for good, if we'll just hang in there with him, trusting, believing, and growing. Becoming "one flesh," in spite of HIV, is possible because the "mystery" of that oneness relates to spirit and soul, long before it relates to the body.

I shudder to think that I could have lived to seventy-five or eighty, with Donna as my wife, practicing cardiac surgery and providing well for her and the kids, *without ever really having a marriage.* My male chauvinistic attitude prevented me from understanding the fact that even though I saw myself as head of the family, I was not really part of it. Perhaps equally devastating would have been for me to die much sooner with all these things unresolved, leaving Donna to carry it all for the rest of her life. So, either way, what has happened is better for her, as well as me. But I want you to understand that this is more a statement about God and his grace than it is about our ability to be what we know we should be.

If I hadn't had this illness, I wouldn't have had the time to really seek God, though he's been seeking me for years. I don't think I ever stopped long enough to be in fellowship with him. My prayer life was like that of many Christians—short, sweet, and superficial—unless I needed something.

Getting infected with HIV gave me the time and the hunger to be in the Word. In fact, my appetite became voracious. I have learned that there is more to being a Christian than just having a personalized ticket to heaven—invaluable as that is. The vulnerability of becoming a patient, physically, carried over into becoming God's patient, spiritually. It taught me to listen carefully to my divine Physician, hear what he had said and was still saying. If only I would repent, believe, and put my faith into action, there was much yet to be discovered in my relationship with him—a renewal of intimacy similar to, but much deeper than, what had occurred with Donna.

This deeper renewal is what I will share with you in my final chapter, hoping that you will choose a similar path in your own efforts to transform whatever difficulty you may face today into an opportunity to grow.

13

Living from the Inside Out

Once upon a time there was a Georgia lad who wanted to become a surgeon so he could stamp out disease and give sick people a better chance at life. Year after year he studied and trained, striving to perfect his skills, driven to be the best he could possibly be.

He was fast. He was good. In everything he tried, he achieved remarkable success. But something was missing. There was a barren place inside the man that neither medicine nor romance could fill—until he heard about another Healer who had brought God's Word to man.

So he believed, and was baptized, and then he turned his attention back to surgery. He thought there would be time, later, to really nurture the seed that was sprouting in his soul. But now he had more pressing things to do.

How would you make a parable of *your* life story? What lessons could it teach, especially about things you regret? The main regret I have about my life is not that I contracted HIV, but that it took the crisis of AIDS to show me I was still a baby Christian, even after all these years. My HIV infection became my opportunity to grow in faith, to see realities as I never had before, to understand truths I had never heard before, and to be healed from the inside out. In effect, AIDS gave me a new lease on life.

These changes didn't happen automatically or instantaneously, as if there were a mystical magic wand to wave or a celestial button to push, through which we could control or manipulate the Almighty. We don't need to manipulate God, because he is already on our side. But if we're going to grow stronger in faith instead of weaker when testing comes, the only way to do so is to consume God's Word like a hungry baby after its mother's milk. And we have to believe all our heavenly Father's promises as deeply as a child trusts everything his earthly daddy says.

Reaching maturity of faith is a growth process, not an event, no matter what some may proclaim. Momentous perceptions and even miraculous events may be part of the process, but these only take us deeper into God's grace and truth. Every answer only leads to another more insightful question.

I have wondered how best to tell you about what I've found in terms of faith. I've tried to put myself in your place, especially if you've been walking along with me mainly because of our common interest in AIDS, but not necessarily because we share a common bond of faith.

If you are a skeptic, I wish we could talk. I would like to hear your side, and I would love to explain how I have come to see that all the questions and all the answers converged roughly two thousand years ago. An itinerant preacher-healer, who was the Son of God, was crucified on a hill called Golgotha just outside Jerusalem, not for his own sins, but to redeem all those who trust in him.

It's one thing to see yourself as a victim of an infernal disease for which there is not now a cure, nor may there ever be. I've had my own Pity Party, but good as it may feel, self-pity can change neither the past nor the future—although it quite effectively poisons the present.

Jesus of Nazareth, by contrast, was a willing victim. His horrid death was the completion, not the interruption, of his earthly task. For this purpose he had come into the world, and he steadfastly set his face to go to Jerusalem, knowing better than anyone else what would happen there. When he had fulfilled his destiny to cure something far more deadly than AIDS will ever be—the disease of sin, both in our world and as it impacts our personal lives—he said, "It is finished."

You can read the inspired account for yourself, in the Gospels. But the main reason I have invested the time and energy in telling you about my journey is because the Savior who redeemed me from the pit of hell wants to do the same for you. As far as I can see, there is no other way to generate and sustain even the *desire* to live more fully in the face of AIDS. The *ability* to do so without supernatural help does not exist in the long term, because in the long term this disease will conquer the most indomitable human spirit. The *power* to triumph in life or in death begins and ends with Jesus, because he showed by his life, death, and resurrection what knowing and trusting God is really all about.

When I first heard the news that I was HIV-positive, I had been cruising along. But after the initial shock, including the low self-esteem, depression, and confusion I've already told you about, I ended up in an emotional and spiritual limbo that lasted for months. During that period, my most intense feeling was aloneness, not just loneliness, which is more a symptom than a cause. I felt isolated, cut off from my profession, feeling like a leper in my own home, and more than a little bit forsaken by God. The illness had shaved my meager faith down to its bare foundations.

I knew from seeing hundreds of people die that we are all just passing through this world. It is not really our "home." I hoped my destination was heaven, but I wasn't very thankful about the possibility of getting there sooner than expected. But what about my destiny? During those first few months, I didn't think I had one anymore. Everywhere I looked, especially as I filled my mind with information about AIDS, everything and everybody, including me, seemed to say, "No. No. No!" This negativism nearly drowned out the "Yes. Yes. Yes!" that was coming from God.

"Yes," he spoke into our anxiety about finances—and the disability insurance was approved in just a few weeks. "Yes," he whispered as we wondered what would become of the kids—and an annuity was established to cover their education. "Yes," he murmured as I struggled with my identity and worth—and the Marshfield Clinic offered to retrain me and was actually insistent that I remain active and useful. Had I been walking by faith and not by sight, I wouldn't have needed this much proof of God's faithfulness.

It took nearly two more years of nurturing along my little faith-seedling before I realized and celebrated with the apostle Paul that ". . . no matter how many promises God has made, they are 'Yes' in Christ. And so through him the 'Amen' is spoken by us to the glory of God" (2 Cor. 1:20 NIV). His word to us is always "Yes," even when it sounds like "No."

The word *Amen* means "so let it be." It's one thing to pronounce this word at the end of a prayer that is thanking God for his faithfulness, which we did, of course, whenever we heard good news. It's totally another matter, though, to say it *and mean it* when the news is not so good, and the future seems nothing but bleak.

To put it bluntly, it seemed in those early months impossible to fulfill one of the New Testament's most difficult exhortations: "Be joyful always; pray continually; give thanks in all circumstances, for this is God's will for you in Christ Jesus" (1 Thess. 5:16–18 NIV). By myself, I never could have manufactured joy or thanksgiving, an "Amen" to God's way with me. It would have to be *his* doing; there was no doubt about that. But for me the key to letting him do this was nestled in the very next verse, "Do not put out the Spirit's fire."

For a while, deep inside me was a vague longing, like a wish you want to put on your Christmas list but hold back because you think it could never happen. I began yearning for something more, something beyond striving to set a new world record for treading water just before I drowned. If faith was worth anything, there had to be something beyond diagnosis, treatment, dying, and then being happy in heaven. Like my first experience with faith, I knew there was still something missing. Finding it took me much deeper into grace than I ever imagined possible.

Going deeper with God began in the same place it begins for everybody, in his Word. Anything else is extraneous, because only the Word of God carries the authenticity, authority, and power to cut through and expose methods, motives, defenses, distortions, and deceptions that so easily spring from the heart of man.

In March 1990 I was asked to teach the Book of Revelation in an adult Sunday school class. I wasn't sure I should accept the invitation; although I had read Revelation several times, it never meant much to me. However, I said "Yes," and again God said "Yes" to me. For nearly six months I immersed myself in this remarkable Scripture, investing at least ten hours a week in study, sometimes a lot more. For the first time in my life, I began to understand what fellowship with God is. It was an exciting, energizing, and revolutionary experience to explore God's final written word to man.

On the other hand, it was also enervating and frustrating to bring in the "pearls" I had collected week after week, only to be greeted by not much more than a yawn by many people in the class. It's entirely possible the problem was the instructor. I mean, how often can you try to express how amazing, exciting, even wild, this book of the Bible has become to you before your listeners either absorb what you're saying and get just as enthused, or simply tune you out?

Despite my frustration, the really important thing wasn't my success or failure in involving others in my quest. The quest itself was its own reward. Slowly, but surely, the Word was coming alive to me—and *in* me—as if God were right there with me, speaking it into my very soul. It didn't matter how others might respond. It only mattered how Ed Rozar responded, and he was hungry for more.

One passage in particular really arrested me and challenged me to quit straddling the fence in terms of faith:

> The Amen, the faithful and true Witness, the Beginning of the creation of God, says this: "I know your deeds, that you are neither cold nor hot; I would that you were cold or hot. So because you are lukewarm, and neither hot nor cold, I will spit you out of My mouth. Because you say, 'I am rich, and have become wealthy, and have need of nothing,' and you do not know that you are wretched and miserable and poor and blind and naked, I advise you to buy from Me gold refined by fire, that you may become rich, and white garments, that you may clothe yourself, and that the shame of your nakedness may not be revealed; and eyesalve to anoint your eyes, that you may see" (Rev. 3:14–18).

Here in words recorded near the end of the first century was a description of this cardiac surgeon near the end of the twentieth century. Before my diagnosis, faith was somewhere in the background noise of my daily existence—important, yes, but not as valuable as what I could do for myself. I didn't know how wretched, pitiful, poor, blind, and naked I was until I got that telephone call in April 1989. My destiny, as I saw it then, had been altered in less than twenty words from a guy I had never met, calling from an office I had never seen. Suddenly I was stripped bare—in more ways than I care to think about—and for a while the vulnerability and helplessness was nearly overwhelming.

But here in Revelation was an offer I couldn't refuse: gold to fill my poverty, white clothes to cover my nakedness, salve to help this blind man see. All I had to do was decide whether God was real and his promises true. Was I willing to quit straddling the fence and trust him with my whole self: spirit, soul, and body? "Amen!" I cried, and he took me deeper still. The Holy Spirit was beginning to erupt like a volcano inside me.

Before this, my whole philosophy of life was task-oriented. Life, including life in the operating room, was one unending assembly line of new challenges. When my battle with HIV began, this approach carried me forward, *at first*. We would face this with hope—and lick it if we really worked hard. But the challenge was just too big. The only way past it was through it, and the only way through it was with God in control.

So I had to quit *hoping* I would get better, because the best I could manage with that approach seemed to be turning this illness into a chronic, long-term ailment. It was like saying, "Maybe I won't be too sick too often. With his help, I will endure and try to carry on until he finally carries me into glory." I felt that approach was the same as admitting I didn't really believe that God would heal AIDS. In fact, as long as I focused on my problem with those "blind" eyes, I couldn't grasp that I could be free of this.

Real faith is more substantial—it is "being sure of what we hope for and certain of what we do not see" (Heb. 11:1 NIV). The King James Version states this even more clearly: "Now faith is the substance of things hoped for, the evidence of things not seen." Were those hoped-for things only spiritual in nature? How could anybody's faith prove things not seen?

It was time for me to cease praying in hopes of seeing some results; even this was faith mixed with doubts—lukewarm faith. Hope had me thinking, *It's going to be great when my body is free of this, when I don't have any more symptoms. My T-cells and macrophages will be reborn, and my HIV test will be negative.* Now, instead of praying about the specifics of the problem, I affirm its overall solution, which already exists in the mind and will of God. "Lord, your Word says it, and I believe it." I began reading books on healing and listening to a tape series on healing. F. F. Bosworth's *Christ the Healer* was one of the foundations from which my journey to wholeness began.

A transformation had taken place that began in my spirit. It was working itself outward to my mind, which had previously been far too cluttered with scientific facts, including symptoms, diagnosis, treatment, and prognosis. Paul describes this far better than I could: "Do not be conformed to this world, but be transformed by the renewing of your mind, that you may prove what the will of God is, that which is good and acceptable and perfect" (Rom. 12:2).

The key issue is not the renewing of our minds, though this is a formidable enough task. We are so conformed to the world's pattern that we can't even see that, until some crisis presents the opportunity to look at our values, priorities, and beliefs with different eyes. This may be doubly difficult for doctors, because the medical system forces its disciples to conform or perish.

The heart of the matter here is that only when I *am* transformed by the renewing of my mind will I be able to discern, test, approve, and contend for God's good, pleasing, and perfect will. As I see it, a slow, wasting death at an early age, leaving a wife and five children to fend for themselves, is not God's idea of Ed Rozar's destiny. If it is not his, why should it be mine?

When the Word says, "by his stripes we are healed," it's either true or it's not. If it is not, then there's nothing else to say. If it is, then we have to get past interpreting the Bible in light of our experiences. Whether we've ever seen a healing, or a demon exorcised, or another spiritual gift in operation—or even whether we think such things are possible in modern times—is not relevant to the truth of God's Word. That's going about it backward, as far as I can see.

You may believe, as I once did, that "by his stripes we are healed" is talking only about spiritual "diseases," especially the ultimate disease, spiritual death. But the way I see it now, *I am healed already,* in my spirit first, through faith in Christ and by his indwelling Spirit. But there's more, because this healing works itself outward, through my soul (including my intellect) and finally manifesting itself in my body. Just as one knows in his "knower" he is saved, I know that I *was* healed: Jesus has paid the price for me. "It" is finished.

I may not yet see scientific evidence that the HIV is gone, but I'm talking about faith—the evidence of things *not seen.* If I have to see it to believe it, what kind of "faith" is that?

Is anything too hard for God? If he can break the power of sin and destroy the works of Satan, eradicating a virus from the body of Ed Rozar should be an easy task. Shall I be a practical atheist? Shall I pray to God, but put all my hope in medicine, when modern medicine is a relatively late pretender to the throne of healing in a realm that has always been God's anyway? This virus has invaded my body from without. So, as Pastor Ed Gungor expressed it to me, "You are a prime candidate for healing."

"Hopeless" is not a word in God's vocabulary. He can do it, and it's right to trust that he will. For me and you, it is done: finished, completed. Positioning yourself to receive it is the hallmark of seeing the physical evidence of his promise. But, before I go any further, I want to make one thing perfectly clear: I'm not bragging, as if my faith is better than yours. My healing is not a divine reward for superior knowledge or actions. I'm not boasting about Ed Rozar, but about the Lord. He promises, and he delivers. We can either stand in his way, or we can believe.

We never have to beg, any more than we would expect to beg a bank teller to let us make a withdrawal from our bank account so we could pay the rent. If the money's in there, we wouldn't expect the teller to say, "Ed Rozar, you're such a braggart, thinking you can just come waltzing in here to claim this cash."

I haven't made it yet, but, like Paul, "I press on to take hold of that for which Christ Jesus took hold of me" (Phil. 3:12). There's nothing about me that should cause God to do a miracle because I somehow deserve it. Then again, if it is true that we who believe have been made "heirs of God and joint-heirs with Christ" (Rom. 8:17 NIV), how can it be boastful to expect our Father to do what he promises? Books by Kenneth Hagin and Norvell Hayes helped me to drink in the reality of God's promises to me.

I'm no saint, at least the way you may think of the word. But the New Testament saints were generic believers who were "holy ones" not because they acted holy; their lives were *made* holy because they were empowered, controlled, and filled by the Holy Spirit. We can either quench the Spirit's fire, or we can let him ignite us. For this to happen, we have to be open to his way.

In the middle of 1991, I started praying at the start of each new day, "Holy Spirit, I welcome you to walk with me this day. Lead me, guide me, fill me, use me." Gradually, as I studied and listened and observed and prayed about it, I came to realize that this Person, who lived within me—this Comforter, Counselor, Helper, and Spirit of truth—held the key to consistency and courage and power and effectiveness for God's kingdom. Two books really helped me understand the ministry of the Holy Spirit: Dr. Paul Cho's book *The Holy Spirit, My Senior Partner* and Benny Hinn's *Good Morning, Holy Spirit.*

By November I was convinced there still was something more, something still missing that—if God wanted to give to me—I would be a fool to resist. More than that, I began earnestly to want everything that was within his perfect will for me. I was learning how to *unveil* this Christianity that had been part of me for seventeen years.

Years earlier, when I was part of a mission team in India, I had witnessed events that didn't correlate either with medicine as I knew it, or with rationalism as I understood it. People were healed, instantaneously and miraculously, right before our eyes. Others were released from the clutches of the Evil One and his agents, through exorcising prayer. But perhaps the most common thread tying it all together was the attitude of praise and worship, consistently marked by prophetic utterances and what is commonly called speaking in tongues.

I have to tell you, as a surgeon, I really didn't know what to think of all these things. I knew something remarkable was taking place through this group of Christian men, and I had never even imagined such stuff could happen. But, instead of studying this phenomenon until I could understand what it was about, I returned to the States and the sterile world of surgery, placing what I had witnessed on a shelf in some compartment of my mind for future reference, marked: unexplained things to pursue when you have time.

Now I had more than time. I had a need, and I had the desire to go as deep with faith as the Spirit of God was willing to take me. The result was renewal, on one level after another, until when everything else was laid bare before God, the only thing left was more fully to know him and be known by him. I wanted to love him and be loved by him to the point where we were one—at least as much as possible this side of heaven.

When it came to that, however, there were no words, at least no words I knew, that could adequately express what I wanted and needed to say. Glenn Klein began to disciple me and reach out to me like no other person short of Pastor Ed Gungor. He knew what I needed. As he is a bold messianic Jew, he would not be intimidated by a cardiac sur-

geon infected with HIV. One day in November 1991, we
spent several hours together over lunch and then in his study
at home. He preached his heart out, and then we prayed for
me to receive the baptism of the Holy Spirit. The most
remarkable thing happened because of that prayer and laying
on of hands: From somewhere deep inside me, sounds and
words I didn't understand burst forth in an experience of
joyful release.

I didn't make it happen, but I believed it would, by faith.
This experience was from God. Even more than that, it was
God speaking to my spirit, God speaking through me. "For
one who speaks in a tongue does not speak to men, but to
God; for no one understands, but in his spirit he speaks mys-
teries"(1 Cor. 14:2).

Again, there is nothing so special about Ed Rozar that
God was obligated to give me this new way of expressing
the inexpressible. His only obligation is to keep his Word.
While I would never say that you must have an identical
experience to prove you are one of God's children, if you
are one of his children, I recommend that you remain open
to whatever gifts he wants to give you. For me, this new way
of praying, which I use almost exclusively in private, has
transformed my inner life almost as much as coming to
Christ in the first place. The peace and joy that the filling
of the Holy Spirit has brought me have been working their
way from the inside out, in a healing that far exceeds everything that has happened or will happen in the future. That is
surely what Job meant when he compared his earlier relationship with God to how he had come to know God more
personally because of his losses: "My ears had heard of you,
but now my eyes have seen you" (Job 42:5 NIV).

I know what you're thinking—not everybody is healed.
This was true in Jesus' day, and it's true now. "And he did
not do many miracles there because of their lack of faith"
(Matt. 13:58). I don't have all the answers, but I do trust
him.

People die. Sometimes they die young, and only God knows why. The answers to many such questions are not easy. But God's Word is true, regardless of what we see. His good and perfect will is what I am pursuing. Through his Spirit, he has rescued me from depression and despair. Helpless before an illness I thought spelled impending death, I had no idea that what it really spelled was *fuller life* and *more authentic faith*. Only God knew that. "Every good and perfect gift is from above, coming down from the Father of the heavenly lights, who does not change like shifting shadows" (James 1:17 NIV).

It has been quite an adventure. I wouldn't trade it for good health and mediocre faith in a million years. I know HIV will finally be eradicated from my mortal body. I have received my healing. God has a destiny for me, and I am committed to fulfilling it in his power. And when the time comes to go to my grave—as it will come for all of us eventually—I will go believing God and confessing his Word. I will not be disappointed when the time comes, for then I will finally be able to praise and worship him forever, without the hindrances that even now still come between us.

I would like to close this book with a prayer, first for myself, but then also for you:

> Father, I lay all my burdens, all my diseases, all my successes before you, at the foot of the cross. Now Lord, mold me in your will. I want to reach the destiny you have for me. I want to be able to stand before you, despite whatever illnesses, problems, or tragedies that have come into my life. I want to hear you say, "Well done, good and faithful servant."
>
> I give you myself—spirit, soul, and body—believing that your promises to me in Jesus Christ are "Yes," and only "Yes." Thank you, Lord, for being faithful. Even more, I thank you for being who you are, my

heavenly Father. You have great things in store for me, beyond what I could dare to ask or think.

Father, in Jesus' name, I pray the words on these pages would be more than words; that they would be a vehicle for your Holy Spirit, to bless, inspire, excite, and energize every person who has taken this journey with me. Amen and Amen.